Varieties of Capitalism and the Political Economy of Differentiated Integration in Europe

NEW HORIZONS IN EUROPEAN POLITICS

Series Editor: José M. Magone, *Berlin School of Economics and Law, Germany*
Founding Series Editor: Julie Smith, *Robinson College, Cambridge, UK*

The *New Horizons in European Politics* series is an invaluable forum for original research across the spectrum of European politics, promoting innovative cross-disciplinary analysis of contemporary issues and debates. Covering a diverse range of topics, the series examines issues such as: the impacts of the severe challenges brought about by the financial crisis; economic issues, including integration and monetary union; the politics of the EU and other governmental and nongovernmental institutions; environmental politics and the ongoing struggle to mitigate climate change; and the politics of trade, energy and security in Europe. Both international and comparative in its approach, this exciting series encompasses theoretical and empirical work from both well-established researchers and the next generation of scholars.

For a full list of Edward Elgar published titles, including the titles in this series, visit our website at www.e-elgar.com.

Varieties of Capitalism and the Political Economy of Differentiated Integration in Europe

Rafał Riedel

Full Professor in European Integration Studies and Head of the Department of Political and Administrative Systems, University of Opole, Poland and Guest Professor at Johannes Gutenberg-Universität in Mainz, Germany

Jakub Anusik

Research Associate, National Center of Science, University of Łodź and University of Opole, Poland

NEW HORIZONS IN EUROPEAN POLITICS

Edward Elgar
PUBLISHING

Cheltenham, UK • Northampton, MA, USA

Published by
Edward Elgar Publishing Limited
The Lypiatts
15 Lansdown Road
Cheltenham
Glos GL50 2JA
UK

Edward Elgar Publishing, Inc.
William Pratt House
9 Dewey Court
Northampton
Massachusetts 01060
USA

A catalogue record for this book
is available from the British Library

Library of Congress Control Number: 2024934464

This book is available electronically in the Elgaronline
Political Science and Public Policy subject collection
http://dx.doi.org/10.4337/9781035319312

MIX
Paper from
responsible sources
FSC® C013056

ISBN 978 1 0353 1930 5 (cased)
ISBN 978 1 0353 1931 2 (eBook)

Printed and bound in Great Britain by TJ Books Limited, Padstow, Cornwall

Contents

Figures

Tables

Acknowledgement

This research was supported by a project generously funded by the National Science Centre (Narodowe Centrum Nauki) within the programme OPUS (grant number: 2020/37/B/HS5/00230), under the title: *Determinants and Dynamics of Differentiated Integration in a Post-Brexit Europe.*

Preface

This monograph is one of the outcomes of a research project that was generously funded by the National Science Centre (Narodowe Centrum Nauki) within the programme OPUS (grant number: 2020/37/B/HS5/00230), under the title: 'Determinants and Dynamics of Differentiated Integration in a Post-Brexit Europe'. The project focuses on the exploration of the dynamics and determinants of differentiated integration in Europe in which the two authors are investigators. The subject of differentiated integration has been growing in the scholarly literature at an enormous pace in recent years. This is due to the fact that that differentiation has become a systemic feature of the European integration project and has been recognized as one of the most salient issues in contemporary Europe along with the fact that it carries significant potential for future transformations of European integration. This fact has been reflected in scientific discussions featuring differentiation as well as its sources, dynamics, determinants, mechanisms, and outcomes.

In this monograph, the authors focus on the political economy perspective on differentiated integration in post-Brexit Europe. Employing the varieties of capitalism framework into the study of the current state of European integration allows for a better understanding of the determinants of differentiation that has become a vital characteristic of contemporary Europe. As such, this publication is addressed primarily to an academic audience: scholars of European integration, area studies, Europeanization, comparative politics, international relations and related disciplines, as well as economic integration scholars. The publication is also expected to serve as handbook both for undergraduate and postgraduate audiences as well as policy makers, officials, journalists, opinion leaders, and general audiences. It could also be used as supplementary reading on courses such as European Integration, (Comparative) Political Science, International Relations, Varieties of Capitalism, International Economic Integration, and many others.

In recent years, the study of differentiated integration has established itself as a key area of the European integration field. The processes of (dis)integration and differentiation in Europe have also generated enormous attention in other social sciences, such as (comparative) political science or international relations. However, there are no monographs that focus systematically on the dynamics and determinants of differentiated integration with a gravity point on the varieties of capitalism. Therefore, we believe that this book fills a significant gap while simultaneously making a contribution to the study of the 'ever loser union', core and periphery formation, as well as the understanding of the nation-states' politics and their influence on supranational developments. The analysis focuses predominantly on the period between the so called 'big bang' enlargement (i.e., 2004 – when most of the Central Eastern European economies joined the European Union) and the onset of the COVID-19 pandemic. While the initial point allows for comprehensive comparisons between the current Member States at that time, the ending point marks the start of the biggest economic turmoil since the Great Recession. Additionally, in 2020–2021, the Brexit process came to an end, at least in its legal dimension, which sets the final date of the time-scope of the analysis.

Crises constitute an important contextual variable of the analysis, since they play an immense role in shaping the socio-economic landscape. At the same time, they open the windows of opportunity for even more differentiation, which makes them important milestones in the process of the political and economic development of the European continent's integration and disintegration. Differentiated integration is an intrinsic feature of the European Union and its neighbourhood, and it has become a baseline in any discussion about the future of Europe. With our research, we wish to make a considerable contribution to the scholarship on the political economy of differentiated integration and, in a broader sense, to the field of varieties of capitalism in the European context.

Jakub Anusik, Rafał Riedel

1 Introduction: The comparative capitalism approach to European differentiated integration

Differentiation and differentiated integration (DI) in the European Union (EU), both internal (intra-EU) and external (extra-EU), is an answer to and a consequence of growing heterogeneity in Europe. Heterogeneity can be grasped in a number of ways, and thus is researched in many various methods, predominantly from the perspective of political science (Schimmelfennig & Winzen 2020). The authors approach it from the political economy perspective, applying the varieties of capitalism (VoC) framework. The authors' enquiry tries to explain the position of a specific country on a particular orbit of differentiated integration system by looking at the characteristics of the capitalism version that is developed in that country's specific national economy.

One of the added values of this publication is that it goes beyond the static models of European integration differentiation built on legal-institutional criteria. It tries to capture the dynamism of the system of differentiation, and, at the same time, it employs a dynamic perspective on the side of explanatory variables, namely the changing system of VoC. The question of how politics affect economic outcomes – and conversely, how economic determinants intertwine with political solutions – is one of the oldest in economics, and these questions have probably been asked for as long as people have been interested in the issues of production, distribution, resources, the organization of political and economic systems, and related fields. Much of the existing European integration scholarship, and predominantly on differentiated integration, is focused mostly on the political dimension (e.g., Euroscepticism) and external factors which determine different paths that the states take on their European journey. This publication offers a different approach, focusing on the political economy of the integration process. That which is novel, along with domestic institutional factors (the economic complementarities that define a specific variant of capitalism), will be taken into consideration as explanatory variables for the dynamics of differentiation. These parameters include both variables of an 'input' and 'output' nature which are shaping different forms of the market economy regime. For example: expenditures on social security relative to GDP would serve as an example of the input variable, while the output would serve as its results (e.g., the percentage of population living under the poverty threshold). Albeit narrowly, comparative capitalism models have already been used in the research on European integration, proving their helpfulness especially after the crisis in the Eurozone. The intersection of the two theories is, to some extent, present in the literature since it underlines the role of Member States' heterogeneity in terms of the capitalism mode they accomplish and the different state interests they follow. The aforementioned factors have been identified by the authors as barriers to further integration and pointed to as a reason for the democracy deficit occurring in the EU. Much of what has been written about as regards the economic aspects of differentiated integration triggers either an issue of structural non-optimality in the European Monetary Union (EMU), leading to a divergence of monetary systems inside the Union, and, interconnectedly, austerity measures and their political implications what is connected to the political problem of reforming the most disadvantaged economies during and after the 2008 financial crisis. Some studies argue that under the EMU the two growth models (i.e., the export-led model specific to the Euroland core economies and the demand-led model of the 'peripheries') have become increasingly incompatible due to the external imbalances which emerged between them (Magone et al. 2016). Moreover, certain political coalitions are forming inside the EMU countries in order to protect the prevailing type of capitalism and growth modus. This often results in clashes with the EU's transnational institutions, as well as with other Member States (MS) and influences the integratory path of a given country.

The main objective of the analysis covered in this book aims to explain the correlations and potential causality between the level, scope, and depth of differentiation in the European integration process on one side, and, on the other, the socio-economic parameters that define the varieties of capitalism in specific EU Member States. These interdependencies are dynamic and reveal many interesting features, especially after the Brexit process. The departure of the United Kingdom from the Common Market has translated into less free-marketeer input in supranational decision making, as well as less liberal ideas in the EU's economic governance in general. It has serious consequences for the map of various types of economic systems inside and outside the EU. The authors observed a reconfiguration of the 'poles' that has salient implications for the economic convergence dynamics in Europe. An increasing shift towards the Coordinated Market Economy (CME) type of management has been observed in the Common Market in recent years, marked with the 'polycrisis' stigma. Inside the Union, the proportions seem to have changed in favour of CME, which is applicable in most MS, especially when measured by 'economic weight'. Yet still, this increased convergence in the modes of economic coordination does not necessarily translate into less diversity among the EU's Member States as regards the propensity to integrate within the EU. Observably, the EU's common policies tend to follow more and more CME-esque logic, which is not surprising since it is the prevalent system in the most influential, EU core countries. On the other hand, there is a second set of countries, composed mostly of the new eastern MS where neoliberal transitions have shaped regimes in that which are more similar to the Anglo-American LME ideal. In such light, the growing disparity and differentiation remains a salient issue to be conceptualized.

The authors, in this book, also deal with the problem of European differentiation in the face of complex interdependencies and constantly emerging crises. Overlapping crises (or polycrises) have become much more than a contextual variable in analysing the process of European integration. Since the moment of their inception, the crises hit the European Communities, and then the European Union. First and foremost, the trauma of the Second World War laid the foundations for the European unification process in general. Then, a series of cascading crises were experienced – e.g., the 'empty chair' crisis in the 1950s, and the Euro-sclerosis in 1980s. In the more recent times of the 21st century, we have collectively witnessed an economic crisis, Crimea-related crises, migration crises, Brexit turbulences, COVID-19 lockdowns and pandemic-related restrictions, and, last but not least, the Russian aggression against Ukraine, which started in 2014 but exploded into a full-scale conflict in 2020. Russia and its aggressive behaviour cannot be treated as just another source of crisis. Moscow is one of the most constant challenges for Europeans to overcome in their attempts to unite. In a broader historical horizon, one could say that it could also act as potential stimuli for unification projects. More than 100 years ago, an Austrian-Italian thinker named Richard Coudenhove-Calergi postulated a 'United States of Europe', not only being inspired and impressed by the American example, but predominantly because of the Eastern threat in the form of the then Soviet Russia. This remains a factor to this day – Russia is an important push factor in the pro-integration attitudes of many Europeans, especially those directly exposed to the East, such as the Baltic states or Poland, or, more recently, Ukraine. From a Russian perspective, the success of the European integration project is an existential threat. It demonstrates to Russian citizens some alternatives to the despotic rulings in Moscow. Even the accession of Ukraine, and its potential success in a political and economic sense, is something that Russia could not tolerate nor afford. For the same reason, Russia supports any political actor (such as, for example, Viktor Orbán), who acts against the European unity, or indeed any progress of the European integration project (Snyder 2019, p. 14).

Among all the crises that Europe has experienced recently, it is Brexit that has contributed the most to sharpening the discussion about flexible forms of integration and a new formalizing of European differentiation. It has stretched the circles of external differentiation, and, as a consequence, even more differentiation is foreseen, anticipated, or maybe even expected. Moreover, the differentiation between a political core-Europe working ever-closer together and a periphery of hesitant members that may join the core at any time is not only a temporary phenomenon. European differentiation is not merely about accommodating increasingly heterogeneous preferences and interests – about *politics* and *policies* – it is also about *polities* and the political order. The structural-institutional make-up of the system and its constitutional fundaments affect the statuses of integrating states and citizens. The system of European differentiated integration creates a situation without applying the same laws to all affected. In the normative vision of a united Europe, a differentiated order in which not all are subject to the same rules and in which different sections are governed by different rules can be in breach of the principles of equality before the law, giving rise to arbitrary interference (Eriksen 2019, pp. 4–5). Despite all these risks, differentiated integration is still treated as a legitimate vehicle of Europe's unification project. Integration is seen in this view as an overall imperative, with differentiation being the instrument to realize it. And the lack of a realistic alternative is fuelling the differentiated integration progress. Any return to Europe of independent states would – under the current circumstances of cascading interdependence – proliferate problems and inter-state conflicts, it would increase transaction costs and negative externalities as well as making it harder to deliver positive balance in any other form of collaboration. The system of differentiated integration is far from perfect, but it is closer to optimal (bearing in mind what is realistic), and core-Europe became the European integration trendsetter and pace-maker. One of the most fundamental issues which add to the dynamism of differentiation is a lack of clarity with regard to what the European integration project is ultimately meant to achieve. Being an open-ended process, it leaves enormous room for manoeuvre for flexible solutions in the space between minimalist inter-governmentalism and more federal supranational ambitions. The EU joins what alternatively – by itself – would have been naturally separated. It binds 27 countries (and a good number of neighbouring states) to a common framework that abolishes interstate aggression, which is vitally important to remember in the context of the heated conflict in Ukraine. It promotes tight cooperation in the building of an economic and political union. On this path to an 'ever closer union', differentiated integration 'disjoins' what should be – by the logic of uniform integration – united. And, at the same time, it keeps the whole system of multiple overlapping groupings together, despite its growing heterogeneity (Eriksen 2019, p. 259).

What is more interesting is that an in-depth analysis of the ways some economies are converging reveals some salient differences. They are most spectacular in the case of some post-communist economies, in this study represented by Poland, the largest state of the EU's eastern flank. After the turbulent post-1989 transformation that was conducted in the spirit of a neoliberal paradigm, the formerly centrally planned economies also incorporated some elements of the CME system. Nonetheless, it does not imply that they subsequently became more similar to the CME that is represented in this analysis by Germany. Even in the case wherein one or a group of parameters suggest an increasing role of the state in the coordination mechanism, it is crucial to interpret them in a particular context as well as conduct an in-depth qualitative analysis that allows an exploration of the full picture of the post-communist economies. The market economy institutions are built in a substantially different way in the post-communist world and, for example, a larger state presence in an economy – which would be typical for the *Rhein model* – may not contribute to more coordinated and inclusive growth, but rather contribute to the development of political patronage and clientelist relations. This could possibly lead to the creation of a distorted, 'illiberal' type of CME.

The European integration system is organized along various levels, each of which coordinates the functions that are performed at this level. Earlier DI literature concentrates on the *legal-institutional* (and – to some extent – political) aspects that generate differentiation. In this meaning, the EU Member States form the core of the European unification system, whereas the non-members form the peripheries. Both the core and peripheries can be divided into sub-categories. The inner core is comprised of states that integrate more deeply, more quickly, and participate if not in all then certainly in most of the EU's policies (including, for example, the final stage of the European Monetary Union). The outer core includes a group of EU Member States that either temporarily or permanently do not participate in the fastest and deepest circle of integration. They take advantage of numerous opt-outs, abstentions, transitional periods, and other forms of differentiation. The periphery is also structured into two sub-groups. One, the inner periphery, consists of states that perform 'integration without membership' – they are formally non-members, but *de facto* they can be described as quasi-members who participate – in an opt-in logic – in most of the EU's policies, including most of the Common Market legislation. Such a status allows them access to the Single Market; at the same time (politically speaking) they are not fully bound by the gravitational pull of Brussels. The outer periphery consists of countries that circulate on an even more distant orbit of European integration. They are not legally bound by any legal-institutional solution such as the European Economic Area (EEA) or *Bilaterale* agreements, and at the same time their geo-economic position makes them interlinked with the Common Market in a substantive way.

The divisions inside the European Union can also be, and quite often are, framed as 'core-periphery relations' (Magone 2008, p. 237; Magone et al. 2016; Gräbner & Hafele 2020; Magone 2020; Riedel 2023a, p. 296). Nevertheless, without neglecting such formulations, the authors position their study in the DI literature, which tends to define all the EU members as the core, and all the neighbouring states as peripheries. The nuances of gaps and divisions within these two groups are captured within the labels of *inner* and *outer* core as well as *inner* and *outer* periphery. The authors are fully aware that there are plenty of other ways of conceptualizing the centre-periphery relations inside and outside of the Union. Nonetheless, for the purpose of obtaining a better understanding of the system of European differentiated integration, they have used the vocabulary of the mainstream literature of the subject field.

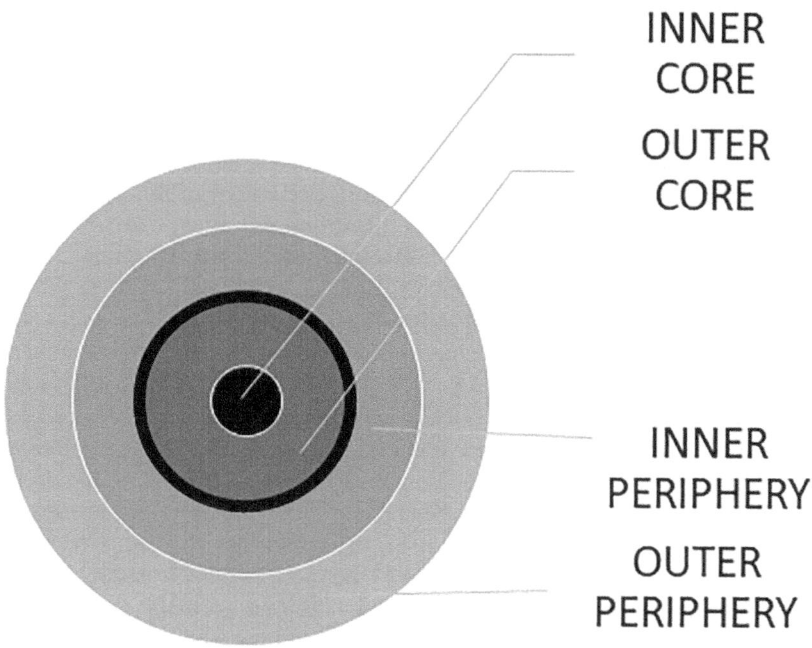

Source: Authors' own elaboration.

Figure 1.1 *The core-periphery model of the EU*

In consequence, the case selection of the four countries representing the critical cases from inside and outside the European Union follows the logic of integrative circles. Germany represents the *inner core* of the European integration process (as a founding member, participating in most supranational policies, and opting for deeper integration). This holds all the more since the 2021 elections, which were won by the liberal-green-social democratic coalition led by Olaf Scholz. The *outer core* is represented by Poland – the largest new EU Member State that participates only in some EU policies and shows, at least under Jarosław Kaczyński's leadership, clear and increasing scepticism towards Brussels and any idea of further *communitarization.* Next, there is Switzerland – formally a non-member and a special case of 'integration without membership' representing the *inner periphery* of European integration. Last but not least, the United Kingdom represents a special category of a former member that circulates on a more and more distant trajectory vis-à-vis the EU, and constitutes a critically important case of the *outer periphery.* What is of vital importance for this analysis is that these four cases represent not only various positions on the map of European differentiated integration, but also represent different instances of the varieties of capitalism. Consequently, through a cross-case study analysis, the authors explore how the socio-economic complementarities of specific types of capitalism constitute the 'tectonic plates' of the system of European integration differentiation.

The ideal types, also defined as poles, are represented by the German (a coordinated social market in the EU's inner core) and British (the outer periphery's free-market) economies. The Polish economy will serve as an example of an outer core case struggling to converge towards the coordinated social-market economy mainstream. And Switzerland, with its liberal economic governance model, will act as an illustration of the inner periphery of the European differentiated integration system. The economic poles, as defined in the varieties of capitalism literature, will also be treated as a subject of permanent evolution. Not only do the peripheral economies 'move' closer or further towards specific poles, but the poles also change their place on the map of economic governance. These moves are understood by the authors as the aforementioned tectonic plates' shifts, which affect the system of differentiated integration that is built upon them. The general assumption behind the research idea to be explored in this research endeavour claims that the type of market economy a specific state develops is crucial for its position in the system of differentiated integration. This is important both internally – as regards the mode of coordination, e.g., in industrial relations or social welfare systems – and also externally; it spills over to and affects relations with its economic partners.

As such, this publication employs the political economy perspective, or – as some would say – the new political economy perspective. What is new in the new political economy? A general definition suggests that it is the study of the intersection of politics and economics. Though such a vague definition may have the virtue of being all-inclusive since it does not really give a sense of what is being studied. If economics is the study of the optimal use of scarce resources, political economy begins with a study of the political nature of decision making and is concerned with how politics may affect economic choices in a broadly understood society (Drazen 2000, p. 5). Since the intense debates about the globalization of the world's economy began more than four decades ago, the demise of the nation-state has been widely predicted. But, whenever political passions and nation-state politics have collided with economic rationality in the last 200 years, political passions and the nation-state have won (Drucker 1997). Political economy is one of the fastest growing fields in studying international relations with the gravity point being on either their political or economic realm. The new generation of political economy deals with the conceptual link between political institutions and economic choices, outcomes, consequences, and vice versa. With this publication, the authors intend to contribute to the conceptual discussion of the corelations between economic interdependencies in some clusters of economies and how they constitute the tectonic plates for the map of differentiated integration. This is why they have employed the typologies of varieties of capitalism trying to grasp the aspects of divergence (institutional complementarities) that are considered crucial to the ways in which advanced economies are regulated. This stream of studies concentrates on the theoretical problems in order to explain cross-national differences in economic policies and performance. The authors intend to shed some light on the processes in which the outcomes are shaped by, or embedded in, previously existing institutions and other factors, such as economic determinants and political interests or ideas. In particular, they test the compatibility of the states' types of capitalism with the mainstream economic governance in the EU. Interestingly enough, the Common Market is considered to be a *Thatcherite* – thus British – project to a large extent. From the moment of its creation to this very day, it remains the most advanced free trade agreement on a global scale (Applebaum 2020, p. 81). And – paradoxically – it is Britain that decided to leave it, predominantly for political reasons and against her economic interests. The key aspect is the incompatibility of the British version of capitalism with its continental counterparts, as well as the mainstream economic solutions dominating the European Union.

The authors' research design explains the concentric circles of European differentiated integration as a dependent variable, and the independent variables to be employed in their explanations consist of socio-economic parameters nested in the varieties of capitalism and institutionalist theorizing. This means embracing its key areas of interest: corporate governance, industrial relations, and the education and training regime. Such an interdisciplinary approach enriches the existing scholarship on European integration studies on the system of differentiation with an in-depth application of the political economy perspective. So far, the economic factors determining European differentiated integration have been integrated into research designs only in a minimalist way (e.g., income levels alone). Authors who attempted to unpack the mechanisms of the differentiation system predominantly analysed political factors as the sources of DI. An example of such a political variable is the level of

Eurosceptism in a given country. In their research framework, such a variable is placed rather as an element of the dependent variable (DI), which the authors operationalize in a multi-dimensional way. Thus, in their optics, it is treated rather as an outcome (the degree of integration). For example, both the Czech Republic and Hungary are located on the outer core of the EU, but – in their approach – the Hungarian society's and its elites' negative attitude towards the EU places the country on a more remote part of the same circle (Anusik & Riedel 2023). Beyond these discursive factors (such as attitudes towards the EU, both of the society and of the political elites), the authors mostly model DI by considering the scope of the legal-institutional differentiation of the countries of interest. This is usually operationalized on the basis of legal opt-ins and opt-outs on the level of primary and secondary law.

In other words, the authors seek to test whether the institutional complementarities of economic systems explain the position of specific states on the legal-political map of differentiated integration in Europe. As such, this study connects the two streams of academic literature that deal with two sides of one coin, namely, the European integration process (and in particular its differentiation) and the varieties of capitalism which provide the explanatory variables of the research. This analysis contributes to the better understanding of differentiated integration by employing economic determinants into the research design. At the same time, it revitalizes the varieties of capitalism scholarship, not only by connecting a post-communist state into the equation, but also by updating the empirical material after the Brexit referendum, and – last but not least – by cross-fertilizing it with the European integration studies. Such an inclusive interdisciplinary approach will allow us to meet at the crossroads of various interconnected scientific discourses, including the literature on differentiated European integration, varieties of capitalisms, as well as some other related debates, e.g., dependent capitalism, centre-periphery relations, development studies, or middle-income-trap literature.

A differentiated integration approach provides us with suitable conceptual tools for capturing adequately what is presently unfolding in Europe. The scope and magnitude of Europe's political, institutional, cultural, social economic, ethnic, and linguistic diversity is profoundly shaping and conditioning the integration process. The more the diverse states and economies are tied together, the more their diversity will be drawn into and reflected in the integration process. Member States have different socio-economic systems and governing philosophies – which implies that the greater the amount and range of Member State input, the more difficult it is for the EU to reconcile these. Increased differentiation entails increased contestation over which socio-economic model to prioritize, and at what level of the multi-level system it should be concentrated (Batora & Fossum 2020, pp. 1–21). In structural terms, the combination of institutions and procedures as well as resources suggests that the specific socio-economic segments may vary considerably in terms of institutional arrangements.

The growing body of European integration literature claims that the European Union has become more diverse as part of a transition from time-bound or temporary differentiation to more permanent differences in European integration. This differentiation also includes ideas, ideologies, or values related to the organization of the economy in each of the states participating in the European integration process. This is why, in this publication project, the authors connect the stream of research dedicated to differentiated integration and the varieties of capitalism. It allows us a better understanding of the relations between the position of specific states on the map of differentiated integration, and the model of capitalism they perform. This interactive relationship that is at the centre of interest of this publication does not exist in vacuum. Indeed, it is quite the opposite; it evolves in various important contexts, and one of the most important is the cumulative crises that Europe has been facing in the past years and decades. The EU, along with the whole of Europe that has emerged from the crises, has become increasingly differentiated. In a sense, a unified Europe crossed the red line of differentiation, and, in the end, the main assumption of differentiated integration was that all movements are in the same direction. Brexit was the strongest wake-up call reminding us that post-crisis Europe is experiencing disintegrative pressures. The crises-driven EU exhibits increased structural differentiation in combination with a highly focused and ideologically driven crisis response (Batora & Fossum 2020, p. 8). The overlapping crises overshadow one another, to the extent that their consequences and implications mix and blur. For example, conventional wisdom lays the blame for the Eurozone crisis on the absence of an optimum currency area in the EU economy. However, some more recent revisionist arguments stress the absence of a common sense of shared social and economic purpose (Tranoy & Schwartz 2020, p. 67) among the parties participating in the European integration process. A system of uniform rules and rule-based policies cannot be applied effectively to a variegated economy on the continental scale. The defining feature of the European segmented political and economic order is that each segment is imbued with a specific repertoire of ideas and ideological predispositions that uphold the given segment's cognitive closure (Batora & Fossum 2020). Because such a segmented order is not a state-like structure, it lacks the magnitude and scope of territorial control across a broad range of functional spheres. As a result, one can observe a variety of socio-economic models spread across the European continent, representing not only various parameters, but also diversified institutional arrangements. With this publication, the authors intend to contribute to the developing debate on differentiated European integration with a political economy perspective. They believe that the book will offer scholars and other observers some valuable insights into the most contemporary developments in European integration, seen as a process that takes place in a particular context of cumulative crises. In this analysis, the authors concentrate on the crises of the 21st century – the time horizon is set mostly on the so-called *big bang* enlargement of 2004 (and the subsequent waves of EU expansion in 2007 and 2013), which makes it possible to go beyond an exclusively Western European context, and also include in the analysis some new Member States from the region of Central and Eastern Europe, namely Poland – the largest country and economy of the EU's eastern flank. Such temporal scope conditions cover: the economic and financial crisis (2008–2012), the migration and refugee crisis (2015), Brexit (2016–2021), the rule of law crisis (ongoing since 2015) which is a consequence of the so-called 'illiberal turn' that some of the European Union Member States took in recent past years, and onwards to the most contemporary crises generated by the COVID-19 pandemic and its related restrictions (2020–2022). During the research process, another great crisis erupted, in the form of the Russian aggression against Ukraine (2022). While the authors acknowledge the importance of this crisis for the European integration project – in military, humanitarian, geopolitical, political, and economic terms – this analysis does not cover it. The reasons are twofold. Firstly, this crisis is still ongoing, and therefore too fresh to be systematically captured in the type of analysis that is provided in this monograph. Secondly, the empirical data on which the statistical analysis is based refer to the most contemporary available data sets updated in 2022/2023, therefore they do not cover the crises related to the war in Ukraine.

Prior to DI becoming recognized as a systemic feature of the EU, the general assumption about the future of European integration was that Member States would integrate at a different pace (the differentiated integration of a multi-speed Europe), but they would all more or less end up at the same destination. Post-crises – or even during the polycrisis – it has become apparent that the EU is less capable of pulling together towards an 'ever closer union'; its future development is far more open-ended than before (Batora & Fossum 2020, p. 2). The new, evolving situation requires intense scientific investigation that will enhance our collective knowledge about its determinants and dynamics.

Consequently, this publication project aims to contribute to the state of research on the political economy of DI in Europe, as well as to integrate various perspectives on it while explaining the dynamics and determinants of the growing differentiation in Europe. This multi-factor analysis leads to the contribution of some insights into the four overarching sets of research questions, the first of which is: What drives and determines differentiation both inside the EU and on its peripheries? Secondly, what are the dynamics of this differentiation? Thirdly, how have the driving forces evolved so far? Fourthly, what are their current trajectories and where are they heading? This group of questions naturally addresses the problem of the trend and the expected implications of the growing differentiation as well as the risks and opportunities attached to it. Directly and indirectly, these questions are connected to the existing theories of international integration (from political science, economics, and other related disciplines) – how they can inform us about the various aspects of differentiated integration as well as how the new developments in European differentiation contribute to the existing theoretical debates (for further details, see the sections on literature review and methodology). A third group of questions is connected with the grand explanatory variables identified in the studies on differentiated integration: time, subject matter, and actors. How (and why) do the various countries, i.e., EU Member States and non-members, integrate differently? Is time (in the longer or shorter term) an explanatory variable and how does it matter? Historically, the evidence shows that differentiation accelerated at some periods and slowed down at others, and that some countries were more integrated whereas some others were much less so, and, finally, that some sectors get integrated more easily whereas some others carry some serious integrative problems. Finally, there is a group of questions concentrating on the nature of differentiation and its consequences for the continuity of the European integration project as such. Has differentiation reached a point at which it carries the potential for disintegration? What does it mean for the supranational institutional architecture? Is there a specific EU Member State strategy as regards the increasing differentiation? How do various forms of differentiation correlate with the various forms of capitalist economies present in the EU Member States?

The above-stated questions are addressed in detail at various stages of this scientific enquiry, using diversified methodologies. They form a complex research problem that has not yet been resolved in a sufficient way. Most of the ongoing investigations in the field are trapped within the boundaries of a single discipline. This publication project proposes the integration of various disciplinary approaches, which has not been delivered satisfactorily to date. In the international literature, only a limited number of studies try to integrate diversified perspectives and they do it in a rather narrow and modest way (De Neve 2009). The European Union, by its characteristics, is an object of scholarly attention that is 'naturally interdisciplinary'. This is why it is investigated by economists, lawyers, political scientists, Europeanists, sociologists, and many other representatives of social scholarships (Riedel 2023a). In addition, integrative approaches are quite common (Puchala 1972).

Featuring interdisciplinary research, the authors have drawn together recent developments in the evolution of European integration differentiation, i.e., its dynamics and determinants. Thus, this book provides a multi-dimensional perspective, starting with a critical literature overview of European differentiated integration, then moving on to an analysis of varieties of capitalism scholarship – both the classical approaches and the more contemporary perspectives. While explaining the dynamic background of the multiple crises that have affected the EU in the 21st century, the empirical heartland of the publication is focused on four countries (Germany, Poland, Switzerland, and the United Kingdom) representing critical cases from inside and outside the European Union.

The research methodology applied in this project is subordinated to predefined objectives and questions. This explorative study requires outsourcing the full explanatory potential of the methodological tools. Taking into account the high dynamics of the union building process as well as its novel character, the methods need to adequately reflect the nature, novelty, and complexity of the analysed object. At the same time, the theoretical-methodological approach needs to be rooted in the established and recognized methodological tools present in the field. Therefore, the methods used partially derive from the scholarly tradition present in similar studies (Riedel 2016), but their innovative and integrative nature go beyond mainstream approaches. Due to the relatively wide scope of project, along with the integrity of the research methodology with the stated goals, specific research questions have been carefully taken into account throughout the research process. In line with the best practices of the art (Mahoney & Goertz 2006), a careful application of the mixed methods is going to be applied. The majority of the analysed determinants are operationalized in the form of parameterized variables that allow for a multi-factor analysis measuring the strength and importance of the determinants in question. The mixed-methods approach is justified from the point of view of the interdisciplinary perspective (political, social, economic), which is the main characteristic of this research project (Puchala 1972).

The authors' research project positions itself at the crossroads of political and economic dynamics and determinants and will require both a quantitative and qualitative methodological toolbox. Quantitatively, the authors mostly explore statistical data outsourced from available databases. It is used predominantly as descriptive statistics to capture the trends, correlations, and causality between selected socio-economic parameters and factors. Qualitatively, they approach the political dimension of European differentiation. Apart from a critical analysis of the secondary sources, a textual analysis is provided – necessary when dealing with documents, including selected elements of discourse analysis (e.g., framing). Such method triangulation guarantees a high-quality, multi-dimensional analysis that will be concluded in a form of comparative study examining the state of European differentiation as well as the evolutionary trajectories of the Member States' economic systems from a political-economy perspective.

The structure of the book proceeds as follows: firstly, this introductory chapter sets up the research design of the whole publication project, describes the background, explains the research questions, and presents the undertaken approach. It introduces the main theoretical concepts to be used, as well as presents the methodological declaration. It also serves as an opportunity to position the presented book project in the wider literature of the discipline. In the conceptual chapters, the authors introduce the VoC literature into the deliberations on differentiated integration. With such a theoretical background, they approach four case studies represented by countries positioning themselves on the four various orbits of the European DI system. The comparative chapter connects not only the two streams of literature but allows one to identify the similarities and differences between the four states in question. The authors wrap up the journey through the overlapping maps of DI and VoC in the concluding chapter, in which they sum up their deliberations and connect them with wider debates of the field.

2 Exploring the crossroads of 'united in diversity' and varieties of capitalism

2.1 THE THEORY AND PRACTICE OF DIFFERENTIATED INTEGRATION IN EUROPE

Differentiated integration (DI) in Europe has always accompanied the process of political and economic unification. Under various slogans, such as 'flexible integration' or 'multi-speed Europe', this feature of the European integration process has been present both in academic deliberations and on the ground in real life, so to speak. At the same, time it raises controversies and sparks vibrant debates about its sources, characteristics, mechanisms, and implications. In scholarly discourse it is rather treated as a neutral phenomenon that needs to be explained, possibly without much normative bias. It is natural that the growing number of more and more deeply integrated states and economies will result in a greater variety of integration modes. Despite the general associations with the European Union (EU) as a standardization vehicle, the Union offers a rich variety of integration outcomes. These outcomes need to be investigated and explained in order to better understand the nature of the integration process as such.

Moreover, this flexibility that can be observed in the European integration process is dynamic and, in various time periods, the authors identify more or less differentiation. Due to the fact that it was the United Kingdom that accumulated the majority of the differentiation cases, the post-Brexit era is characterized by less differentiation compared to the times when London struggled for its opt-outs as an EU-member. This provides a new perspective on European differentiated integration, since the absence of the UK opens some new horizons for differentiation – both internal (intra-EU), and external (beyond the circle of the EU). This is specifically salient from an economic point of view, because Britain represents the type of capitalism that is labelled as that of a liberal market economy (LME) and it promoted this model in various instances and occasions when it was a member of the Single Market. After Brexit, the coordinated market economy (CME), which dominates in continental Europe, lost any counterbalance in the scale of the Union. This brings about serious consequences for the evolution of the default economic model for the entirety of the Common Market. As such, it is also important for the system of differentiation, because economy type is an important predictor of the specific position of the country on the map of differentiated integration. Brexit consolidates the EU in terms of internal differentiation, and at the same time it expands the circles of external differentiation by bringing about less differentiation inside and more differentiation outside of the Union. The EU without the UK is an EU without the greatest proponent of differentiation. So, in the face of no new treaties, no new enlargements (that used to be the 'moments of differentiation'), and no UK, it means less space for differentiation, at least in the legal meaning of this word.

Historically speaking, rounds of enlargements used to be the main drivers of differentiation in the EU. The most important event that generated most of the treaty-level differentiation was the Eastern enlargement. However, it is true only when one adds up the legal cases of differentiation opportunities, and it does not reflect the economic gravity of specific differentiation cases. It rather reflects the fact that the Eastern enlargement consisted of a big number (almost half of today's Member States: ten in 2004, two in 2007, and one in 2013) of small, relatively poor and incompatible countries. In this sense, DI can be treated as an enlargement tool which helps new Member States to synchronize with extant Member States. Or, in other words, it is a mechanism of keeping the new, less wealthy, lower-capacity Member States out of the inner core.

Differentiation is also not a big thing quantitatively: 6–7% of treaty articles are not implemented uniformly, and 3–4% of the legal acts contain some cases of differentiation in the case of secondary legislation. And the long-term trend, where legislation is concerned, is actually towards less differentiation. Bearing in mind the growing number of laws and the growing number of Member States, proportionally less differentiation is observed over time. The countries associated with most of the differentiations were the UK and Denmark, with London being clearly dominant. Paying attention to the economic burden of Britain, it is legitimate to say that the UK stands (or stood) behind most of the differentiation.

Even before Brexit, Schimmelfennig et al. (2015) underlined that the EU as a system of differentiated integration has two vectors of differentiation. On the one hand, there is the existing vertical differentiation which manifests itself by the means in the levels of centralization, but there's also a variation in territorial extension known as 'horizontal' differentiation. 'Differentiation has been a concomitant of deepening and widening and has increased and consolidated as the EU's powers, policy scope, and membership have grown' (Schimmelfennig et al. 2015, p. 766). Turning to an explanation, these authors attribute the figure of differentiated integration in the EU to the interrelation of interdependence and politicization. According to Leuffen et al. (2013), polities can be conceptualized as a three-dimensional configuration of authority. This level of centralization manifests itself in the following manner: first of all, the level of centralization has to be pre-existing, because polities that monopolize authoritative decisions in the centre have a maximum level of centralization, whereas decision-making authority dispersed across a multitude of actors indicates a low level of centralization. In addition to the first condition, the functional scope varies between authority over a single issue and authority over an entire range of policies. Many countries are loosely integrated with the EU both horizontally and vertically. Vertical differentiation refers to policy areas that integrated at various speeds and reached various levels of centralization over time, whereas horizontal differentiation means that many integrated policies are neither uniformly nor exclusively valid in all EU Member States (Schimmelfennig et al. 2015, pp. 764–782). For example, the UK did not participate in all EU policies (horizontal differentiation) but in some others it did – while still a member – at its own speed and extent (vertical differentiation).

There is plenty of outstanding scholarship that has significantly enriched our knowledge on differentiated integration in Europe. However, they all take a different focus than the study offered in this book. An excellent study by Frank Schimmelfennig and Thomas Winzen (2020) focuses on the inherent legal and institutional aspects. They address the state, dynamics, and determinants of European integration differentiation based on sophisticated theoretical models. Schimmelfennig and Winzen's works provides a comprehensive conceptual, theoretical, and empirical analysis of differentiation in European integration, but they place emphasis on explaining differentiation in EU treaties and secondary legislation and focus on differentiated integration as a legal instrument that the European governments use regularly to overcome integration deadlock in EU treaty negotiations and legislation. Their book shows that differentiated integration has facilitated the integration of new policies, new members, and even non-members, and it has been mainly 'multi-speed' and inclusive – most differentiations end after a few years and do not discriminate against Member States permanently (Schimmelfennig & Winzen 2020).

Other studies, such as the edited volume by Gänzle et al. (2019) and a monograph by Duttle (2016) are also key contributions to differentiated integration research. They take into account the Brexit factor; however, their focus is much more on assessing the consequences of Brexit on EU policies, institutions, and members. This is a different emphasis compared to the authors' project, which explores the varieties of capitalisms (VoC) that are important factors in explaining the European integration differentiation dynamics. Other contributions also discuss the significance of differentiation for the future of European integration, nevertheless they are usually written from a pre-Brexit perspective. None of the pre-existing studies makes the leap from analysing legal or institutional aspects of differentiation and dive deep into specific polities exploring specific VoC and important economic determinants salient for the European politics of the selected countries. This study is the first to focus specifically on VoC as the important factors in explaining the dynamics and specificities of European integration differentiation.

The European system of differentiated integration developed organically as a pragmatic response to the gridlocks, risks, and turbulences that challenge the European integration process. Differentiation has become a way of holding together a dynamic system in times of cumulative crises. Handling the system does not come without costs and consequences, however – various statuses of EU membership (internal differentiation) and non-membership (external differentiation) affect identities and power structures as well as the integrity and viability of the EU. Many politicians fight against supranationalism and opt for more differentiation in the name of freedom and democratic self-rule. Nonetheless, the consequences of what seems to benefit sovereignty and independence can, in fact, lead to the very opposite (Eriksen 2019). Differentiation is not merely an innocent instrument for handling conflicts and tensions stemming from growing heterogeneity. Flexibility and differentiation may work as a way to strengthen the autonomy of the (non) Member States and citizens' self-rule up to a certain level, but only if they are applied smartly. Beyond the red line, disintegration starts, and the British case is highly illustrative in showing the limits of differentiated integration. Some observants speculate that the EU actually needs more flexibility to revitalize itself, some others claim that it is almost conditional that the EU embraces greater differentiation, or it will face potential disintegration. Yet some others criticize European differentiation for creating unequal statuses not only among the (non) Member States but also, and somewhat more problematically, among its citizens (equal freedom for all – as the first principle of the self-ruling republican polity). When a state's subjects do not have the same rights and duties, and when different policy fields and groups of states are governed by different rules, there is a risk of legal uncertainty, chaos, arbitrary rule, and dominance. Asymmetries arising from differentiation translate into an asymmetric distribution of power and resources (Eriksen 2019, pp. 2–3). The systemic effects of European differentiation may lead towards segmentation and hegemony both inside and outside the EU. Segmentation appears when policy fields are selectively integrated, and hegemony occurs when one segment wields power over other units. The EU is not in itself a hegemon, but it may consolidate a hegemonic structure of power inside and outside. It occurs when one of the parties in a cooperative scheme has the power to arbitrarily modify the rights and duties of others. It may work directly through instructions, directives, or powerful constraints, or indirectly through removing the possibilities for actors to make free choices and decisions. Hierarchies become systems of domination when those affected are excluded from the decision-making process. The rules are unjust when they are subject to forms of rule that are arbitrary, non-transparent, and/or generally inattentive to democracy and legitimacy (Eriksen 2019, pp. 14–15 and 48).

Fancy metaphors about differentiated integration are floating around in political discourse. They are often used and misused with specific political connotations and are without much conceptual clarity or understanding. Multi-speed Europe suggests there is a group of pioneers and a group of stragglers. A core-periphery distinction suggests there is a group of core countries which strive to keep the peripheries out. Undoubtedly, differentiated integration in Europe has reached the very top of the agenda both in scientific and public discourses. Even though it has been present in the European integration project for decades, never before has it gained so much attention due to its saliency and dynamism. Brexit and the shift in French and German attitudes towards differentiation (namely becoming more open, permissive, accepting, and even welcoming) changed the 'ever closer Union' paradigm substantially. Britain's leaving of the EU widens the circles of integration, and, at the same time, the Franco-German engine is determined to deepen integration, and the two dynamics will most probably result in a new system of differentiation, unknown so far in the history of the European integration project.

Deeper integration creates more room for differentiation. Some scholars even see the history of European integration as a story of its deepening and widening (Schimmelfennig & Winzen 2014). These two dynamics have found the mechanics of differentiation so far – consequently, the progress in integration meant an increase in differentiation over time. However, the most recent political and economic developments in the EU and beyond clearly show that differentiation gained its momentum, and its dynamics have accelerated (Gänzle et al. 2019), especially when we do not limit ourselves to the legal prism of understanding differentiation. Alexander Stubb's (1996) early and influential typology proposed the labels 'multi-speed', 'multi-tier', and 'multi-menu' differentiation. Multi-speed differentiation is determined by time, in which differentiation is a transitional, or temporary, phenomenon, converging towards uniformity in a definable period. Multi-tier differentiation is differentiation across space – it steadfastly distinguishes groups of states by their level of differentiation. Last but not least, multi-menu differentiation is structured by policies. In this particular differentiation form the depth of integration within each policy area is roughly uniform. The participating states vary, however, from policy to policy. Member States 'pick and choose' from the 'menu' of policies, and each state puts together its own set of 'courses'. Another important diversity in the DI typologies is the distinction between *de iure*, that is, legally codified differentiation, and *de facto* differentiation, resulting from a flexible and unequal implementation of, or informal cooperation beyond, legal obligations. *De facto* differentiations are much more difficult to measure than *de iure* differentiations, and *de facto* differentiations should be analysed from the point of view of their real implementation and not only how differently they are applied, but also what different (direct and indirect) consequences they bring forth.

Taking into consideration the above-mentioned diversity of flexibility in European integration, it needs to be recognized that differentiation also occurs in the implementation (transposition and practical application) of EU legislation by Member States. To the extent that EU law allows Member States to make choices during implementation – this creates another possibility to differentiate between Member States. This approach is called 'flexibility in implementation', as it entails EU law offering flexibility to Member States during times of implementation. When Member States make use of this flexibility, it results in actual patterns of 'differentiated implementation'. By giving Member States discretion during implementation, any differences between Member States can be taken into account (Princen et al. 2022).

This synthetic literature review shows that DI is not a simple process – actually a lot of variation in the various DI modes can be observed. Altogether, this diversity allows for a recognizing of the value of having various integration paths and paces and outcomes. In many cases, it is necessary to implement DI in order to achieve an effective approach to overcome contentious issues in a diverse EU. On the other side of the coin, it generates plenty of negative externalities, including the risk of too much variation – at the cost of a level playing field in the Common Market. Still, bearing in mind all its pros and cons, it is treated as the norm in contemporary Europe. Uniform integration is much more the ideal, however, than the aforementioned norm in contemporary Europe. The vision in which all the agreed rules are uniformly adopted in all Member States is much more a legal doctrine than an actual practice.

2.2 EXAMINING THE DYNAMICS OF DIFFERENTIATION – CENTRE-PERIPHERY RELATIONS

There are many ways of analysing DI as a multifaceted phenomenon, from an analysis of primary and secondary law, through multilateral negotiations, up to and including party politics in domestic contexts. It can be studied as a phenomenon, concept, process, or as a system. The complexity and plurality of approaches is justified by the very nature of differentiated integration. In this chapter, the authors intend to intertwine the dynamic nature of DI with a broader debate on centre-periphery relations.

This system of differentiation is changing, but it is not a temporal characteristic of European integration. DI has become the dominating model of European integration in general. Further internal differentiation of the EU has become a structural and essential element of the development of European integration. At the same time, the fundamental core of EU reform revolves around the Eurozone. Membership of the Eurozone has a direct influence on the position of a state in the EU. The other important point of reference is the principle of democratic rule of law which is the basis for cooperation within the EU and its effectiveness (Barcz 2018, p. 21). At the same time, other sectoral policies exemplify *de iure* or *de facto* differentiation, e.g., the climate and environmental package.

Not only is the system of differentiation in Europe dynamic, it also reflects some characteristics of hierarchical order on a broader scale. Differentiation corelates with other ways of structuring international relations in general. It tackles the question of domination and hierarchies between and among states and their economies. Some groups of countries create rules and norms that are binding for others who do not participate in generating these rules. In other words – there are the producers and the receivers of specific regulatory frameworks. This features the relationship between the core and periphery, where the core is understood as a group of EU members, and the periphery as a cohort of EU non-members. At the same time, DI is an answer not only to the diversity of preferences but also to the diversity of capacities inside the EU. It allows one to overcome all these situations in which a number of the Member States are unable or unwilling to integrate further. It disables veto-players or laggards. A driving ambition of some Member States may not be blocked by the opponents from other Member States. An EU of concentric circles becomes a coalition of the willing and able.

As a scholarly concept, DI is a relatively new phenomenon in European studies (Andersen & Sitter 2006). It grew together with the growing saliency of real-life differentiation (opt-outs, exemptions, enhanced cooperation, constructive abstention, special clauses, additional protocols, etc.). In recent decades, differentiation has been a dominant feature of European integration (Börzel 2005). Studying differentiated integration undoubtedly contributes to a better and more refined theoretical and empirical understanding of the European integration process as such. Differentiated integration can be best understood as a legal and institutional response to the increasing heterogeneity of Member State preferences and capacities resulting both from the widening and the deepening of the EU (Leuffen et al. 2013; Schimmelfennig 2014). In the case of some countries (the UK being a good example) it is not the capacities but the *preferences* that keep them outside of the European core. They simply belong to the category of less willing countries, together with outsiders like the quasi-members – e.g., Switzerland. Some Member States opt out (internal differentiation), whereas some non-Member States opt in (external differentiation) which results in the need for reconciling heterogeneity inside and outside of the Union.

When looking at DI in a broader historical context, it is possible to identify the political idea of differentiation already in the famous Tindemans Report (1975), whereas as a legal concept it appeared in the Single European Act (1986). Academic debates on the topic find their roots in Dahrendorf's formulation of Europe à la carte (1970s). Already by the 1980s, scholars had identified several variations of differentiated integration, and the scientific discourse has exploded ever since. From that moment on, many various conceptualizations can be traced in the literature, including flexible integration, a multi-speed Europe, Europe as an empire, a Europe of variable geometries, concentric circles, hemispheres, etc. (Jensen & Slapin 2012, De Neve 2009, Zielonka 2007, Kölliker 2001). Yet differentiated integration is understudied in comparison with the huge literature on integration as a whole. The reason for that may be because it has been limited by an assumption that differentiated integration would erode over time (Leruth & Lord 2015), that Member States (and their neighbourhood) would converge over time, and that the same variously applied policies would find their cohesive end. This assumption was, however, challenged by a series of cascading crises (Schimmelfennig 2024). A new assumption suggests that we are heading towards some more diversified forms of integration. It is John Eric Fossum who claims that the EU of tomorrow may combine all three of the following: accelerated integration for some, outright disintegration for others, and greater differentiation for the rest (Fossum 2015, pp. 799–815).

The idea that differentiated integration amounts to little more than a process of convergence on similar outcomes at different speeds seems increasingly questionable. Instead, the authors observed a growing consensus among observers and analysts that differentiated integration is a permanent organizational principle of the EU. The need to manage divisions or disagreements will not simply vanish (Leruth & Lord 2015, p. 754). The system of European integration is subordinated to the principle of differentiation, is in a permanent state of evolution, and adapts to any ongoing internal and external changes. Over the past decades, various forms of differentiation have been proposed in response to the (growing) heterogeneity among Member States in the EU. Differentiation is seen as a way to increase both the efficiency and the legitimacy of EU decision making in the face of the challenges raised by the increasingly diverse membership of the EU. One may anticipate three sources of variation within Europe: differences in institutional arrangements for making decisions common to all, differences in the integration of members and non-members to specific EU policies and institutions, and differences in assumptions of fact and value within particular policy segments (Lord 2020, p. 244). All three sources have become important with regard to the challenge of managing the incompatibilities of interests, will, and capacities to integrate. Integrating Europe can be described as a plurality of polities at different levels

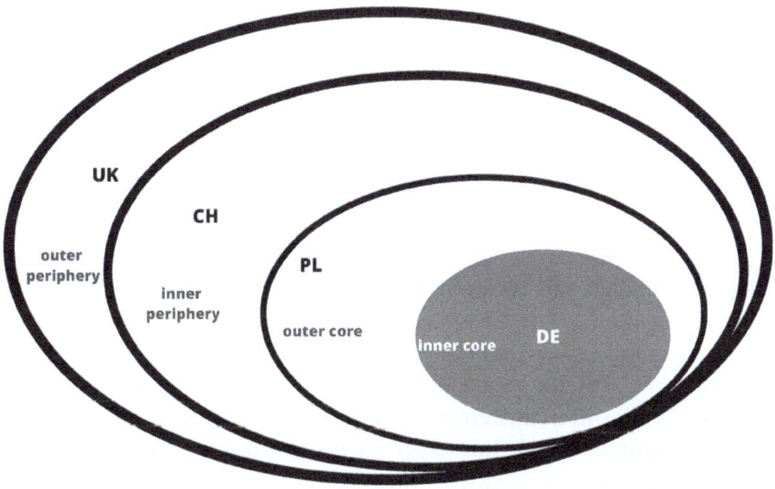

Source: Authors' own elaboration.

Figure 2.1 *A core-periphery model of differentiated European integration*

of aggregation. There are some important variations in the decision-making rules, practices, and outcomes of integration. Sometimes the Union merely and softly coordinates the preferences of its members, whereas sometimes it synchronizes the norms in a hard manner.

The conventional wisdom shared by historians of the European integration process claims that it evolves from one crisis to another. More precisely, it adopts in an evolutionary process to any emerging critical situations, be they external impulses or internal gridlocks. Even the founding fathers of the communities were convinced that 'Europe will be forged in crisis …' (Monnet 1976). Nonetheless, the observers of European integration would not agree that it constitutes more than the sum of the decisions taken during episodes of crisis. Bearing in mind the developments in past decades, one needs to take into account the cumulative nature of the crises – from the European Union's constitutional crisis, through the economic and financial crisis, the migration and refugee crisis, the Brexit critical juncture, up to the most contemporary crises generated by the pandemic and related restrictions and, finally, the rule of law crisis as a consequence of the illiberal turn that some of the European Union Member States have taken in recent years. On top of that, one cannot forget the so-called 'mother of all crises' which is the Russian aggression against Ukraine, which is beyond the temporal scope of this book. As the war is still ongoing, it is too early to judge its impact on the European system of differentiation.

Coming back to the intra-EU scale in analysing DI developments, one needs to recognize that it was Brexit that has triggered a novel process in European integration; namely, differentiated *disintegration* – the selective reduction of a Member State's level and scope of integration. Any attempt to evaluate the potential crisis impulse of Brexit as regards the European integration project, and in particular for differentiated integration, should start with the assumption that the UK was the first country to leave the EU, but the last of a long list of close neighbours and remote countries which have asked for preferential access to the Union's Single Market (Eisl & Fabry 2020). This means that the United Kingdom shifted from the sphere of internal differentiation to external differentiation. Over the years, the EU has developed a system of highly diverse modes of differentiated integration frameworks, corresponding to the specific momentum of the European integration project. While most of the existing studies focus on Brexit as the main milestone in the evolution of differentiated integration (Gänzle et al. 2019), the authors of this monograph offer a dynamic perspective in which Brexit itself is understood as a process which took place in a particular setting consisting of several determinants. While scholars have provided outstanding insights on the legal-institutional explanations of differentiated integration on the supranational level (Schimmelfennig & Winzen 2020), they still know little about the economic determinants that are critical for a better understanding of the process of differentiation.

Moreover, it is important to remember the historicity of differentiation's evolution. It was the Maastricht Treaty (1993) that brought about a serious deepening of European integration – it extended the EU's authority over a wide range of issues, made it much easier for people to work in another country, created a common currency, and turned nationals into EU citizens (Hooghe & Marks 2019, p. 113). The Europeans entered the 21st century in a totally renewed set of circumstances. Moreover, after 2004's big bang enlargement, the territorial and population width of united Europe expanded. This parallel instance of deepening and widening brought about more and more heterogeneity, and, as a consequence, more differentiation. At the same time, a series of crises were witnessed that were both the symptoms and syndromes of ongoing changes and the subsequent tensions that were generated. Furthermore, it is argued that the cascading crises actually strengthened the trend in differentiation. The crisis of 2008 intensified the process of creating a so-called 'multi-speed' European Union in the sphere of financial and fiscal policies. This policy model develops an increasingly visible hierarchy between the central and peripheral states. The central states are larger and stronger within the political system of the EU. However, in connection with the intensification of the integration processes and an increase in the number of participants and diversity, the European Union faces the threat of disintegration. At the same time, the application of flexible integration to the integration process is a necessity (Lasiewicz 2015, p. 100). There is widespread consensus among scholars originating from the Central and Eastern European region that crises impact development and disparities within the structure of the EU across various levels of its functions. As such, the crises have contributed to differentiations of the EU's policies. In some sense, this is contrary to the concept of European integration developed in the 1950s, which assumed that the EU Member States need to move forward at the same speed and demonstrate equal participation in integration projects. Crisis situations have contributed to the differentiation of the European Union. In order to fight a crisis, actions are taken which are aimed at preventing a crisis, such as the fiscal compact, but the potential outcome is the differentiation and fragmentation of the Union, the marginalization of supranational institutions, and the creation of a separate budget for the Eurozone. Consequently, the European Union is thus subject to numerous divisions and tensions (Lasiewicz 2015, p. 91). However, it is important to remember that differentiation does not create different unions – institutionally the EU remains uniform. It is a very limited number of narrow policy regulations which accommodate most of the differentiation cases. These are the so-called 'core-state powers', such as the monetary policy, foreign policy, or interior policies. Bearing in mind that the most important stances of differentiation position themselves in the domain of monetary policy and the Schengen Agreement, joining the Eurozone and Schengen Area practically qualifies a country to join the inner core.

When conceptualizing core-periphery relations, we tend to imagine them in a hierarchical way, and the hierarchies are often visualized as a pyramid. This pyramid depicts a small number of countries on the top, or, in other words, in the core. However, in the case of European differentiated integration, it is the opposite. The inner core consists of most of the EU Member States, and a relatively small number of (relatively small) countries that form the outer core or (semi) periphery. In this backdrop, Poland – which is one of the four cases examined in this study – positions itself in the outer core of the European integration system. Based on the legal-institutional criteria of differentiation, the deepest integrated inner core consists of 14 countries: Belgium, France, Germany, Italy, Luxembourg, Netherlands, Greece, Portugal, Spain, Austria, Finland, Estonia, Slovakia, and Slovenia. They represent very little differentiation in EU treaty articles and more variation in differentiated legislative acts. Its members tend to systematically participate in all key differentiated 'clubs' established under EU law (the Economic and Monetary Union, Schengen, PESCO, EPPO, etc.) and international law (the Fiscal Compact, the European Stability Mechanism, and NATO), with rare exceptions. The outer core is formed by seven countries, including Poland, and it exhibits a higher level of differentiation and internal variation, approximating the core in certain respects (e.g., EU law) but the periphery in others (e.g., international law) (Chiocchietti 2023, p. 15).

Certainly, there are a number of ways in which the core-periphery can be defined, and various states may be categorized as belonging to various groups depending on the criteria applied. Among the states selected in this analysis, it is generally recognized that the UK and Switzerland belong to the centre of global economy, but in the system of differentiated European integration they are qualified as being in the periphery. They chose not to belong to the group of EU members and therefore are seen as being outside the core. At the same time, some other countries – such as Poland for example – are defined as the (outer) core due to their EU membership. The Polish position in the global economy is relatively weaker than those of the Swiss or British, and therefore by many it is categorized as being semi-peripheral. Nonetheless, applying the standards of differentiated integration – which are at the heart of this analysis – one should consider Poland as the outer core of the European system of differentiation (as explained in the introduction). At the same time, the authors are fully aware of some different views present in the literature. A good illustration is Tomasz Zarycki's edited volume which consists of contributions in which various authors define Poland differently in the centre-periphery spectrum. While in Salvadore Babones's writing, the division between semi-peripheral and peripheral countries is important – and what is noteworthy, Poland is included in his text as semi-peripheral country. However, in Tomasz Grosse's concept (2016), Poland is treated as a peripheral country. In other places in Zarycki's edited volume, such categories as contact periphery, new periphery, and many other categorizations of periphery and semi-periphery appear. The criteria of such categorizations are salient. Tomasz Grosse in his text 'The Tragedy of Peripheral Countries, or Poland's Geopolitical Dilemmas in the European Union' performs a two-level analysis. Firstly, he identifies the most important threads of a theoretical discussion on the geopolitical role of peripheral countries. Secondly, he verifies the most important conclusions of this debate in relation to the Polish case. The pessimism contained in the title is intensified by the article's conclusions in which the author notes that participating in the process of European integration only strengthens Poland's peripherality (economic dependence, strategic inertia, and limited options in Europeanized public policies). Krzysztof Jasiecki ('The New Periphery in the Perspective of the Diversity of Capitalism. The Example of Post-Socialist European Union Countries'), in turn, refers to a part of the world literature devoted to the variety of capitalism and related discourses. Akin to Grosse's chapter, the one by Krzysztof Jasiecki is full of quite negative conclusions about the 'development drift' of Poland and other countries in the CEE region. In the other part ('Poland as Contact Peripheries'), the editor of the volume refers to a piece of work by Stein Rokkan and Derek Urwin (1983) which differentiates external and contact peripheries. The author polemicizes with politically articulated development concepts, both on the pro-core recognition of semi-peripheralism as a development ideal, and the anti-core idealistic pursuit of autonomy. Tomasz Zarycki concludes that Poland's location can be read as a contact point, and what is more, it is a contact point that generates definitely more negative tensions than positive. The Polish case exemplifies how many various ways a state can be categorized on the map of the centre-periphery relations, depending on the criteria applied. In this study, the authors have employed the European differentiated integration framework. It is undoubtedly dynamic in the sense that was described above, and is in contrast to some earlier paradigms, for example the thesis that is well-established in the literature (Wallerstein 1974) about the systemic rigidity of world hierarchies and rare cases of changes in the location of individual national economies in the core-periphery's structure.

2.3 MAKING SENSE OF THE POLITICAL ECONOMY APPROACH TO (DIFFERENTIATED) INTEGRATION IN EUROPE

Applying the political economy perspective to study the EU is not a new undertaking in European integration scholarship (Callaghan & Höpner 2005; Menon & Schain 2006). What is innovative in the proposed research volume can be summarized in two points, the first of which is that the new political economy perspective has never been applied to this problem in a comprehensive way (Laursen 1995). The vast majority of similar studies have been exclusively nested in political science or economic disciplinary boundaries (Keohane 2002), with few attempts made at integrating their methodologies and conclusions. The ambition of this scientific undertaking is to search the explanations at the crossroads of political and economic determinants (Riedel 2016). The authors' approach provides a truly cross-disciplinary analysis building bridges both on theoretical and methodological levels. By doing so, it provides a better understanding of the holistic picture of the multi-dimensional processes that cannot be fully explored when approached from a reductionist, single-disciplinary perspective (From & Sitter 2006). Secondly, this analysis focuses on contemporary 'state of the art', which goes beyond previously conducted studies that were historical in essence (Colomer 2011, pp. 395–411). In this research project, past developments provide an important historical background. However, the main gravity point is put on the present situation. Additionally, a predictive component is also included in the concluding part allowing for some forecasting and speculation about the future trajectories of the European integration project.

Moreover, the saliency and topicality of this problem stems from the uniqueness of the contemporary state of affairs in Europe (Börzel 2005). The series of crises and challenges that the EU, representing the Western world's norms and values, has been confronted with in recent times is totally unprecedented, and their cumulative nature creates a situation of a critical juncture (as understood in a historical institutionalism paradigm; see: Olsen 2010), starting with the economic crisis in 2007, followed by the outburst of illiberalism in the 2010s, the migration and refugee crisis of 2015, COVID-19 and the pandemic-related restrictions of 2020, and, last but not least, the Russian aggression against Ukraine in 2022 with the accompanying energy crisis. These have increased inflation and brought about many other related implications – and all these developments have overlapped – and their transformative power cannot be overestimated. This polycrisis, or quasi-permanent crisis, poses new circumstances for the Union. Therefore, the socio-economic developments are going to be analysed through the analytical prism of political economy (Bongardt & Torres 2022) in order to provide a full and sharp picture of the economic foundations that lay under the system of DI in Europe.

To study the political economy of the European system of differentiation, the authors plan to analyse the most critical elements of this process. Such a broad research agenda includes several interconnected dimensions, including a historical context, geopolitical background, and socio-political determinants. However, they intend to focus on the VoC (Zhang et al. 2022) that constitutes the critical aspect of the European differentiation as seen from the political economy perspective. The political economy approach implies a mixed-methods analytical framework. Originally, economics as a discipline was called political economy. Those studying it accepted outright that economic decisions are made in the political world. But today's new political economy is much more than a political context taken into account in an essentially economic analysis. It is the exploration of various processes and phenomena at the crossroads of political and economic determinants. Its utterly multi-disciplinary nature allows one to analyse the objects of investigation in their full complexity. This is why the intersection of economics and political science is highly productive in providing explanations to composite problems. From Adam Smith's *Wealth of Nations* in 1776, until at least John Steward Mill's *Principles of Political Economy* in 1848, what we now call economics was called 'political economy'. This terminology in large part reflected the belief that economics was not really separable from politics. And it was much more than an administrative classification of disciplines, it rather arose from the widespread view that political factors are crucial in determining economic outcomes. So the historical view is that political forces are not only influencing economic outcomes, they are often the determining influence (Drazen 2000, p. 3). More broadly, political economy examines the relationship between politics and the economy, and more precisely the effects of non-market institutions on the operation of markets. Applying the political economy perspective means exchanging theoretical vehicles, i.e., some elements of political science theories in the realm of economics, and vice versa (Regini 2006, p. 517).

Obviously, the authors could not proceed much further without being more precise about what they mean by the term 'politics'. In the political science discipline, politics is defined as the study of power and authority, and the exercise of power and authority. One of the most important observations in political economy is that actual policies are often quite different from optimal policies (the latter defined as being subject to technical and expertise-driven, but not political, constraints). The term 'political constraints' refers to constraints due to conflicts of interest and the need to make collective choices (Drazen 2000, p. 67). And since they are often far from cost-benefit calculations, non-rational choice explanations are deployed. On the other side of the coin, economic determinants are much more often incorporated into political science explanations with, however, the noticeable exception of studies on DI. If the economic rationale appears in European DI investigations, it is usually quite facile and perfunctory. Rarely does a thesis go beyond cursory statements such as: 'high-capacity, wealthy countries are more homogenous and instrumentally less differentiated'. This example illustrates a functionalist logic, and – this being important to notice – the most recent studies have actually leaned towards post-functionalism which features political factors even more, i.e., party preferences and identities becoming the drivers of differentiation. This means a return to classical political science explanations, and a move away from integrating and fine-tuning some economic variables.

Having said that, the authors do not question any statements that relate to economic rationale and that appear in the DI literature, such as: 'the richer the country is (GNI per capita), the less likely it is that it will experience discriminatory opt-outs' (more differentiation). The data confirm the above statement, but at extremally low levels of statistical significance. And such conclusions never connect to broader economic debates, an example being that one of the assumptions of the political economy of growth is that everything that rises must converge (Drazen 2000, p. 457). Such explanations connect to the authors' way of thinking about the political economy of DI in that the transaction costs are smaller in more homogenous groups of countries – therefore they are more likely to build an economy of scale, which should lead to less differentiation among them. This assumption lies the foundation of the authors' study, and at the same time it connects to the grand economic discourses, e.g., Marx-inspired claims stating that the economic structure of society is the real foundation on which arises a legal and political superstructure. Relationships of solidarity in Europe are established and based upon perceived differences between Member States and their populations, not only upon differences of income, of life chances, of welfare, or of economic growth, but also other differences, including the differences of power that constitute the differentiated space of Europe (Michailidou & Trenz 2020, p. 139). Segmentation consists in ideological variation in how problems and solutions are framed and understood within the same political order. It occurs when different policies within one polity depend on contrasting assumptions of fact and value about the economy, or society, or on different normative justifications or standards of validity (Lord 2020, p. 243).

Consequently, this study focuses on a largely neglected aspect of European DI studies, that is the comparative dimension of the EU's national economies across time and space. In past decades, the EU has evolved far beyond the standards of international organization, yet it is distant from the classical nation-state as we know it in the post-Westphalian version (Eilstrup-Sangiovanni 2006). Some scholars treat the EU as a *sui generis* supranational organization (Archibugi et al. 1998), some others see in it a quasi-federal governance structure (Radunz & Riedel 2024), yet some others claim it reached the stage of that of a regulatory state long ago (Majone 1994, p. 77). The European treaties promise an 'ever closer Union' with a clear suggestion that unification remains an open-ended process (Kölliker 2001) along with the promise of a converging trend.

The concepts used, similar to the standard ones exploited in the DI literature, range from the *Europe à la carte* metaphor, through a Europe of different speeds, concentric circles, differentiated geometries, up to the diversified hemispheres of integration. More and more analysts, experts, and academics claim that the observed increase in differentiation hit the limits in which it carries the potential for disintegration. And here the Brexit case returns to the spotlight – the British exemptions from the Eurozone and Schengen Area have already been quite prominent examples of differentiation (Schimmelfennig & Winzen 2019). But undermining one of the four freedoms (the free movement of people), which was the case in the (in)famous Brexit referendum, attacked one of the fundamentals, and questions the very idea of the European integration project. Openly opposing the very core of the Single Market changes the direction of Europe's integration trajectory (Riedel & Gierlich 2021), at least in the case of the UK.

In the political science discourse, the positive and negative aspects of DI are hotly debated. Very often they are labelled under the slogan of flexible integration or a multi-speed Europe. Critics of DI claim that it may lead to further divisions within the EU; Member States may not be treated equally. It seems unavoidable that some states will be 'in' or 'out'. All the more, it is hard to predict which 'in' or 'out' they would be, as many functional spheres of Member State cooperation could evolve. DI could dismantle solidarity, as those who become outsiders would not be able to take part in the core of the decision-making process. More DI would make the decision-making process even more complex than it is now. Structures within structures could arise, competencies would overlap, etc. Even federalists would not accept it (Grosse 2015) – they would prefer to have a transparent, coherent structure of the EU. On the other hand, the main arguments for a differently integrated Europe can be described as follows: first and foremost – Eurosceptics would not be able to slow down the integration processes. Those who want to integrate more closely, to be avant-garde and to wish to build a stronger Union – shall have a chance to do so, The flexible integration concept is intended to make the EU more efficient, dynamic, and capable of facing its challenges (Umiński 2017, p. 14). EU Member States are different and represent a high level of heterogeneity. For instance, not all of them 'fit' into the Eurozone, as their competitiveness differs, inflation rates are not the same, some of them need a devaluation of currencies, etc., so their economic policies can hardly be harmonized. Diversity requires differentiated approaches to integration.

Certainly, analysing such a multifaceted phenomenon like European integration from a single-disciplinary perspective is a reductionist undertaking. Previous investigations of differentiated integration were dominated by political science approaches. There is an old saying that goes: 'for one who possesses a hammer, everything seems like a nail'. This is why the authors have tried to enrich this discourse with more economic input, but the economists are often 'one-eyed' too (Holst & Molander 2020, p. 79). Experts are too often overconfident of their own competence, especially when trapped in their own discipline identification. They tend to frame problems so that they fall within their disciplinary matrices and paradigms (Holst & Molander 2020, p. 79). Therefore, the authors have applied the political economy approach which allows one to integrate both political science and economic perspectives when studying DI in Europe.

2.4 TWO DECADES OF VARIETIES OF CAPITALISM: TIME TO REVISIT?

The varieties of capitalism (VoC) approach has gained much attention since the early 2000s due to its usefulness in terms of making international comparisons between different capitalistic economies. This trend in the political economy literature has become so prominent that it is sometimes used as a synecdoche of the entire direction of comparative capitalism studies. Nevertheless, worth remembering is the fact that the discipline has been seriously prolific since the 1960s. Hence, much of the original VoC framework's critical accounts can be addressed by drawing on existing resources. The authors thus opt for building an eclectic comparative framework; mostly inspired by the VoC school, but utilizing other authors' achievements as well. This chapter first briefly tells the history of the comparative political economy of capitalism before the VoC appeared in 2001. Then, the main features of the original VoC framework and the authors' modifications of it are discussed. Finally, the authors trace the story of an uneasy relationship between the VoC research strand and the research theme of European integration.

After the Second World War, Keynesianism dominated both economic policy and economic thought. This meant almost three decades of intellectual stagnation for institutional economics. Economic policy makers were mostly occupied with welfare-state building, the 'active management' of aggregate demand, and market failure internalizing. Nevertheless, the question of rebuilding Western economies after a global conflict inspired researchers to elaborate comparatively on the variety of modernization paths that were available. Analysing the situation of European countries and the USA in this context, the British economist Andrew Shonfield (1965) wrote about the 'national varieties of capitalism'. His research framework was shaped by a historical context as the leading theme at the time was the challenge of balancing private and public initiative in rebuilding the economy after the war. He paid particular attention to the question of the new types of state interventionism and its long-term effects for development. It applied mainly to so-called 'indicative planning' which consisted in the creation of desirable incentives by the means of government subsidies, grants, or tax preferences. Shonfield created, on the basis of a comparative analysis of the United Kingdom, Germany, France, and the United States, a simple typology of industrialized capitalist states. He distinguished between free-market-based liberal capitalism, partnership-based corporatist capitalism, and state capitalism managed *via* extensive intervention. The groundbreaking nature of Shonfield's work lies in stressing the importance of the economy's institutional environment for the success of development strategies. A case study of Japan's post-war economy led another early comparative political economy author, Chalmers Johnson, to develop the concept of the 'developmental state' (1982). This, in essence, is a mode of market capitalism based on the state's active management of the economy, social mobilization, and a specific kind of economic nationalism. This notion became important for the fostering of the field in the following decades. Firstly, it extended previous comparative studies to include countries from outside the Western (Euro-Atlantic) circle. Secondly, the developmental state model has attracted the attention of numerous researchers. Utilizing it, they have tried to characterize the type of capitalism emerging after the Second World War in other developing economies, such as China (Strange 2011), or Latin America (Schneider 2015). The chaos of the stagflation in the 1970s re-established the dominance of the neoclassical schools which were then led by monetarism. Much of the criticism levelled at the Keynesian doctrine concerned the inefficiency of the institutional system that was promoted by the welfare states. This marked the return of institutional thought to the science of economics and the flourishing of comparative political economy and new institutional economics (NEI) as well as the rebirth of economic sociology (Nee & Swedberg 2005, pp. 789–818). NEI places institutional governance in the centre of analysis together with its components: state, law, markets, and firms. It also pays a great deal of attention to firm-level analysis (i.e., contract theory, agency theory, etc.). In terms of its methodology, NEI seems to complement the neoclassical paradigm (Brousseau & Glachant 2008, pp. 1–19), while 'old' institutionalism rather opposed mainstream views. Thus, NEI upholds fundamental assumptions about the competitive nature of the market and capitalism. The difference is that it introduces greater nuance with the notion of rationality by emphasizing the cognitive limitations that characterize human beings.

During the Cold War, the ideological rivalry between capitalist and socialist blocs was also reflected in the social sciences. At that time, disputes about the superiority of one system over another took place in the field of comparative economic systems. The vacuum of this strand in literature, which appeared in the aftermath of the events post-1989, gradually began to be filled by the expanding achievements of comparative capitalism research. The method of constructing typological comparisons and the level of systematizing the methodological and theoretical assumptions in comparative capitalism has evolved significantly since the 1990s. In a book written by Michael Albert (1993), the Anglo-Saxon model was contrasted with the Rhenish model. The former was to be characterized by the dominance of free-market solutions, while the latter was to be played by trade unions and the state. Interestingly, the tendency to draw a dichotomous division according to a similar axis continues in the literature to this day, despite the enormous changes that have occurred in researchers' approach to making comparisons. Albert's work did not have a strict theoretical and methodological framework, and the very comparison of Anglo-Saxon capitalism (based on the USA and the United Kingdom) with Rhine capitalism (Germany, the Netherlands, and Switzerland) was developed in terms of broadly understood cultural differences and values, but also via advantages resulting from geography and available resources. The undeniable legacy of the work in question is the penetration into academic discourse of the names with which these two types of capitalism were assigned by the author. Subsequent works did not differ from each other in that they limited their analysis only to developed countries – most often wealthy societies in Western Europe, the United States, and Canada – and sometimes also to Japan and South Korea. The set of analytical criteria that the authors often used in this period included: the everyday life of citizens, the importance of work, attitudes to capital groups, employee-management styles, negotiation tactics (Hampden-Turner & Trompenaars 1993); conditions for profit maximization, the mobilization and accumulation of capital, and the interaction of domestic economic institutions with their foreign equivalents. David Coates (2000) went beyond the dual typology, proposing the following triad: the market model (coinciding with the Anglo-Saxon), the consensual (identical to the Rhenish model, although its additional representatives were also Scandinavian countries), and the state-led Asian model (Japan, South Korea, and Taiwan). The macroeconomic perspective was adopted to a greater extent by André Sapir (2006) due to the inclusion of values typical for this area, i.e., the economic growth and stability index, balance of payments, budget situation, unemployment and employment, interest rates and inflation, competitiveness and productivity, etc. As a result, he distinguished four models which coincided roughly with the geographical coordinates of the countries: the Nordic, southern, continental, and Anglo-Saxon models, which, interestingly, also included Portugal. Until the end of the 20th century, comparative capitalism research did not manage to develop uniform methods and theories that could be used to comprehensively compare countries in terms of the uniqueness of their economic institutions. The works of the authors from that period seemed to oscillate around several concepts related to the current conflicts between work and capital on various levels (the labour market, production, and culture). So they were: corporatism, communitarianism, liberalism, statism, patrimonialism, etc. (Becker 2009). However, all the theories described thus far lacked concepts that would consolidate these disputes out of context. A new stage in the development of comparative capitalism studies was opened by the birth of the VoC research programme at the beginning of the 21st century.

The VoC approach consolidates and incorporates the above-described attempts to create an analytical framework for comparing countries according to the type of capitalism they pursue. Its creators, Peter A. Hall and David Soskice, proposed (2001) for this purpose a scheme more theoretically coherent than those previously used. In the works of comparative capitalism, one can often find the statement that VoC takes a more microeconomic perspective as it is 'firm-oriented'. This is, however, only partially true. The analysis also takes into account a broader set of factors, such as the state's competitiveness in international markets (reflected in the concept of 'institutional competitive advantage'). However, and especially in the early contributions, it was not pronounced enough, in a sense ignoring the findings of the international political economy. An introduction to the VoC analytical framework should begin with listing the criteria against which comparisons are made. There are five main elements of the 'institutional matrix' of a country to be analysed. These are the crucial areas in which companies face coordination problems:

- Corporate governance (how firms coordinate rules for managers' access to funds);

- Industrial relations (how firms coordinate the wage bargaining process);
- Education and vocational training (how firms coordinate the process of employing qualified employees and improving their skills);
- Relations between entrepreneurs (how firms coordinate their relations with other firms e.g., suppliers);
- Relations between employees (how firms coordinate the process of hiring employees who strive to achieve a company's goals).

Firstly, based on advanced market economies, two main 'ideal types' have been proposed: Coordinated Market Economy (CME) and Liberal Market Economy (LME). They differ in terms of the dominant 'coordination mechanism' that regulates the above-listed areas; it is market rivalry in terms of the LMEs and the multi-actor cooperation in the case of the CMEs. The liberal type is based on the flexibility of the labour market, the short-term orientation of capital, the general skills of workers, and competing with 'radical' innovations. Alternatively, CME relies less on purely market-based solutions. Its comparative institutional advantage is the creation of 'gradual' innovations, mainly consisting of the improvement of already-existing products. It should be remembered that the original analysis from the beginning of the 21st century was prepared on the basis of a sample of highly developed countries: old EU Member States, the United States, Canada, Australia, and Japan. According to the original results obtained with the use of this theory, Anglo-Saxon countries were considered examples closest to the LME ideal, while Germany and Austria were assumed to be a close emanation of the CME model. Over time, this literature was expanded to include other geographic regions and income groups; Andreas Nölke and Arjan Vliegenthart (2009, pp. 670–702) proposed extending the typology to include the Visegrad Group countries, arguing that they pursue a specific model of a Dependent Market Economy (DME). This type is based mainly on relatively low labour costs and the inflow of 'hot' capital from abroad. As a result, DMEs' comparative institutional advantage is achieved through connecting their economies to international supply chains. In the case of Central and Eastern European countries, it is mainly a multi-segment industry in Germany, for which they supply components, that makes them 'assembly platforms' for Western economies. The VoC approach has been further developed for other countries and regions. In the context of Southern European countries, attention was paid to the hybrid nature of the institutional system and the ineffectiveness of the solutions prevailing there under the Mixed Market Economy model (MME, Molina & Rhodes 2007) which was developed on the basis of Spain and Italy. The role of interest groups and clan connections was highlighted in extending VoC by another type: Hierarchical Market Economy (HME), which is supposed to be the case in Latin American countries (Schneider 2013), and Turkey (Kıran, 2018) and the Balkans (Saucedo-Acosta et al. 2019). Table 2.1 provides a synthetic summary of the constitutive features for the above-mentioned models of capitalism. It is not difficult to notice that the authors put enterprise in the centre of the perspective – in this convention, it is the main plane (looking inside it) and the vehicle (looking outside) of socio-economic life. Nevertheless, company behaviour is shaped by wider institutional conditions. In turn, this wide environment is set – at least in terms of formal institutions – by state policies. As was mentioned, the key reference point that allows the classification of a country under consideration is the kind of coordination mechanism utilized in particular areas. This concept is partly related to the degree of the importance of the state in the economy and allows one to determine whether the functioning of a specific matter is coordinated by competitive-and-market or consensual-and-administrative solutions. Obviously, the VoC framework and its underlying concepts should not be understood simply as a tool serving to measure the scale of state intervention in the economy, since the non-market type of coordination is much more than the taking of actions by the state itself. Yet, it may be argued that, at least until the dichotomic scheme is to be maintained, the CME model entails a more interventionist governmental approach. Early VoC scholarship was criticized for neglecting the role of the state in such incentive-creating areas such as taxation, public investment, or industrial and social policies. It is worth reflecting on the older traditions of comparative capitalism (like Shonfield's contribution) and to alternative frameworks and schemes (Esping-Andersen 1990; Amable 2003) in order to address this issue. The authors stress that the state also plays a significant role in organizing and supporting innovative activities, as well as research and education which have a significant impact on the direction of economic and social development. The same goes for the influence of political institutions, democracy, and the rule of law. Thus, the authors attempt to combine both micro- and macroeconomic perspectives in their analysis.

The glue that connects partial considerations (conducted at the level of each institutional area) into the whole is the concept of institutional complementarity. Different configurations of differently coordinated (market or non-market) areas ultimately result in different types of institutional systems. Complementarity in institutionalism is such an important slogan that it requires a more elaborate commentary. The history of the term goes back several decades (Lachmann 1979) and has been applied to various fields of social sciences. A huge contribution to the theory of institutional complementarity should be attributed to the Japanese economist Masahiko Aoki (1994, 2001). He used a highly formalized argument in his works, mainly using game theory. According to the most common definition, two institutions are complementary to each other if the existence of one increases the effectiveness of the other. Empirical examples of the complementarity of institutions that can be found in the literature are, for example, the vocational education system in Germany (in German, *Ausbildung*), which effectively functions in a wider, CME-type of institutional system, but attempts to 'transplant' it to other countries failed (Nölke 2019, p. 3). This stems from a lack of complementarity between types of education system and other institutional areas. Focusing on the specific skills of employees is better suited with a long-term oriented labour market and a more sophisticated type of manufacturing, so it does not fit to the LME-like form of industrial relations.

Figure 2.2 illustrates the authors' take on the concept of institutional complementarity which they have applied in the 'case studies' section. The authors have mostly examined the internal (country-level) complementarity between distinct institutional areas: corporate governance (concerning financial system), industrial relations (concerning the labour market and welfare state), and the knowledge creation system (concerning public policies oriented toward providing education and training). In the spirit of previous comparative capitalism studies, the authors perceive these three areas as crucial for understanding modern capitalist formations. The arrows on the picture represent the feedback loops of interactions between the three main institutional dimensions. Of note, the authors have attempted to capture the internal (in) complementarity (resulting in effectiveness or lack of it) both qualitatively in the national case studies (see Chapters 2–5) and quantitatively (see Chapter 6). Nevertheless, the authors have tried to develop this concept, since the whole book covers different countries' '(in)compatibility' with the emerging institutional regime of the EU. This can be seen as a wider understanding of institutional complementarity.

An important point should also be made in relation to the immanent dispute between institutionalists practicing comparative capitalism and representatives of the so-called 'convergence approach' in mainstream macroeconomics. Comparative capitalism is designed to build various typologies of possible institutional systems in capitalist economies. Thus, they assume their initial heterogeneity and even go to great lengths to make these differences more pronounced. It can also be stated that most of this literature anticipates further institutional divergence, which is conditioned by a number of factors. This is in contrast to the position of contemporary neoclassical macroeconomics, in which the convergence school assumes the so-called 'catching-up effect'. According to this effect, under economic growth, relatively poorer countries reduce the gap between themselves and top-income countries. It is happening as a result of their economies regularly achieving higher GDP growth than that in advanced countries. This would be related to, *inter alia*, the diminishing marginal product of the economy in a macro scale. This brings another assumption that, as a consequence of the decrease in development differences (measured quantitatively), the economies – in the long term – would strive to

Table 2.1 VoC extended typology

Area of analysis	LME	CME	DME	HME
Distinctive coordination mechanism	Competitive markets and formal contracts	Inter-firm networks and associations	Dependence on intra-firm hierarchies within transnational enterprises	Dominance of family-owned, diversified business groups
Primary means of raising investment	Domestic and international capital markets	Domestic bank lending and internally generated funds	Foreign direct investments and foreign-owned banks	Foreign direct investments and foreign-owned banks; bank credit to state-owned enterprises
Corporate governance	Outsider control, dispersed shareholders	Insider control, concentrated shareholders	Control by the headquarters of transnational enterprises	Control by family conglomerates
Industrial relations	Pluralist, market based, few collective agreements	Corporatist, consensual, sector-wide or even national agreements	Appeasement of skilled labour, company-level collective agreements	State-regimented and weak system of industrial relations
Education and training system	General skills, high research and development expenditures	Company- or industry-specific skills, vocational training	Limited expenditures for further qualification	Low skills and human capital
Transfer of innovations	Based on markets and formal contracts	Important roles of joint ventures and business associations	Intra-firm transfer within transnational enterprise	Limited transfer of innovation via multinational corporations
Institutional comparative advantage	Radical innovation in technology and service sectors	Incremental role of joint ventures and business associations	Intra-firm transfer within transnational enterprise	Non-market and hierarchical interaction between business groups; state intervention
Country	UK, USA, Australia, New Zealand, Ireland	Germany, Austria, Belgium, Japan	Poland, Slovakia, Czechia, Hungary	Turkey, the Balkans, Latin American economies

Source: Authors' own elaboration based on Nölke and Vliegenthart (2009) and Schneider (2013).

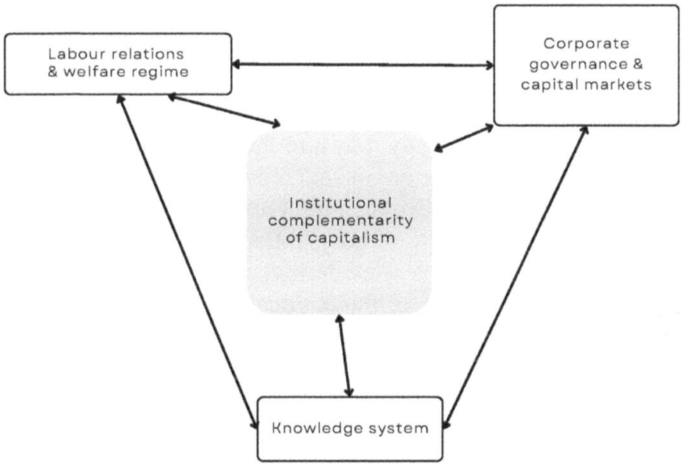

Source: Authors' own elaboration.

Figure 2.2 The concept of institutional complementarity

achieve a coherent stage of development in the qualitative sense (which also means institutional convergence). However, the evidence is not conclusive. In light of empirical studies, income-level convergence occurs in most OECD countries, but it is not the case, for example, in some Latin American countries such as Venezuela, Argentina, or Uruguay (Derviş 2012, pp. 10–14). Although the VoC scheme has been gradually improved in the last two decades, there are still some controversies over its construction and methodological assumptions. The framework has been used primarily to extend the typology to the new EU Member States, as well as non-Western or non-developed economies such as China. Also, it was employed as an analytical platform for more narrow, specific topics which include a wide range of issues from bank re-domestication to the effectiveness of CSR. Hence, the VoC has to be perceived most of all as a research programme. This study admits to the latter strand as it aims to take advantage of comparative capitalism methods in order to determine the internal set-up of market institutions which is presumed to be a relevant driver of an economy's mode of integration into European structures.

European studies have already recognized the role of the heterogeneous preferences of state actors in integration processes (see: Hooghe 2003;

Steenbergen et al. 2007). However, until recently, the diversity of attitudes of integration participants was not linked to the diversity of their economic models. Conversely, and for a long time, comparative studies of market economies have utterly ignored the subject of European integration. Andreas Nölke (2019, pp. 135–151) believes that the literature of comparative capitalism developed in three stages, which he refers to as successive 'waves'. The first wave focused on the seminal work of Hall and Soskice at the turn of millennia. At that time, attention was mainly drawn to the clear differences between the 'ideal types' of capitalism. The dominant prediction in this trend spoke of the inevitable divergence of these two regimes. Further liberalization of the liberal type and an even greater scope of cooperation in the coordinated type was anticipated. These expectations were formulated in isolation from external processes such as globalization or the regionalization of national economies. The second wave aimed primarily at extending the dichotomous typology to also elaborate on countries that were not included in the scheme before (and also on those less developed) and to consider previously overlooked factors in the analysis. In addition to the impact of globalization, the decreasing importance of the industrial sector (at the expense of services) in the modern economy has also been noticed. A stronger emphasis was placed on the role of individual state policies. However, it can be said that the works of both the first and second waves did not pay enough attention to the interaction of the parallel processes of shaping the national institutional order and the Europeanization of economies. In the few works that have considered this important context (see: Sharpf & Schmidt 2000; Menz 2008), rather optimistic views have come to the fore, claiming that the coexistence of different national varieties of capitalism does not contradict the pursuit of deeper economic integration within the EU. This idea was based on the observation that the Europeanization of economies is increasingly implemented in a differentiated integration mode, which allows individual countries to follow their own path of institutional development.

A new trend of studies at the intersection of comparative capitalism and European integration appeared as a response by researchers to the events of the global financial crisis and the debt crisis in the Eurozone that occurred after 2007. This time, those researchers' expectations regarding the possibility of reconciling the different types of capitalism with the process of deeper integration were much more pessimistic. This third wave of comparative studies on capitalism retains some of the building blocks of the previous theories, but also revises some of the assumptions and ways of conceptualizing different types of market economies. The scholarship connects the achievements of the 'comparative' and 'international' strands in modern political economy. The authors of third-generation comparative capitalism suggest that in the course of economic integration, two basic ways of achieving economic growth have developed in the pre-Brexit European Union. They are the so-called 'growth models':

- *The export-led growth model*, represented mainly by Germany and some Northern European countries;
- *The consumption-led growth model*, represented mainly by the southern peripheries of the Euro area: Italy, Portugal, and Greece, but also partly by the United Kingdom.

The first of these two models prioritizes export growth, mainly of high-quality industrial goods. This type of market economy, best represented by Germany, largely corresponds to the type of CME known from previous generations of typologies of capitalism. It is based on a compromise between key actors in the field of industrial relations (government, enterprises, and employees), which results in keeping unit labour costs at a relatively low level. This arrangement allows the domestic industry to achieve a competitive advantage on international markets. On the other hand, limiting the growth of wages in the economy has a negative impact on domestic demand. The export-based model, like the CME, is characterized by fiscal discipline and tends to generate budget surpluses. In light of the research, this model is also represented by Central European countries (including Poland) and the Baltic countries (Bohle 2018), and Ireland (Regan & Brazys 2018). An important component of all these systems, however, is the inflow of foreign direct investment (although their source and nature are different for each of these regions). The second model, which achieves growth through domestic consumption, corresponds to a lesser extent with the traditional dichotomy known from VoC. Its driving force is not international trade, but internal consumption, mainly in the non-tradables sector. Domestic demand is stimulated by an increase in wages and/or debt. As a result, these economies do not develop strong institutions for coordinating wages (such as collective bargaining) or effective mechanisms to limit credit growth. These features were additionally strengthened after the entry of countries with a pro-demand economic profile into the Economic and Monetary Union (EMU). It is worth noting that in times of prosperity these economies achieve higher GDP growth rates. However, this growth is more unstable and more vulnerable to collapse in the face of external macroeconomic shocks. It was not until the shift towards growth models that the literature of comparative capitalism began to fully include the aspect of European integration in its analyses. However, most of the work focuses exclusively on integration within the EMU. According to the authors of the third wave, before the establishment of the EMU, the potential for reconciling different types of capitalism was greater in Europe. The relatively harmonious coexistence of the two main models was allowed by the monetary sovereignty of the Member States and the resulting mechanisms for mitigating macroeconomic disturbances. In the EMU, the basic instruments of monetary policy (interest rate and exchange rate management) were transferred to the transnational level, increasing the scope for growing imbalances in the current and capital accounts of some economies. Eurozone countries with strongly rooted institutions of coordinated capitalism (based on robust coalitions of industrial producers) are able to suppress inflationary pressures by means of so-called 'wage (or social) dumping'. As a consequence, they enjoy a more competitive real exchange rate, which in turn leads to the accumulation of regular surpluses (in the current account) and deficits (in trade with the southern periphery of the EMU).

The Eurozone – in its pre-crisis form – found itself in a situation where most of the positive effects of integration accrued to the pro-export CME economies. However, this took place at the expense of countries pursuing the second method of achieving growth. In addition, the comparative perspective of capitalism research on the issue of British-EU relations and the process of Britain leaving the community is also interesting. This country was classified, in the first generation of comparisons, as the closest empirical example of an ideal LME model. Interestingly, Lucio Baccaro and Jonas Pontusson (2016, pp. 175–207) point out that the British economy also fits into the consumption-driven growth model. In their opinion as regards in the British economy's case, we are dealing with the 'duality' of the economic model. The reasons for this state of affairs are deindustrialization (associated with the period of Thatcherism) and an education system focused on general qualifications (with a *de facto* lack of vocational training). As a consequence, export-oriented industries occupy high-tech niches characterized by high added value (such as electronics and financial services), while the country's low-skilled service sector predominates. Although a number of measures have been taken to popularize higher education and to increase the participation of workers in high-paid industries, the massive immigration resulting from European integration (from the east and south of the continent) has stifled the wage (and employment) growth of low-skilled workers. According to comparative researchers, the above process is a catalyst for the dissatisfaction of the working masses and a factor which, combined with traditional *exceptionalism*, was supposed to lead to the British monarchy leaving the EU. Christian Schweiger (2014, pp. 81–106) points out that these 'work-fare state' policies were pushed by the British government on the EU forum both when adopting the Lisbon Strategy and the subsequent Europe 2020 development strategy. This agenda referred in particular to the concept of the 'third way' (see: Giddens 2013) and was to consist mainly in professional activation of citizens by the state. A large part of these solutions has been incorporated into community policies. This is interesting because in previous decades, the

United Kingdom did not actually participate in the creation of the so-called 'European social model'.

2.5 IS THERE AN 'EUROPEAN VARIETY OF CAPITALISM'?

In this section, the issue of whether there is a divergence or convergence in terms of the models of capitalism among EU countries is addressed. Moreover, the authors ask the following question: Is it possible to assess whether the general agenda of the Union 'promotes' any specific kind of institutional order? In other words: If convergence occurs, what is its direction?

The intuitive solution to the problem would consider the power relations inside the organization. One could assume a tendency of converging to the coordinated model, since Germany leads the process of European integration and has an enormous influence on the overall direction of policy making. Yet the problem gets more complicated when one considers the changing poles on the map of differentiated integration since the 'policrises' period started with the Great Recession and the Eurozone crises, 2015's migration crises, 2016's Brexit referendum, the COVID-19 pandemic, and the outbreak of Russia's full-scale military invasion of Ukraine in 2022. Another issue is the changing paths of integration of the new Member States, which joined the Union after 2004. The issue of capturing the scope and direction of capitalism convergence in the European Union needs to be evaluated more deeply.

Looking from the perspective of world economy research, the EU, when treated as a whole, appears to be a region with specific features of economic order. At such a high level of generality, the community remains in stark contrast to other major actors of globalization such as China or the USA. In particular, the latter country sharply differs from the EU. In almost all typologies of comparative capitalism, the liberal foundations of American capitalism are emphasized, with the big role of the so-called 'short-term' ('impatient') capital in corporate financing, a strong preference for risk-taking, and the tendency to create radical types of innovations being good examples. The USA is a natural reference point for Europe due to its cultural proximity and the level of economic development. Clear differences are manifested primarily in areas such as the attitude towards transnational corporations (especially the issue of taxing them), the protection of consumer rights, and environmental challenges or equality issues (Pontusson 2005; Ülgen 2022).

A polycrisis-based reality forced the EU to change via different channels of influence. The rise of populism after the Great Recession led to what was called 'the crises of globalization', making the Western leaders rethink the rules governing global trade. The COVID-19 pandemic accelerated the energy and digital transformations, and also restored the role that the state has to play in these matters. Nevertheless, in the authors' opinion, all of these factors followed the original impulse for the EU to change, that impulse being the occurrence of Brexit. It created gaps in the balance of power within the EU structure, particularly among states that supported the free-market paradigm. It's also essential not to understate the fact that Brexit led to the departure of a country from the EU that had previously shown strong resistance to further integration (the 'ever closer Union' principle enshrined in treaties was frequently attacked by British opponents of EU membership). However, the Eurosceptic camp in the European Council and the European Parliament has now been significantly weakened. This opens the door to various integration initiatives that were at odds with the UK's position, such as financial matters or defence. An example could be the expansion of the scope of common bonds issued by the European Commission to finance the Recovery Fund, as well as financial regulations, including the EU Capital Market Union project.

A closer examination of European integration reveals a rich tapestry of diverse capitalist models within the EU Member States (Callaghan 2006). Scholars in the field of comparative and international political economy have conducted extensive research to understand how the European integration process impacts the economic systems of individual nations. This influence takes shape through various mechanisms and has significant implications for the economic landscape of the European Union. One of the key aspects of European integration is monetary integration, exemplified by the establishment of the Economic and Monetary Union (EMU). The adoption of the euro as a common currency by a subset of EU countries represents a profound step towards economic convergence. It has both benefits and challenges, such as fostering trade within the Eurozone while requiring participating nations to adhere to common monetary policies set by the European Central Bank. Another vital aspect is the facilitation of international financial and capital flows, as well as the mobility of workers. The free movement of capital and labour is a fundamental principle of the EU's Single Market. This allows businesses to access larger consumer bases, leading to increased competition and economic growth. For instance, a French company can easily invest in Germany, and workers from Poland can seek employment in Spain, benefiting from the EU's open borders. Moreover, European integration involves the harmonization of fiscal rules and the oversight of budgetary discipline. Instruments such as the Stability and Growth Pact, the so-called 'six-pack' and the 'two-pack', play crucial roles in coordinating economic policies among Member States. They aim to maintain financial stability and fiscal responsibility within the Eurozone, helping prevent economic crises such as the one experienced during the European sovereign debt crisis. The EU also promotes specific solutions through its development strategies, such as the Lisbon Strategy or the objectives of the Europe 2020 programme. These initiatives set targets for areas including research and development, employment, and education. By fostering cooperation and investment in these areas, the EU seeks to enhance overall economic competitiveness among its Member States. For example, the Europe 2020 programme aims to boost innovation and increase employment rates across Europe. Lastly, European integration influences national regulations in critical areas such as competition law and tax law. The EU sets standards and guidelines that Member States must follow to ensure a level playing field for businesses and consumers; the European Commission closely monitors mergers and acquisitions to prevent anticompetitive practices that could harm the Single Market. Additionally, the EU's Value Added Tax (VAT) system harmonizes tax rates on certain goods and services, simplifying cross-border trade within the EU. The process of European integration is a multifaceted endeavour that impacts various aspects of the economic landscape in EU Member States. From monetary integration to fiscal discipline, development strategies to regulatory standards, these mechanisms shape the diverse forms of capitalism present within the European community, ultimately contributing to the economic stability and growth of the EU as a whole.

The existence of the above-listed channels of influence results in the fact that the architecture of the national institutional order is shaped by a much larger number of actors than assumed in the first wave of research on comparative capitalism which was limited to an analysis of the behaviour of domestic entities, mainly enterprises and trade unions. These pro-convergence aspects of European integration can be regarded as conscious activities of the community, which are aimed at promoting (macro)economic convergence. Convergence at the institutional level seems to be a more complex process and a more difficult one to grasp analytically. Two important points must be made. Firstly, the very scope of capitalism convergence in Europe is under discussion. While some authors prove the existence of divergence tendencies (Farkas 2016), others point to the achievement of almost full convergence, at least in some institutional areas. Mariusz Próchniak (2019) points to a significant level of convergence in the EU in the area of product market competition. The same goes for the sphere of financial systems and capital markets (Borowski et al. 2022). This is an intuitive result, considering that the common market for trade in goods is the foundation of the integration process in the old continent. Secondly, assuming that institutional convergence in the EU is a fact, the question arises about its direction, i.e., which model of capitalism is *de facto* promoted at the level of community policies. Ben Clift and Sean McDaniel (2021, pp. 1–19) suggest that, in comparative studies, one can distinguish two stages of thinking about this issue. At the initial stage, the researchers based their analyses on the analytical scheme associated with the first two waves of comparative literature on capitalism, mainly with the original (dichotomous) VoC convention. As part of these analyses, it was shown that European integration favours the evolution towards the Anglo-Saxon, liberal type of capitalism. Martin Höpner and Armin Schäfer (2007, 2012) argue that the nature of European integration (after the Maastricht Treaty) is part of a broader project of neoliberal reforms and embodying the postulates of the Washington Consensus. This would concern, among others, promoting the liberalization of the rules for conducting mergers and acquisitions of enterprises, relaxing banking supervision standards, or exerting pressure to make labour markets more flexible. They refer to these processes as the 'post-Ricardian era' because the relative strengths (i.e., competitive advantages) of heterogeneous economic models were to lose their importance in light of the process of convergence to some uniform type of 'European capitalism'. It was also expected that the institutions of coordinated capitalism would be gradually dismantled under the influence of the 'pro-liberalization' actions of the EC and the CJEU. The global financial crisis was an important context in which later works were created. They attempted to determine the direction of convergence of capitalism within the framework of EU integration. Importantly, these analyses were carried out using a wider range of theoretical tools developed in the course of the development of the third wave of research on comparative capitalism. According to these authors (Johnston & Regan 2018, p. 4), the process of European integration, especially after the experience of the crisis in the euro area, favours convergence to a growth model based on exports, similar to the German example. These authors even state that the vector of European integration after the crisis shifted towards the German ordoliberal model, using this term interchangeably with coordinated capitalism. In fact, ordoliberal ideas have been an important element of European integration almost from its very beginning (see, e.g., Nedergaard 2013).

However, it is a much broader concept and, for the sake of clarity, the authors have used narrower terms derived from the comparative literature on capitalism. The shift towards the German model is evidenced by both the original design and directions of the reforms of the monetary union (i.e., the penalization of economies with trade deficits) as well as the nature of the recommended (often as a condition for obtaining financial assistance) structural reforms based on austerity policy, budgetary discipline, and the pursuit of cost competitiveness. While these dynamics are most relevant to EMU countries, the cited authors argue that this 'technocratic agenda' is guiding the overall integration process. According to the researchers, in the realities of crisis, this programme was pushed mainly by Germany and other relatively wealthy countries in the north of the continent which wield massive political influence in the EU. According to some authors, the UK's exit from the EU also causes a number of 'tectonic movements' in the distribution of preferences of individual Member States of the community. Grzegorz Lewicki (2019) points out that, in the absence of Britain, Northern European countries (such as the

Netherlands) become the largest advocates of a free-market (but also fiscally conservative) agenda. This is reflected in the emergence of new regional cooperation initiatives, e.g., the so-called Hansa 2.0, an informal alliance comprising the Netherlands, Ireland, and the Nordic and Baltic countries, was an obvious consequence of the new political landscape post-Brexit. The increased cooperation of these states, which emphasize strict budgetary discipline on the one hand yet are reluctant to embrace the social and protectionist agenda within the European Union on the other, is a response to the noticeable shift of political weight towards the south.

In the tumultuous year of 2020, European Union member countries responded to the crisis triggered by the COVID-19 pandemic with an extraordinary scale of public aid to their entrepreneurs and industries. This monumental effort not only represented a significant financial commitment, exceeding a staggering EUR 2 trillion, but also underscored a growing acceptance within the EU for a more pronounced role of the state in shaping economic outcomes. This shift towards greater state intervention in the economy was not solely defined by the sheer magnitude of financial support; what was equally crucial was the new-found flexibility in granting aid, a change that marked a pivotal departure from previous norms. What set this evolution apart was the Commission's emphasis on transparency and comparability in how Member States provided support to their economies. Consequently, discernible differences emerged in how various European capitals approached mitigating the economic repercussions of a pandemic that had affected all EU countries in a similar manner. The increased visibility of these disparities lent weight to the argument for improved coordination at the EU level, especially concerning support for entrepreneurs and industries.

This transformation in the approach to public aid and state involvement in the economy was not solely a reaction to the pandemic. It also reflected a broader shift towards greater freedom of action at the national level and expanded support for industries at the EU level. EU industrial policy began to manifest more visibly, particularly in the realms of digital and green transformations. This shift was propelled by several factors. Firstly, EU funds were channelled into the 'reconstruction and strengthening of resilience' for EU economies. These funds sought to reduce the cost of capital for select sectors or companies and bolster research and development initiatives. Secondly, EU tools were increasingly harnessed to both support Member States' actions (on the offensive side) and counter the actions of third countries (on the defensive side). This marked a significant change, particularly given the historical criticisms that deregulation and liberalization had eroded traditional state tools for conducting industrial policy, thereby limiting the state's role to fostering international expansion and exports.

The transformation of EU industrial policy encompassed two principal dimensions. Firstly, it revolved around sectoral priorities, with digital and green transformations emerging as central to the EU's new economic approach. These priorities were evident not only in the projects funded but also in their far-reaching impact on various facets of EU activity. For instance, the strategy for COVID-19 vaccines underscored that strengthening the EU pharmaceutical industry necessitated the development of 'green production' and the utilization of shared data. The second dimension of this transformation pertained to cross-border projects, which assumed paramount importance. Gradually, the portion of the EU budget not allocated to pan-European projects witnessed an increase. A notable example was the substantial rise in funds allocated to scientific projects under the Horizon Europe programme. However, it was not merely the financing from the EU budget that mattered; equally significant were joint actions by multiple countries in specific industrial sectors.

This transformation represented a departure from the traditional model that had prevailed for many years. These policy initiatives heralded a transition from a model of 'negative' integration, which primarily focused on dismantling barriers to the internal market, promoting liberalization, and advocating openness, to a model of 'positive' integration. In this new paradigm, the goal was to leverage EU regulations to provide EU citizens with access to various public goods. These public goods encompassed a broad spectrum, including social justice, the protection of workers' rights, public health, privacy safeguards, environmental quality, and financial stability. Notable examples of such initiatives included regulations concerning posted workers and elements of the mobility package, topics that sparked extensive discussions, particularly in countries such as Poland.

The evolving role of the EU, increasingly oriented towards the provision of diverse public goods, underscored the comprehensive nature of modern integration processes. The original vision of the EU's founders had envisioned creating robust economic interdependence among Member States as a means to ensure prosperity and peace across the continent. Market-driven integration was intended to underpin economic development through economies of scale while concurrently reinforcing the common interests of European capitals. However, since the 1980s, a key objective of EU integration had been to curtail the role of the state in the economy and employ EU law to streamline market processes. This drive was evident in the EU's efforts to open up critical economic sectors, such as energy, air transport, and finance, through initiatives from the European Commission and jurisprudence from the Court of Justice. For example, the famous 'Cassis de Dijon' case pertained to the introduction of a product to the German market.

However, exclusive focus on economic objectives had its drawbacks. On the one hand, the EU succeeded in granting consumers greater choice and lower prices. Yet, on the other hand, the failure to consider the broader social context in EU regulations exposed the Union to criticism from populist movements, particularly in countries that had grappled with debt crises. The imbalance between market deregulation, which undercut the foundations of the social state in Member States, and social welfare measures within the integration framework left the Union open to criticism as an institution that fostered negative neoliberal and globalization tendencies.

This shift in approach necessitated the adaptation of EU policy tools. Until recently, the dominant vision had revolved around regulations designed to create equal conditions of competition in the market, particularly in sectors falling under the exclusive competencies of the Union. The primary goal had been economic efficiency, centered on improving consumer well-being by delivering lower prices and a broader array of choices. However, the contemporary evolution of the market approach emphasized bolstering the significance of non-economic objectives, including climate concerns and social consequences. It also prioritized a greater integration of activities across different levels, encompassing both the EU and national spheres, thereby affording EU institutions greater latitude to act. Consequently, this transformation heralded a shift towards more specialized regulations, supplanting the previous horizontal approach that promoted liberalization irrespective of the sector.

Several key factors have accelerated and deepened these changes in the EU's economic framework. These factors include the new goals articulated in the European Green Deal, the response to Brexit which marked the leaving of a prominent advocate for a liberal economic approach, and Member States' concerns about third-country entities dominating their markets. Consequently, interventionism and protectionism, both at the EU and national levels, have assumed significant roles in reshaping the market's operational landscape. This transformation also aligns with the preferences of many citizens who express apprehensions about the consequences of deregulation and globalization. Crucially, this new approach is predicated on ensuring that market operations contribute to the creation of public goods and are subject to regulations set at the EU level. The emphasis is on guiding and influencing market processes rather than attempting to control or replace them. These developments are unfolding in an economic environment characterized by near-zero interest rates, which muddle traditional market signals and diminish the relevance of conventional monetarist economic approaches. As a consequence, the EU is progressively redefining its objectives towards a 'Union that protects'. This vision of protection primarily extends to safeguarding the interests of employees against the adverse effects of excessive liberalism, shielding consumers from the dominance of large market players, and offering strategic support for a new socio-economic model through an active state role.

In summary, the transformation in the EU's economic policies represents a departure from a previous emphasis on market liberalization towards a more interventionist and protectionist approach. This shift is driven by evolving macroeconomic conditions, crises such as the pandemic, and the aspiration to provide public goods to EU citizens. Consequently, the compatibility of Member States' institutional frameworks with the evolving EU approach to economic governance is coming under scrutiny. This brings us to the forefront of the research in comparative capitalism, where the authors discern a shift in the type of market economy promoted by EU policies. This shift has transitioned from a predominantly liberal model before the crisis to one that is more coordinated, fiscally consolidated, and export-oriented in the post-crisis era. There exist multiple points of convergence between varieties of capitalism (VoC) and Differentiated Integration (DI) theories, which offer rich avenues for further research.

Firstly, it's essential to acknowledge that the field of political economy recognizes the challenge posed by the increasing heterogeneity among European economies and attempts to correlate this phenomenon with the growing diversity in integration levels. However, this diversity is often examined through the lens of economic structure, such as the weight of specific sectors such as agriculture or industry in a country's GDP, or basic macroeconomic indicators such as the average wealth of citizens. What is needed is a more comprehensive analysis that prioritizes the specificity of a country's internal institutional order as a central variable. While this presents a significant research challenge, the domain of comparative capitalism, especially in its third wave, provides typologies that can effectively operationalize the concept of the institutional order. In this regard, a wealth of potential for merging concepts is to be found related to differentiated integration and comparative capitalism research.

Secondly, certain tools from the study of differentiated integration can be employed to operationalize the parameter of a state's *propensity* to integrate. The extent of a state's participation in the European integration process is a multi-dimensional issue that demands a multifaceted modelling approach. Therefore, evaluating the degree of integration of a given country within the European community should encompass more than just the economic dimension. In addition to economic factors, this evaluation should consider the legal and political dimension, reflecting the actual state of integration with the EU, as indicated by the number of exclusions and delays in primary and secondary EU law. The social dimension, which gauges citizens' attitudes towards European integration through public opinion polls, is another vital aspect that warrants inclusion.

Thirdly, it's worth noting that the mainstream of the European integration process has undergone significant changes over the past two decades, having been triggered by multiple crises. Simultaneously, the vectors of convergence among the variants of capitalism in EU Member States have shifted. Consequently, the authors align with the observations of third-wave comparative researchers. However, combining these insights with the preceding points raises questions about the alignment of a country's institutional order with the ideal-typical European order promoted by the EU's most significant policies. Are states moving towards a more liberal institutional framework somehow being nudged towards the periphery of EU integration? After all, the mainstream trajectory of the EU has been shifting towards greater coordination and state interventionism.

Fourthly, the time period covered by the empirical analyses in subsequent stages of this work is essential to consider. This timeframe spans from the neoliberal period of global economic development in the 1990s and 2000s, marked by a significant eastward expansion of the EU. During this era, the diversity in the variants of market economies among Member States increased substantially. The upper limit of this temporal scope extends to around 2021, which corresponds to the United Kingdom's formal departure from the EU. It was during this timeframe that the EU's mainstream trajectory pivoted towards greater coordination. This leads to the premise that countries moving in a liberal economic direction during this period may become progressively less compatible with the EU community, consequently experiencing reduced integration.

To distil the core thesis of their book, the authors contend that during the neoliberal period, states adhering to the Liberal Market Economy (LME) model before the mid-2010s were more closely aligned with the EU's core, given its compatibility with the Union's prevailing paradigm. However, the landscape changed following the global financial crises and the ensuing 'polycrisis' period, during which more coordinated or even interventionist public policies gained favour on the EU agenda. Consequently, in this later period, countries transitioning towards a Coordinated Market Economy (CME) model, or those slowest to dismantle it, gravitated closer to the core of European integration. This realignment underscores the dynamic relationship between economic models and the shifting contours of EU integration.

2.6 THE EXPLANATORY POTENTIAL OF THE MIDDLE-INCOME TRAP AND DEPENDENCY THEORIES

In this chapter the authors explore the concept of the middle-income trap (MIT) embedded in the dependent market economy literature as an explanatory vehicle in examining some aspects of differentiated integration in Europe. More precisely, it is illustrated in this study with the case of Poland (Chapter 4) that – among the selected and analysed national economies in this monograph

– belongs to this group. The MIT is acknowledged to be a justified approach in examining centre-periphery relations. Consequently, in this chapter, the authors present the conceptual linkages explaining how the position that a state holds in the economic hierarchies may be important for the position it occupies on the map of differentiated integration.

In this book, the MIT problem is associated with one of the Member States in question, namely Poland, but its explanatory potential goes far beyond this empirical exemplification, and it stems from the concept's relations to the dependent market economy literature that is nested in dependent capitalism and VoC debates in general. At its heart are the centre-periphery constellations, hierarchical orders, and various forms of interdependency that define the position of a given economy in the global system. In this publication, the authors are interested in the European scale, therefore they have used these theoretical vehicles in order to shed some light on the positions some states take in the system of integration differentiation. Consequently, this chapter provides an overview of the MIT concept and then connects it with the dependent market economy and dependent capitalism literature. As a whole, it delivers some theoretical lenses that are useful in understanding some aspects of centre-periphery relations in an integrating Europe.

The debate on the MIT originates from concerns about slower growth rates observed in many catch-up economies (Riedel 2020). The academic deliberations on the MIT are most often rooted in growth theory, sustainable development, convergence studies, and many other streams of economic analysis (Li & Cheng 2019). Much less frequently, they focus on the political determinants or on the European integration context. Despite the lack of a precise definition, the term 'middle-income trap' has made its way into political and economic discourse and has attracted enormous interest in studies on politics and economics. Surprisingly enough, some analysts are sceptical even about its existence (Im & Rosenblatt 2015), whereas other scholars have built analytical models exploring this category. Those postulating its non-existence will point to the argument that after the Second World War, most countries did not attain high-income levels. It is statistically and logically expected that most growth trajectories will stagnate at average levels. Others show evidence of middle-income traps based on descriptive and econometric studies (Ye & Robertson 2016). Nevertheless, it is an empirical fact that over the last six to seven decades, many formerly poor economies were able to reach intermediate positions on the global income scale, and only a marginal portion of them have achieved high income levels. Although deeply heterogenous, most of the middle-income countries have progressed in terms of education, health, and also poverty reduction. However, despite these visible changes, only around ten out of more than 100 economies previously classified as middle income had achieved a higher-income status by the end of the first decade of the 21st century (Andrianjaka & Rougier 2019). East Asian economies, such as Japan, Taiwan, South Korea, Singapore, Hong-Kong, or China, often described as examples of an economic miracle, grew by 6–7% annually (on average) during their catch-up development. By contrast, in sub-Saharan Africa, the standard of living has been stuck for decades, whereas in South America it even dropped by three quarters in the life of one generation (Chang 2016). A number of emerging economies have grown rapidly at low-income levels and were ultimately unable to move beyond their middle-income status (Eichengreen 2000).

The concept of MIT was introduced to the literature with a World Bank report entitled 'An East Asian Renaissance: Ideas for Economic Growth' co-authored by Gill and Kharas (2007). It launched a new research stream, which has been put forward to advance our understanding of sources and the implications of growth slowdowns (Shiraishi & Sonobe 2019). The effective transformation from simple commodity production to higher value-added activities is at the heart of the transition from a middle-income to a high-income economy (Paus 2020). Research on the MIT generally focuses on economic determinants (Zheng 2020), and it is very often ignored that the MIT is not exclusively an economic phenomenon, nor an 'economic law'. Its non-economic dimension remains marginal in relation to the majority of the approaches. To fully understand the concept of the MIT, essentially it is first necessary to define middle income by international statistical standards and then to define the trap itself. Middle-income countries are commonly defined as the middle of the distribution of countries ranked by per capita income (Riedel 2017; Topal 2020; Iammarino et al. 2020). By World Bank standards, it translates to incomes up to 12,275 USD. Other authors or institutions will set their ranges differently (Chang 2016; Filipe et al. 2017; Bresser-Pereira et al. 2020). The MIT, then, is a special case of slowdown in economic growth which makes the transition from middle- to high-income levels difficult. It is characterized by modest growth and slow (or non) convergence with better-developed counterparts. The last relative aspect deserves further emphasis – it is not growth *per se* but its relation to some other comparable economies of the region or block. At the same time, it needs to be noted that there is huge imprecision to be found in the concept of the middle-income trap. Income is not growth – they are correlated but are not the same (Riedel 2018). Income growth may be periodically higher or lower than output growth. Still, the standard measurement of the MIT, widely recognized in the scholarly literature (Tugcu 2015; Ye & Robertsone 2016; Lee 2019), is simple – the level of per capita gross domestic product expressed in purchasing power parity. The scepticism is huge among the analytical community both about the GDP per head as a measurement of economic development as well as about the purchasing power standard. Leaving all the arguments aside, in the end most analysts agree that since there is no better parameter available, GDP per capita PPP remains dominant and widely accepted (Bulman et al. 2014, Dabus et al. 2016; Harding 2020). Additionally, in the European context it would be recommendable to set the points of reference slightly differently than those on the global scale. Indeed, the European Union constitutes a club of rich economies, and even those that are relatively poor inside the EU bloc belong to the rich North by international standards.

In this study, the question itself is whether a country like Poland belongs to the group of MIT economies. Some scholars (Michalski 2018) claim that since Poland exceeded the old threshold as defined by the WB, it now belongs to the highly developed countries, representing income levels well above the world average. Other scholars argue the opposite; according to Sachs' classification (2015, p. 67), Poland belongs to the category of middle-income countries that represent so-called positive economic growth (it is not stimulated exclusively by low-hanging fruit, such as fossil fuel extraction), in which economic decline (before COVID-19) happened only in the times of the transition time from the bankrupt communist system to the market economy. The authors, in this study, take the position that a country like Poland is representative for the relative MIT. The term 'relative' questions the point of reference – wherein on a global scale Poland belongs to the so-called 'rich North', on the European scale its economy notes average levels, and by EU measurements it belongs to one of the most underdeveloped economies in the bloc. The purchasing power parity standard hardly explains these differences, and comparing the GDP growth slowdowns in Central Europe and sub-Saharan Africa makes little sense at all. The authors rather suggest that the economy and the dynamism of its catch-up growth trajectory should be analysed in relation to the ecosystem to which it belongs. One could claim that all the economies participate in globalized exchange, which is true. Nevertheless, the authors argue that the specific national economy should be predominantly seen in the context of its neighbours, its main partners, and the position it holds in the hierarchy of the most immediate economic ecosystem. For a country such as Poland, this ecosystem is the Single Market and the wider European Economic Area (EU+EFTA). Observing Poland's economic parameters in this background leads to the conclusion that it is in a relative MIT since its convergence towards the EU's average levels is slowing down and stagnating.

In the scientific literature there is no consensus on the question of whether the transition from middle-income to high-income levels is no different than any other transition, for example, from low income to middle income (Lee 2019). It is natural that low-income countries grow faster – it is predominantly the result of a low base effect and imitation gains. The more they converge with the better-developed economies, the slower the pace of convergence (Riedel 2017). But some economies manage to close this convergence gap and some get stuck at the middle-income levels. Therefore, scholars have searched for the determinants of this phenomenon (Czerniak 2014; Keiro et al. 2017; Leven 2019). The low base effect logic would suggest the correlation that growth is related to the level of development. At certain phases of development, growth has a tendency to accelerate, while stagnating at others. The transition economies reveal some interesting common trends. Most of the formerly planned economies experienced economic recession from 1989 to the mid-1990s (Shelburne 2016). Then, most of them recovered after 1993–1995. From that moment on, their economic parameters started to diverge with the more developed countries.

The word 'trap' suggests that middle-income stagnation may be the result of some internal or external barriers, from which an economy needs to free itself (Riedel 2020). The very notion of a 'trap' is derived from Nelson's concept of 'low-level equilibrium trap' (1956) that was used to characterize the low-income economies unable to accelerate their growth (Leven 2019). The classical textbook example is the following – individuals in low-and-middle-income economies are not effectively incentivized to invest in education, because only very few of them can be suitably employed in an economy that is relatively simple, if not primitive. Consequently, the companies operating in such regimes cannot level up to some more innovative activities, since there is not enough high-quality human capital. The same could be said as regards infrastructure and other potential barriers such as corruption or inflexible labour markets. This logic suggests that the middle-income trap is basically a coordination problem (Staehr 2015). In past years, the phenomenon of the MIT has not only gained more and more scholarly attention, but it has also sparked political debates. There are even critical voices questioning its very existence. Rapid growth rates are good predictors of slowdowns (Kasjanovs 2015; Lee 2019; Riedel 2020), and the concentration of slowdown episodes in the middle-income range is simply a reflection of regression towards the mean because middle-income economies caught up to the average. They can be understood as statistical convergence forces. For instance, Barro (2016) argues that the transition (from middle-income to upper-income status) is challenging, but there is no evidence that this second transition is more difficult than the first (from low income to middle income). In this sense, a middle-income trap is no different from a low-income trap. Therefore, some other authors (Glawe & Wagner 2020) use a more neutral term – middle-income range (MIR). Alternatively, some other studies identify other types of traps, such as the liberalization trap or technological trap (Bresser-Pereira et al. 2020; Andreoni & Tregenna 2020), while some other observers (Im & Rosenblatt 2015; Keiro et al. 2017) see various types of traps complementary to the main MIT phenomenon.

Theoretical definitions understand middle-income trapped countries as those that are unable to compete with the production output of low-income economies while at the same time being unable to face the competition of highly developed countries that are characterized by innovative, knowledge-intensive products and services. MIT countries are, essentially, stuck between the two (Gill & Karas 2007). The related empirical definitions are either built on absolute or relative approaches. The absolute approach focuses on the middle-income threshold. The relative approach deals with the ration of income per capita of an economy to the national income of the country at a steady-state GDP level, like the US or any other point of reference (Topal 2020). Quantitative definitions focus on the GDP per capita range (e.g., staying between 10–50% of US per capita income for half a century, see Bulman et al. 2014), or on the growth slowdown by using average growth rates (Eichengreen 2000). Economies are considered to be in the MIT when their growth rate per capita income in seven average years is at least 3.5% with a minimum of 2% decline. Some new approaches define the MIT as an aggravation of slowdowns due to inadequate responses (of primarily the governments and, secondarily, the private sector), such as the adoption of counterproductive policies or the failure to adopt policies conducive to growth (Keiro et al. 2017).

Much of the scholarly work on the MIT starts from the assumption that the following factors increase the probability of being trapped at middle-income levels: a rise in wages incompatible with productivity growth, high dependence on exports (its geographical and content structure), regional income disparity, household income inequality, and an aging population (Gill & Kharas 2007; BWP 2013; Im & Rosenblatt 2015). Other authors also emphasize energy dependency (translating into higher energy prices – killing competitiveness) (Kasjanovs 2015). Exposure to external impulses is especially important in the case of small, emerging economies (Dabus et al. 2016). Numerous studies (Andrianjaka & Rougier 2019; Andreoni & Tregenna 2020) have been developed verifying various variables nested in structuralist assumptions, including: natural resources and the methods of their exploitation, the availability of production factors, and structural barriers (Eichengreen 2000; Dabus et al. 2016; Shiraishi & Sonobe 2019). There is, however, one symptom that is dominant in most of the studies – the position of a middle-income economy within the global supply chains. In other words – the ability to go beyond low-skilled, labour-intensive activities, in order to build innovation systems that allow competition with highly developed countries on the markets for more sophisticated products and services. Additionally, there is also empirical evidence that the long-lasting growth slowdowns have often occurred after the economic (especially financial) crisis (Staehr 2015), which suggests that the dependence on financial capital flows from high-income countries plays a significant role in the risk of being trapped at middle-income levels. MIT-risk countries include those exhibiting growth rates that rely on low-skill-labour-intensive production, natural resources and/or low added-value export. The features of

MIT risk-free countries include those with an accumulated stock of capital (especially human capital), high and rising total factor productivity, high skill labour, and capital- and knowledge-intensive production (Leven 2019). While these arguments are consistent with the standard theories of economic growth, the same theories predict that growth slowdowns are inevitable in the long run because of convergence forces. The best-known convergence force is diminishing returns to capital (neoclassical growth theory). Another widely recognized determinant is the diminishing pool of readily copiable technologies or ideas. Innovation by imitation is possible only at the early stages of economic development. This 'follower economy' model implies the existence of a more advanced leading partner as a potential pool for outsourcing. It is built on the 'advantage of backwardness' assumption and it predicts an inevitable slowdown once higher levels of development are reached. Some countries may converge to lower income levels, and others to higher income levels (still in the range of the middle-income margin which is quite broad). Those converging to relatively lower levels are often described as experiencing premature slowdown (Keiro et al. 2017). The most common explanations to the question of why state and economies fail to achieve substantial growth often focuses on one, very often domestic, factor. However, something as complex as national economy has too many elements interlinked into one system to presume that only one thing can go wrong. Problems occur in various parts of the economic machinery and can cascade, thereby bringing the machine to a near halt (Sachs 2015, p. 56). The MIT framework allows one to also see the broader context – the ecosystem in which a national economy functions and the place it holds in its hierarchies. The position a country holds on the map of differentiated integration is linked to the position a state holds in the economic hierarchies with its immediate partners. It is specifically visible in the case of those states that decided to opt out or derogate from monetary integration in the EU. They do not participate in many decision-making formats (e.g., Euro group) and remain (self)marginalized in the institutional meaning of this word as a result. At the same time, they decide not to take part in some enhanced integrative circles, since they do not feel strong enough economically. This mutually influencing mechanism consolidates existing hierarchies and the positions that states hold in the system of differentiated integration.

Connecting the MIT issue with the dependent market economy debates, it is natural to start with classical VoC literature. VoC is the leading approach in the comparative political economy scholarship of the last 20 years (see, e.g., Hall & Soskice 2001; Lane & Myant 2007; Hall & Thelen 2009; and Peck & Zhang, 2013). Its starting assumption claims that the basic institutions of capitalism differ from one national economy to the other, and that these differences are linked to strong institutional complementarities. Although the literature is very rich, with a number of complex capitalism categorizations and typologies, most analysts depart from the juxtaposition of CMEs and LMEs, since they grasp the most important differences between the basic ideal types of Anglo-Saxon LME versus Rhenish CME models. The two crucial notions of the rich VoC discourse are: the coordination mechanism – the way in which economic activity is organized (generally choosing between market-oriented or state-oriented coordination); and institutional complementarity – the manner in which different elements (corporate governance, financial system, education & training, industrial relations, etc.) of the capitalistic system fit with one another and, as a consequence, create a certain institutional comparative advantage for a given economy. One basic variety of the market economy (synonymous with 'capitalism') is LME (typically represented in the literature by, e.g., the UK, USA, Australia, etc.) which is based on a market type of coordination (competition and formal contracts) and has institutional comparative advantage in terms of 'radical innovations' (creating new products). Another variety is the CME (e.g., Germany, Austria, and Japan) which promotes state (or strategic) coordination (such as inter-firm networks and associations) of the economy and specializes in 'incremental innovation' (improving already-existing products). The third variety, initially proposed for the Visegrad Four (V4) and later for other ECE countries, is DME which relies on attracting foreign direct investment (FDI) and being, as Nölke & Vliegenthart put it, 'an assembly platform for semi-standardized industrial goods' which makes for their institutional comparative advantage. Here, the specific coordination mechanism would come down neither to the state nor to the market, but to the intra-firm hierarchies that prevail within transnational enterprises.

Given the fact that the origins of the VoC research programme come from an analysis of the USA, Japan, and Western Europe's developed economies, the fall of communism brought about a group of transition economies and the need to position them within the typologies of capitalist systems. In the context of global political economy, the V4 countries differ from Russia or Ukraine, or even Romania and Bulgaria, in many substantial ways. They are considered to be the success stories of economic and political transformation (even though there has been some serious democratic backsliding in Poland and Hungary) and Europeanization. Nevertheless, there has not been any agreement in the literature on whether they converge towards one particular type of capitalism known from the Western European context. While some scholars claimed that the ECE states show more and more similarities with the CME type (McMenamin 2004; Lane 2005), others argued that they converge rather towards the LME model (Cernat 2002; Crowley 2005; Baboš 2010). Yet, the third group claimed that they represent a sort of hybrid type combining the features of both types (Iankova 2002; Mykhnenko 2007).

As argued by Nölke & Vliegenthart (2009), such conclusions are not only confusing but also challenging towards the basic assumptions of the

VoC approach claiming that the strong institutional complementarities exist between the core elements of a specific type of capitalism performed in a given national economy. The central thesis of this body of literature argues that the character of institutions within an economy is mutually reinforcing, balancing, and complementing. Consequently, any hybrid form – in contrast to a coherent variety of capitalism – would lead towards some suboptimal outcomes. Many premature conclusions – based on exclusively quantitative approaches comparing some basic characteristics of ECE economies with the two leading models: CME or LME – generated methodological artefacts (King & Sznajder 2006). A more sophisticated application of VoC approaches was needed in order to paint an understandable picture of the institutional complexity of ECE capitalisms. By focusing on the most crucial institutional complementarities within the VoC models, Nölke & Vliegenthart (2009, p. 672) concluded that ECE capitalism does not fit with the established typologies since fitting in would entail an exclusion of the central characteristic of the region that is its external dependency. DMEs in the ECE have comparative advantages in the assembly of relatively complex consumer goods that are based on skilled but cheap labour, and the provision of capital delivered by FDI.

An increased level of attention on the topic has been observable again since around 2015. This date marks two political events of crucial importance for the region. Firstly, the so-called migration crisis became one of the major topics of public debate. Secondly, on the canvas of the campaign influenced by this crisis, the Law and Justice political party (PiS) commenced its rule in Poland. From this point, the V4 countries again started to be perceived as a homogenous bloc because what came to the fore was their assertive attitude towards the solutions offered to the Member States by the European Commission. These events also re-attracted the attention of researchers of the developmental issues faced by the V4 countries, partly thanks to the need for finding some explanatory variables of the observed 'populist backlash'. Interestingly, the growth of popularity of the conservative parties and governments in the region has been approached in literature (Pavlínek 2016; Krpec & Hodulák 2019; Feldmann & Poppa 2022) as an effect of societies' discontent with 'neoliberal' policies of the formerly ruling political class (and of the EU) that led to the creation of the DME regime, together with its harmful consequences such as rising spatial inequalities. On the other hand, the populist governments have themselves been labelled as 'neoliberal' by critical political economy authors (Fabry 2019), which was supported by the arguments connected to, *inter alia*, the COVID-19 pandemic's crisis management. Nevertheless, it was reassessed in the literature that the similarities among V4 countries are limited mainly to the variety of dependent capitalism that they perform and that they vary significantly in terms of the kinds of responses or attitudes towards this state of affairs. In the political dimension, Poland and Hungary seem to have more in common because of the 'illiberal turn' of their governments, which have attempted to transform their political institutions. Yet, for the whole group of V4 countries, a similar response to the migration crisis remains the only vivid and stable tangent point. It is worth adding that many other Member States have proved to be critical to the migration policy of the European Commission. Hence, although the specific position in the international division of labour (and issues resulting from it) make a common denominator for V4 countries, their socio-political strategies of escaping this situation are definitely different. Also, a low level of economic cooperation between these countries has been observed (Jasiecki 2020), making their similar institutional order and ties with Germany their biggest commonality.

Germany exemplifies the inner core of the DI in this study, whereas Poland is classified by this study's standards as the outer core. In fact, going beyond the nomenclature used in the literature of differentiated integration, it is necessary to acknowledge that German-Polish relations resemble classic centre-periphery relations (even if Poland is labelled as semi-periphery, it is predominantly in contrast to even more peripheral states in the east, such as Ukraine). This centre-periphery constellation reflects the asymmetrical dependency relations between Germany and Poland. However, the map of DI visualizes the position of other economies (namely the Swiss and British economies) as being even more distant from the EU's core. Switzerland and the UK undoubtedly belong to the global core in economic terms, but in relation to core European integration processes they circulate on more and more distant orbits vis-à-vis Brussels. Therefore, the MIT and DME theorizations are much more productive as interpretative vehicles when explaining the position in centre-periphery relations of transition economies, including Poland.

3 Germany as a coordinated market trendsetter at the core of European integration

3.1 GERMANY ON THE MAP OF DIFFERENTIATED EUROPEAN INTEGRATION

Germany has always been positioned at the very centre of the European integration project (Beck 2013; Muenkler 2015). This has been the case since the very foundation of the European Communities in the 1950s when, at that time, West Germany became one of the most important 'founding members' and since then has been labelled as the 'engine' of European integration (Dehio 1955). This role has been shared with France in the form of the so-called 'Franco-German tandem' for a couple of decades. Nevertheless, due to the relative decrease in France's power (Giddens 2013), Germany – especially after reunification (Kundnani 2015) and the financial crises – remained alone in this position (Blome et al. 2015). Today's Germany – despite the recent economic slowdown – is the politically strongest, economically richest, and most pro-European oriented Member State of the European Union. In the era of Chancellor Angela Merkel, she was referred to as 'Frau Europa' or 'the Empress of Europe' which shows the pro-European attitude of the German leaders, but also reveals some fears and concerns in the context of German domination in the European Union. 'Hegemony' or 'locomotive' – these are terms which have been attributed to Germany in opinions regarding its role and position in a united Europe. The European route has been the way to return to the international community for the Federal Republic of Germany since the inception of the state in 1949, the axiom of *raison d'état* and the foundation on which it built its new statehood and new identity.

By DI standards, it is generally agreed that Germany occupies the inner core (Schoellgen 1992, 2003; Muenkler 2015) of the system of European integration differentiation. It is the outcome of a number of interrelated factors, including historical legacies, economic power, political gravity, geopolitical localization (Röpke 2008; Wolf 2004) as well as the general consensus in the German public discourse about the role of Germany in Europe and, vice versa, the important functions that the European integration process plays for Germany (Habermas 2015). With the exceptions that are described in this chapter, the Eurosceptic narrative remains marginal in Germany, and the mainstream political parties, as well as the vast majority of German citizens, do not question the core position that Germany inhabits within the EU.

Interestingly, this central place that Germany naturally takes in Europe does not translate automatically into a self-accepted (by the Germans) leadership role, at least not in an acknowledged way (Schwarz 2005). For a number of reasons, and with the shadow of history still seeming to be one critical factor (Bousquet 1980), Berlin tries to avoid a leadership role (Stephens 2013) and the accompanying risks of being accused of holding a para-hegemonic position. As a result, the authors can identify a gap that is created in the space between the German size, potential, and gravity on one side, and the self-perception of 'reluctant hegemon' (Schönberger 2012) on the other.

In order to understand Germany's position in the inner core of the European integration project, several issues need to be taken into consideration. Firstly, one must take historical legacy into account – the European integration project was built on the ruins of the Second World War and the trauma stemming from it. Germany's post-Second World War self-limitation *Politik* resulted in, among other things, the 'Europeanization of Germany' paradigm. Secondly, and more contemporarily, the monetary union is of crucial importance for German relations with other EU partners. Despite the fact that it was not a German project by design, two decades after the introduction of the Euro it is undoubtedly the German economy that gained the most out of it, in relative (vis-à-vis other Eurozone members) and non-relative terms. Anthony Giddens (2015) claims that Germany managed to achieve economically much more than they could ever (historically) dream of as regards relative power. Thirdly, the green transition reached the very top of the EU agenda, and it is not a coincidence that it has also been Germany's priority for decades. The European Green Deal is one of the most ambitious objectives announced by the German EU Commission President Ursula von der Leyen. Last but not least, the migration issue – which is so very salient from the point of view of this analysis. It is not only one of the crises that is present in this study as an important contextual variable, but it is also the attitudes towards migration that are so closely interlinked with support for the European integration project. All these aspects are crucial for exploring the German position on the map of European DI, and they are discussed below in a more in-depth manner.

The reunification of Germany in 1990 caused many fears about the growing dominance of the country along with shifts in the balance of power in Europe. Trying to assuage these fears, German politicians assured their fellow Europeans that they respected the values on which the EU was built, and that Germany was absolutely subordinate to decisions taken at the EU level. Thus, attempts were made to create an image of a state that did not want to arouse any suspicions or fears of a return to superpower politics in the European arena. At the same time, however, the significance and importance of Germany in the EU was unquestionable – increasingly so – by ascribing to it a 'leading function'. However, this usually occurred in the context of talking about a sense of responsibility (even increased responsibility) for the fate of Europe and the world. The constitution of the Federal Republic of Germany, as one of the few such in Europe, contains provisions relating directly to European integration. Article 23 of the said constitution refers to the transfer of some portion of the state's sovereignty to the European institutions, which was and still is intended to prove that Germany does not seek hegemony in Europe. It reads: 'For the realization of a united Europe, the Federal Republic shall cooperate in the development of the European Union, which is bound by democratic, state, social and federal principles and the principle of subsidiarity, and guarantees fundamental rights protection comparable in principle to this Basic Law.' As a result, deeper integration – namely binding the German economy with the pan-European monetary union – was the answer at the time; an advanced economic union sharing a common currency.

Historically speaking, the ideas about creating an integrated European space have appeared in the political thought of German intellectuals and thinkers since the earliest of times, with some researchers even tracing them back to Emperor Otto III. Until 1945, Germany's conceptual involvement in European integration could be read mainly as the creation of projects aimed at expanding the German sphere of influence by annexing new territories and connecting them under German leadership. It was Germany that was to play a special role in these processes (*Sonderrolle*), to be the carrier of European values and to defend them against anti-European forces. From Emmanuel's Kant's concept of a republican federation of free nations, all the way up to Friedrich Nauman's *Mitteleuropa*, Europe has witnessed a great deal of German visions of integrating Europe.

Immediately after 1945, the West German integration doctrine did not verbalize Germany's national interest. It was very much to the contrary – the 'Europeanized Germany' paradigm was dominating both domestic and foreign policy discourse in Bonn. The pursuit of European integration gained – mainly thanks to the involvement of Konrad Adenauer – the rank of a constitutional obligation. The policy of the so-called 'restraint and self-limitation' of West Germany manifested itself in depreciating that which was national and emphasizing the importance of what was European. Successive German governments expressed their will to act for European integration, and the country was unequivocally attributed with a pro-European political culture and was considered one of those countries most intensively supporting this process. The issue of transferring sovereign rights to the Community/EU level and sharing the power of national governments with the institutions in Brussels was supported by successive German governments. In the first period (after 1949), when West Germany could not conduct a sovereign foreign policy, the country could only gain by agreeing to transfer powers of attorney on common economic policy to the European level (supranationalization). In the later period, this readiness to cede powers to the EU level did not weaken, but it should be noted that Germany at the same time made sure that its voice, as the demographically and economically strongest country, was sufficiently strong in the EU's institutional apparatus.

At the same time, the main characteristic of Germany's European policy was, and still remains, its pragmatism. West Germany co-created the first European Communities and, together with France, was the driving force behind the integration process. Today – as a united state entity – it has become its authentic leader, with a decisive voice on the most important issues. The great importance attached to the concept of European integration that started in the late 1940s was a direct result of the post-war geopolitical situation in which the West German state found itself, and was also due to the desire to break its isolation in the international (mainly European) arena. Germany's economic power, demographic and geopolitical potential, as well as German soft power, predispose Berlin to play the role of political and economic leader in Europe. Moreover, in the post-war period, many German politicians proved to be outstanding personalities and politicians who, while enjoying great authority, have been and are able to steer the integration processes in the desired direction for Germany. Their negotiating skills, along with their ability to lead to a common position and make compromises, enable them to occupy leading positions in EU institutions and exert a significant influence on the decisions made.

All of the above does not mean that the German political landscape is free from Euroscepticism – this would be totally unnatural. In its early stages, the German version of Euroscepticism was rising mainly in the liberal-conservative political spectrum and expressed itself in economic nationalist rhetoric; the migration crises finally 'touched a nerve of national identity because it asked Europe's populations to harbor culturally dissimilar people' (Hooghe & Marks 2019, p. 1122). In 2015, immigration became the most important issue in almost every country within the EU and rising public support for nationalist parties made it more difficult for government leaders to work out deals at the European level. In early 2016, electoral pressure 'to shut the door appeared irresistible' (Hooghe & Marks 2019, p. 1122). Angela Merkel's popularity dropped rapidly to a four-year low, reflecting concerns over the influx of refugees and migrants to Germany. In this sense, the so-called German 'locomotive' or 'engine' for European integration seems to have stalled the process itself via overexpanding the very peripheries of

European integration, and also within its own society. 'It was a strong decision on a matter that continues to divide EU Member States today. The decision by the German chancellor Angela Merkel also played a major role in setting the stage of the United Kingdom's (UK) popular referendum on the country's membership in the EU' (Gänzle et al. 2021, p. 9). Following the referendum, Merkel dropped her long-standing opposition to a Europe of different speeds and noticed the necessity of differentiated integration and the courage for some countries to go ahead if not everyone wants to participate. 'A Europe of different speeds is necessary, otherwise we will probably get stuck'. When referring to Germany's place and role within European integration, it is not without contradictions in its claim to be the leader of a united and strengthened Europe. Back in 2014, in the wake of the Russian annexation of Crimea and the war in the Donbass region, Angela Merkel's government, together with France, put forth a tough stance on sanctions against Russia and a desire for deeper integration in common foreign and security policy, which would enable the EU to react uniformly to external shocks. Further, in the government's opinion, an energy union should decrease individual states' vulnerability regarding energy dependency on Russian oil and gas. But it turned out to be, in time, quite to the contrary; Germany rowed back, even actively cooperating with Russian pipeline politics in the case of North Stream II, which undermined EU cohesiveness in the energy sector. After the outbreak of the full-scale war between Russia and Ukraine in 2022, Olaf Scholz, the designated German chancellor of the new social-democrat-liberal-green *Ampelkoalition*, proclaimed a *Zeitenwende* in the German parliament in February 2022. This *Zeitenwende* stands for a new understanding of German political leadership in Europe, releasing EUR 100 billion and thereby adapting to the reborn realism of power politics in Europe. But, rather, this amount of public spending was intended to restore the state's own military which had been strongly neglected in the decades before. The first half of 2022 was especially characterized by (inter)national disputes about Scholz's coalition's hesitation to contribute to the Western-backed supply of weapons for the purpose of defending Ukraine. Public support was broad for initiating a turn in Germany's strategic role in a changing environment. The German president, Frank-Walter Steinmeier, spoke to the people about defending their allies and nation. Therefore, he stated, a strong army would be necessary – 'and the army needed the respect and support of German society. As a strong country at the heart of Europe, Germany had a duty to meet. Germany needed to become capable of handling conflict' (after: Quinville 2022). At the same time, Olaf Scholz – after taking the chancellor's office from Angela Merkel – declared 'the initiation of *Zeitenwende*' (incidentally, *Zeitenwende* was declared 2022's word of the year by the German Language Society), meaning 'turning point'. After the full-scale Russian aggression against Ukraine, the new chancellor announced that a new set of relations between

Europe and the wider world would be needed, and also a new intra-European order. It still remains an open question whether the first centre-left government after the Merkel era harbours enough internal and external capacities to shape a path for a further deepening of European integration, or whether its parties will open the door to differentiated integration as another solution to the challenges to cooperation and solidarity among EU Member States and societies. Nevertheless, Germany's determination to remain in the EU's inner core is unquestionable. Equally clear are the Germans' visions for the future of Europe, which Berlin envisages as being more deeply integrated, more federalist, and, most probably, more differentiated.

While from Warsaw's perspective the idea of ever-tighter EU integration has seemingly faded, the German government led by social-democrat Olaf Scholtz has actually enshrined it in the coalition agreement. The coalition parties of the social-democratic SPD, the Greens, and the liberal FDP have pledged to further develop the European Union towards a 'federal European state'. An extremely ambitious goal, it seems, compared to all other U-member states; no other European government goes as far in its vision as Germany does in its coalition agreement. Lofty visions of the future of the European Union have a long tradition – already in the Treaty of Rome of 1957 there was talk of a 'definite will to lay the foundations for an ever closer union between the peoples of Europe'. The 2009 Lisbon Treaty also calls for an 'ever closer union'. Jacques Delors, president of the European Commission between 1985–1995, believed that Europe must go further and further towards integration, comparing it to a bicycle: 'Stop him and he'll fall over.' Such a full affirmation of deep European integration is rarely heard of today. On the contrary, Britain's exit in 2020 was the strongest rejection yet of the EU. And many other EU Member States are openly opposing this idea, or certainly silently not supporting it. While Germany wants to federalize the EU, which would legitimize its dominant role, Poland is pushing for its further enlargement – in this sense Poland took the traditional British role in the discussion about the future of Europe. In other words, by promoting a European federation, the German government creates a natural space for potential differentiation which will result from a deepening of the integration project. However, deepening European integration would mean supranationalizing foreign policy or building European defence capacities, or even transferring to the community level some other competences that would build a European federal quasi-state. As regards the focus point of this publication – that is, the type of economic model – most of the instruments are already at the disposal of the community. In this sense, Germany is of double importance in this process: firstly by the gravity of its economy – it simply is the largest and therefore most important state and economy in Europe; and secondly by its role in Brussels, where Berlin's decision-making power is proportionally higher. If one adds that to the fact that the financial crises proved the supremacy of the German type of economic governance in Europe, we clearly see that the coordinated market economy model (CME) that is favoured by Germany (see the section below) is becoming the default for the whole of Europe.

Despite the fact that various political parties in the German political system opt for various socio-economic policies, and therefore for different economic governance models, one needs to notice that as regards the mainstream parties (CDU/CSU and SPD as well as, to a lesser extent, the FDP), they are surprisingly close to one another in their economic ideas and ideologies – they all support slightly different versions of the same CME (*Sozialmarktwirtschaft* – as it is framed in the German constitution). This could come to a head with other parties' economic governance preferences in Germany, such as the AfD *(Alternative für Deutschland*) with its more libertarian view, or *Die Linke* (The Left) which is much closer to the extreme leftist pole. Nevertheless, most of the mainstream political spectrum in Germany opts for CME types of economic governance, sometimes called German ordoliberalism, which represents a more socially imbedded ideology (Tranoy & Schwartz 2020).

3.2 RHENISH CAPITALISM: THE COORDINATION ROLE-MODEL

The dynamics of modern capitalism have undergone significant transformations in response to the complexities of globalization, technological advancements, and shifting economic paradigms. Among the diverse landscapes of global economies, Germany stands out as a prominent example of a CME as understood within the conceptual framework of varieties of capitalism (VoC). Rooted in institutional arrangements that emphasize collaborative industrial relations, vocational training, and long-term corporate strategies, the German model has been celebrated for its robustness and stability.

In the wake of the devastation caused by the Second World War, Germany embarked on a remarkable journey of post-war reconstruction. Central to this endeavour was the concept of Rhenish capitalism, which gained prominence during the 1940s and 1950s. Shaped by the economic philosophy of ordoliberalism, and influenced by the historical context of a war-torn Europe, this period saw the emergence of a distinctive economic model that would come to define Germany's economic success. The Rhenish capitalist model emphasized a balanced approach that sought to marry market efficiency with social equity. This perspective drew from the experience of the Rhineland region's historical cooperative practices, which encouraged collaborative relationships between business, labour, and the state. Michel Albert's seminal work 'Capitalism vs. Capitalism' (1993) elucidated the characteristics of this model, highlighting its emphasis on stability, long-term planning, and a strong welfare state. This approach was particularly salient in contrast to the individualistic, shareholder-focused orientation of Anglo-American capitalism.

At the core of the Rhenish model was the idea of a 'social market economy', championed by key figures such as Ludwig Erhard, the architect of Germany's post-war economic miracle. This concept aimed to mitigate the excesses of unfettered capitalism by incorporating social protections, collective bargaining, and cooperative labour relations. The model prioritized full employment, labour rights, and social safety nets, fostering a sense of economic security that resonated deeply with the German populace after the hardships of war. Furthermore, Rhenish capitalism emphasized the role of industrial policy and the state in guiding economic development. The notion of ordoliberalism, rooted in the works of Walter Eucken, underscored the importance of maintaining competitive markets while preventing monopolistic practices that could undermine broader economic welfare.

This philosophy laid the foundation for a regulated market economy that aimed to ensure equitable access to resources and opportunities. Eucken and other proponents of ordoliberalism advocated for the importance of competitive markets as engines of economic growth. However, they recognized that markets left unchecked could lead to negative outcomes, such as monopolies and inequalities. To address these concerns, the ordoliberal approach emphasized the necessity of a regulatory framework that restrained market power while promoting competition. This philosophy found expression in Germany's social market economy, which aimed to harness the benefits of capitalism while mitigating its potential drawbacks. The regulatory principles of ordoliberalism manifested in Germany's competition policy, which remains influential to this day. Antitrust measures and anti-monopoly laws were implemented to prevent market domination and to encourage a level playing field for businesses. Moreover, the emphasis on a competitive market structure was closely intertwined with Germany's commitment to preventing inflation and maintaining monetary stability.

In the shaping of post-unification Germany's capitalism, policy decisions focused on revitalizing the East's economy and integrating it into the larger German and European economic landscape. Infrastructure investments, vocational training programmes, and labour market reforms were aimed at addressing regional disparities and fostering economic growth. The role of the state was pivotal in coordinating these efforts, reflecting the country's historical commitment to guided market principles. The challenges of integrating two distinct economic systems demonstrated the adaptability and resilience of the social market economy model. By leveraging its institutional strengths, Germany managed to navigate the unification process while maintaining core principles of collaboration, social protections, and market efficiency. The lessons learned during this period continue to inform Germany's economic strategies and contribute to its positioning within comparative capitalism frameworks.

This chapter embarks on a comprehensive analysis of the evolution of German capitalism since the early 2000s, utilizing the lens of the VoC framework to provide insights into how this paradigmatic CME has navigated through multifaceted challenges and opportunities. Over the past two decades, Germany's economic landscape has witnessed transformations driven by factors ranging from technological revolutions to shifts in political power. This analysis aims to shed light on the degree to which Germany's historical institutional arrangements have adapted or evolved in response to these changing dynamics, while also examining the potential continuities that persist amidst the flux. Against this backdrop, the chapter aims to provide a nuanced exploration of how Germany's CME model has adapted to meet the demands of a rapidly changing global economic landscape. Central to this endeavour is the identification of key drivers that have influenced the trajectory of German capitalism and the extent to which these changes resonate with or deviate from traditional CME attributes. Scholars have extensively examined how Germany's CME characteristics have contributed to its economic success while also exploring the challenges and adaptations faced in the 21st century. One pivotal aspect of the VoC analysis is the role of industrial relations in shaping economic outcomes. Wolfgang Streeck (1992, pp. 301–330) underscores the importance of Germany's cooperative industrial relations in enhancing economic stability and innovation. The concept of co-determination, whereby workers are represented on company boards, has been a hallmark of German labour relations and has attracted considerable attention from researchers assessing its impact on corporate governance and firm-based performance.

The literature has also delved into the vocational training system as a cornerstone of the German model. Anke Hassel (2007, pp. 253–277) has highlighted how Germany's skill-intensive workforce and dual education system have been pivotal in maintaining the country's competitive edge in industries requiring highly specialized labour. Moreover, discussions around corporate governance within the German model have been a key focus. Bottenberg et al. (2017, pp. 165–180) have examined the balance between stakeholder interests and shareholder influence within the two-tier board structure. This structure allows for the representation of different stakeholders, including labour representatives, in decision-making processes. As the German model navigated the challenges of globalization and digitalization, researchers have explored the country's strategies for maintaining competitiveness in the face of changing economic landscapes. A study by Kathleen Thelen and Marius R. Busemeyer (2012, pp. 68–100) sheds light on the adaptability of vocational training in the context of globalization. Additionally, discussions around the introduction of the statutory minimum wage in 2015 and its implications for labour relations and income inequality have fuelled debates on the adaptability of the CME framework. Scholars such as Werner Eichhorst et al. (2022) discuss the challenges posed by digitalization as regards the German labour market.

Like many countries around the world, Germany confronted corporate governance scandals in the 1990s that underscored the need for public discourse on its established corporate governance framework and the fact that it was dominated by influential banks. Historically, German banks played a dual role, serving as essential sources of external financing through loans due to underdeveloped stock and bond markets, while also acting as central nodes in cross-ownership networks termed 'Germany Inc.' (*Deutschland AG*). Furthermore, banks engaged in proxy voting on behalf of individual shareholders. Yet, economic and regulatory changes have challenged this system profoundly since the early 2000s (Larcker & Tayan 2016, pp. 16–32). As globalization gained traction, Germany recognized the requirement for market-oriented finance, driven by factors such as post-unification economic growth, shifts in political dynamics, and the EU's financial integration initiatives. Simultaneously, changes in the German banking sector, focusing on internationalization and fee-based services, coupled with regulatory efforts supporting market-based financing, restructured the funding landscape and induced corresponding shifts in corporate governance.

Recent research (Gugler & Peev 2023, pp. 84–107) revealed that despite almost three decades since the initiation of the global corporate governance revolution, German individuals, families, and other domestic companies continue to maintain a significant presence as primary blockholders in the leading 20 firms (constituting 65% of these firms), the top 100 firms (comprising 54%), and publicly listed German companies (making up 53%). However, non-traditional stakeholders in the *Deutschland AG*, such as foreign blockholders and widely held companies, collectively represent a share of 25% in the top 20 firms, 36% in the top 100, and 36% in publicly listed German companies.

Over the past 30 years, German non-financial industrial companies have significantly increased equity portions within their capital structures, amassing substantial shareholder funds. This shift is evident in the German stock market's expansion, with capitalization amounting to around 2.37 trillion USD in mid-2023 (statista.com n.d.). Despite this, the German stock market's size remains relatively small compared to its population. In comparison, in the period after the Great Recession (from 2014 to 2019), the market capitalization of German equity markets relative to GDP still stood at only 52%, notably lower than the US's 151% and the OECD's 111%. Germany's 52% is even lower than in other CME-leaning countries (World Bank 2023). The transformation in the German corporate landscape stems not only from increased equity positions among companies, but also from remarkable growth in corporate bond volumes, a near-absent facet 30 years ago. Among the listed companies, corporate bonds now play a more significant role in financing than traditional bank loans, particularly after financial crises. This comprehensive shift highlights a broader trend towards equity and market-oriented funding sources for German businesses. Various factors contribute to this shift in the financing landscape of German companies. What is unmissable is the role of tax reduction acts in Germany, such as the 2001 and 2008 Tax Reduction Acts, which have aimed to counter the historical debt bias by lowering corporate tax rates and enhancing the appeal of retained earnings.

Amid evolving business conditions over the past three decades, globalization and the inception of the European Single Market in 1993 prompted a notable internationalization of corporate business models. This transformation is evident in the median German non-financial listed firm's surge in international sales share from one third to about one half. Simultaneously, heightened global competition drove German firms in high labour-cost settings to embrace greater innovation, as evidenced by significant growth in R&D expenditures relative to GDP. This shift unfolded amidst increased uncertainty and operational volatility, with German firms evolving their business models to prioritize risk-sharing considerations. Consequently, equity financing gained momentum, supplanting debt financing as a favoured funding avenue, shaped by interactions between tax reforms, evolving business dynamics, and a need for adaptability in an ever-changing economic landscape. Nevertheless, recent developments in German capital markets have not been favourable, particularly regarding initial public offerings (IPOs) in the equity market. In the mid-2010s, there were only about a dozen IPOs annually, partly due to German entrepreneurs' reluctance to relinquish control. The shift towards market-based financing was further influenced by regulations aimed at the banking sector, resulting in higher costs for corporate borrowers and diminished bank profitability. Notably, the Basel Committee on Banking Supervision imposed heightened equity requirements on banks, known as the Basel Accords. Additionally, German banks embraced internationalization, focusing on fee-based services and spurred by the growing global reach of the financial services industry. Moreover, the introduction of the Euro currency stimulated the development of European bond markets, which had been previously underrepresented (Goergen et al. 2008, pp. 175–193).

Another primary objective of the legal reforms aimed at transforming German corporate governance was to fortify the rights of minority shareholders. This endeavour led to the introduction of measures to increase transparency, prohibit the use of multiple classes of voting shares, and regulate insider trading and transactions involving related parties. Another significant goal was to enhance internal governance, particularly the efficiency and accountability of the supervisory board. This was pursued through the enactment of pivotal laws such as the Corporate Sector Supervision and Transparency Act (KonTraG), the Transparency and Disclosure Act (TransPuG), and similar initiatives (Hopt 2015). These measures not only expanded the scope of responsibilities but also heightened the potential legal liability of non-executive directors. This concerted effort aimed at enhancing the functionality and oversight of supervisory boards demonstrates a commitment to constructing a robust corporate governance framework. Moreover, there was a noticeable shift in incentives for German executives, moving them towards a more market-oriented landscape. Notably, the introduction of stock option plans gained traction. Interestingly, stock option plans only became a viable option for German companies in 1998, enabled by the enactment of the KonTraG. This change marked a significant departure in structuring executive compensation, aligning it more closely with market dynamics and shareholder interests (Vitols 2009).

Untangling the complex networks of cross-holdings presented two major challenges, the first of which was the prevailing tax structure creating substantial 'lock-in' effects due to the appreciation of ownership stakes over time, making them subject to capital gains taxation upon sale. To address this, the German Social Democrats, under the leadership of Chancellor Schröder, introduced the Tax Reduction Act in 2001. This legislation allowed corporations to divest ownership stakes without incurring capital gains taxes. This move coincided with the rise of globalization, regulatory changes, and technological advancements, all fostering the concept of economies of scale within the financial industry. Consequently, financial institutions significantly reduced their cross-shareholdings in subsequent years, leading to the dissolution of cross-ownership networks. Simultaneously, the number of board seats held by bankers experienced a sharp decline, diminishing the primary avenues through which banks exerted influence over the corporate sector. In 2002, the German Corporate Governance Code (GCGC) was introduced. Inspired by the 'comply-or-explain' framework of the British Cadbury Report from a decade earlier, the GCGC represented a form of 'soft-law' regulation. These initiatives resulted in a notable internationalization of corporate ownership in German firms and a significant reduction in the overall concentration of ownership within these firms over recent decades. These changes signify a dedicated effort to align corporate governance practices with international standards while fostering enhanced transparency and accountability in the German business environment (Cromme 2005, pp. 362–367).

As a consequence of these transformations, German capital markets have evolved, and the German stock market has successfully attracted international investors and has expanded in size and scope. This growth is evident in the one-third increase in total market capitalization as a percentage of GDP when comparing the 1990s to the first decade of the 21st century. German regulatory authorities didn't merely replicate a market-oriented legal framework; instead, they enhanced the existing model, integrating its distinctive local characteristics, while also introducing shareholder-focused elements aimed at facilitating the operation of market forces. This approach entailed a deliberate effort to find equilibrium between the traditional German corporate governance system and the evolving requirements of a more market-driven context.

The subsequent decade saw Germany turning its attention to education policy aligned with the Europe 2020 strategy. Priorities included an early, high-quality education, particularly for children from immigrant backgrounds. To achieve this, comprehensive measures were undertaken, encompassing pre-school and early school infrastructure development, a lifelong learning framework for teacher training, youth health promotion, and inclusive education solutions for individuals with disabilities. The nation's steadfast connection between education and the labour market endured, with vocational education embracing the 'dual education model' – a blend of theoretical learning and practical experience in workplace settings. This model bolstered workforce preparedness and bolstered organizational competence, drawing parallels with approaches in other CME-oriented countries: Austria, Switzerland, and Denmark serve as examples.

In Germany, vocational training plays a significantly more important role in the development of skills compared to countries that are following the LME-like patterns. In 2022, the share of upper-secondary students enrolled in vocational programmes was almost 49%, which is 6.5 p.p. more than in an average OECD country (OECD 2023a). This vocational training system operates on a dual basis, incorporating both educational institutions and businesses. Apprentices divide their work time between receiving general instruction at specialized vocational schools (*Berufsschulen*) in order to attain certified and standardized occupational skills and acquiring specific skills through practical experience in their workplaces. This approach to building human capital is a collaborative effort involving employers, labour unions, and the government. It furnishes Germany with a competitive edge over nations with less developed vocational training frameworks. This model generates significant pools of skilled labour, cultivates a versatile workforce, and ensures a consistent influx of personnel equipped with uniform theoretical and practical qualifications. Additionally, this system contributes to a relatively low rate of youth unemployment by facilitating the smooth transition from education to the job market. As the statistical data suggest, for the whole period since the Great Recession, the German unemployment rate remained below those rates of the LME, general-skills-oriented countries (understood as the UK, the US, and Ireland).

Nevertheless, this training approach has faced challenges in recent times due to a consistent shortage of training positions provided by businesses. Numerous explanations have been put forth to account for this trend. Some suggest that the training system's origins in manufacturing make it ill-suited for the requirements of the private service sector. Additionally, heightened global competition has made companies more conscious of the expenses associated with training. Employers have expressed dissatisfaction with the declining quality of applicants, while labour unions have accused employers of lacking dedication. Other analyses view these developments as part of the broader trend of liberalization within the German political economy. With the decentralization of collective bargaining and diminishing bargaining coverage, companies have prioritized their individual interests over the formerly collective approach to training. Simultaneously, there has been a rise in the significance of higher education alongside the decline of vocational training (Busemeyer et al. 2012; Thelen & Busemeyer 2012). Examining the period between 2000 and 2015, one study points out that the number of students entering apprenticeship programmes declined from over 600,000 to around 500,000 annually, while enrolment in higher education programmes increased from slightly over 300,000 to around 500,000 (Benassi et al. 2018). This shift from skill development through vocational education to the higher education system signifies a transfer of this policy domain from employment relations institutions and diminishes the sway of labour unions.

While the formal structures of industry-wide collective bargaining have endured in Germany, declining coverage and increasing decentralization have far-reaching implications for both the institution of collective bargaining and the societal outcomes it delivers. Initially, the decrease in coverage means that labour unions and employers' associations have lost their ability to establish wages and working conditions throughout the entire economy, effectively removing wages from competitive influences. This has led to a significant rise in pay disparities and, subsequently, to inequalities in working and living conditions.

Germany's legal framework outlines the representation of employees' interests through co-determination via works councils (with its origins rooted in the Weimar Republic) at the workplace level, and through collective bargaining carried out by labour unions at the industry level. Subsequently, decentralization blurs the lines between collective bargaining conducted at the industry level and co-determination practised at the enterprise level. This shift grants more authority to works councils and management at the expense of labour unions and employers' associations. They now play an increasingly pivotal role in regulating substantive and distributive matters through works agreements. This elevated responsibility places additional demands on works councils and raises questions about the strict peace obligation that bars them from engaging in industrial action. Nonetheless, only a minority of employees presently benefit from these arrangements. Indeed, a significant portion of the workforce is affected, with 37% of employees in the western region and

48% in the eastern region lacking coverage by any collective agreement and lacking representation through a works council (Ellguth & Kohaut 2019, pp. 39–66). This substantial disparity in representation serves as evidence that the current institutions have been so undermined that it is no longer appropriate to describe the employment relations system as that of a coherent, unified structure nationwide.

Around the mid-2000s, some unions began advocating for a universal minimum wage, while others, including most other unions, employers' associations, and labour economists, staunchly opposed the idea. Governments were divided on the matter and struggled to reach a consensus (Mabbett 2023). Consequently, the social partners agreed upon industry-specific minimum pay levels within the service sector. A critical turning point occurred in 2014 when the government enacted legislation to establish a statutory minimum hourly wage. The minimum wage itself undergoes regular adjustments based on recommendations from the minimum wage commission (*Mindestlohnkommission*). This commission consists of representatives from labour unions, employers' associations, and independent experts, aiming to maintain a balanced perspective in determining minimum wage changes. The statutory minimum wage was introduced in 2015, making it one of the last nations in the EU to implement such regulation. Historically, a statutory minimum wage was deemed unnecessary due to the extensive coverage of collective bargaining. It was also believed to impede unions' and employers' autonomy in determining work conditions without governmental intervention. However, collective bargaining coverage has substantially waned. Additionally, unions found it challenging to secure satisfactory wages through collective bargaining in sectors with few members and limited bargaining power. This led to a notable increase in low pay instances (defined as incomes below 60% of the median pay). The concept of the 'working poor', i.e., individuals who work but still earn incomes below the poverty threshold, emerged as a pressing issue (Backhaus & Müller 2023, pp. 216–232).

The issue of wage and income disparities is also worth discussing from the perspective of gender inequalities. The involvement of women in the German labour market is on the rise and their participation rate is steadily increasing. By 2021, the difference in participation rates between women waned to about 7 p.p. (World Bank 2023). Various state policies either uphold or challenge the single-breadwinner model. For instance, the taxation of married couples jointly acts as a deterrent for married women's participation in the workforce. Conversely, recent expansions in public childcare and the implementation of a fathers' quota in parental leave have contributed to altering gender norms and have increased the labour force participation of mothers (Zoch & Schober 2018). Nevertheless, substantial and persistent gender disparities still exist, especially concerning pay and leadership roles. The unadjusted gender pay gap has tended to decrease. In 2021 it was 17.6%, compared to 22.7% in 2006. Despite this fact, it remains one of the highest among developed countries and significantly higher than the EU average of 12.7% (Eurostat 2023a). In 2022, women occupied 29% of executive roles in Germany, placing the country in the lower third among all EU Member States in terms of gender diversity in executive positions (although it did show a slight increase of 2.6 percentage points over two decades; Destatis n.d.). Progress has been more noticeable in board positions, particularly on supervisory boards, with a legal gender quota introduced in 2015, leading to a surge in female presence on these boards from below 10% in 2008 to about 28% in 2019 (Kirsch & Wrohlich, 2020). The pace of change in women's participation in the labour market and their representation on boards underscores the role of state policies in promoting greater gender equality.

Driven by concerns of excessive indebtedness, Germany introduced the 'debt brake' (*Schuldenbremse*) regulation after 2008's global economic crash. A notable component was the wage-subsidizing *Kurzarbeit* programme, a form of job sharing during economic downturns. Rooted in the belief that economic downturns are transient and that retaining skilled employees outweighs the costs of hiring new ones, this programme maintains demand levels while ensuring a smoother transition through economic troughs. Germany's family policy underwent subtle transformations, addressing welfare state structures that inadvertently disincentivized women's participation in the workforce, particularly those women with single breadwinners. Contemporary cohorts of women are progressively opting for full-time employment and employing childcare services, ushering in a shift that acknowledges changing work dynamics. Amidst these changes, the German welfare state remains rooted in insurance principles and work-centric social welfare ideals. While suggestions for a liberal-social-democratic hybridization of the German welfare state have arisen, the measured nature of German policy shifts and the meticulous process of consultations among stakeholders – including employers' associations and trade unions – underscore the nation's commitment to a balanced, informed approach. With institutions offering factual information and analyses, the German welfare state evolves through prolonged and diligent processes. These changes are further solidified by a succession of political coalitions that align decisions with the strengths of the nation's economy, ensuring the model's compatibility with the broader economic policy landscape (Seeleib-Kaiser 2016, pp. 219–240).

While a noticeable trend towards liberalization is evident, it doesn't signify an overall shift towards the LME. The foundational legal framework supporting the employment relations system remains largely unchanged. Over time, key players in the realms of business and politics have advocated for alterations to institutionalized coordination, without advocating for its complete dismantling. Consequently, a movement towards differentiation is unfolding. Traditional structures persist in essential domains, but they no longer extend collective benefits across the entire economy. Employment practices in various sectors (such as traditional manufacturing versus the private service sector), between enterprises (small businesses versus large corporations), and within core and peripheral labour market segments do exhibit differences. An outcome of this growing diversification is an escalation in inequality, manifesting in both wage disparities and the prevalence of low pay. On both fronts, Germany surpasses the average of CMEs and is approaching levels akin to numerous LMEs (Jackson & Sorge 2012). Time will reveal whether the process of liberalization, decentralization, and differentiation in employment relations will persist, or whether emerging efforts to bolster the influence of works councils and collective bargaining will impede this trajectory of change. The global economic crisis wrought by the COVID-19 pandemic had a relatively mild impact on Germany, with the nation deftly manoeuvring through them. Germany adopted a comprehensive set of measures steeped in Keynesian economics to safeguard its economic stability – the package including strategies to shield the export-driven industrial production sector, notably the key sectors of the automotive, energy, and transportation industries. Moreover, these measures simultaneously facilitated a shift towards environmentally friendly restructuring.

3.3 THE GRAVITY OF GERMAN *SOZIALMARKTWIRTSCHAFT* AT THE HEART OF EUROPE

The interplay between Germany's economic sphere and its position within the European integration landscape is a complex and dynamic relationship that has evolved significantly over time. The country's economic power has influenced its political standing within differentiated European integration, shedding light on the intricate connections between economics and politics. Germany's post-Second World War economic reconstruction laid the groundwork for its eventual political resurgence within Europe. The concept of 'Rhenish capitalism', rooted in collaboration between business, labour, and the state, emphasized stability, long-term planning, and a strong welfare state. This unique economic model, centred on the 'social market economy', allowed for the rebuilding of its shattered economy while fostering economic security and social equity among its citizens.

Germany's economic strength served as a powerful political driver, enabling it to assert itself as a leading force within the EU. As the largest economy in the EU, Germany has wielded considerable influence over EU policies and decision-making processes. Its robust economic performance has bolstered its credibility as a key player in shaping the direction of European integration. The influence of ordoliberalism, with its emphasis on competitive markets and regulatory principles, has been instrumental in shaping economic policies that have translated into Germany's stance on EU economic governance. Germany has consistently advocated for fiscal discipline, structural reforms, and sound monetary policies within the EU, reflecting its commitment to preserving a stable economic environment. The challenges posed by German reunification showcased the adaptability of its economic model. Through strategic infrastructure investments, vocational training, and labour market reforms, Germany not only stabilized its own economy but also contributed to the broader European integration process. This played a significant role in strengthening Germany's political position within the EU.

Germany's economic model has afforded it a leadership role within the differentiated landscape of European integration. As the driving force behind the Eurozone, its economic stability has been crucial in managing the Eurozone crisis and steering the EU's economic policies. Its leadership in issues related to financial stability and fiscal responsibility has solidified its position as a key architect of European integration. In the 21st century, Germany's CME model has faced multifaceted challenges and opportunities. Industrial relations have played a crucial role, with collaborative practices enhancing stability and innovation. The vocational training system, characterized by dual education, has been pivotal in maintaining Germany's competitive edge in specialized labour. Corporate governance discussions have examined the balance between stakeholder interests and shareholder influence, while policy changes have reshaped the financial landscape, reducing cross-ownership networks and increasing market-oriented financing.

Education policy aligned with the EU strategies has focused on early and high-quality education, vocational training, and inclusive education solutions. The dual education model, combining theoretical learning with practical experience, has contributed to building a skilled workforce and to low youth unemployment. However, challenges have arisen, such as a shortage of training positions, particularly in the private service sector, and a shift towards higher education. The labour market and industrial relations have seen changes in collective bargaining coverage and decentralization, leading to pay disparities and inequalities. The introduction of a statutory minimum wage in 2015 did address some issues, but it also raised new questions about labour relations. Gender disparities persist in pay and leadership roles, despite improvements driven by state policies, such as parental leave reforms. The German welfare state, rooted in insurance principles and work-centric ideals, has undergone subtle changes to address disincentives for women's workforce participation and shifting demographics. The nation's commitment to a balanced, informed approach is evident in policy shifts and consultations among stakeholders. While a trend towards liberalization is noticeable, the foundational legal framework supporting the employment relations system remains intact. Reforms are occurring across sectors, enterprises, and labour market segments, leading to increased inequality. The response to the COVID-19 crisis showcased the country's economic stability and commitment to environmentally friendly restructuring. The German variety of capitalism has evolved in response to global challenges while preserving its core principles of collaboration, social protections, and market efficiency. It remains at the least an influential model, and possibly a role model for the other Member States. Interestingly, one could firmly argue that 'going with the flow' is the secret of Germany staying in the EU core both before and after the global financial crisis. This means that before all the economic turbulence, when the EU was promoting rather a liberal type of economy, Germany liberalized its economic institutions (which is most vivid in the financial-system dimension), while maintaining its coordinated 'spine'. After the crises, as interventionism went on the rise, Germany revived its interventionist and ordoliberal traditions of economic governance. However, Germany's economic and political dominance in Europe has not been without challenges and tensions within the EU. Some Member States have expressed concerns about excessive German influence and the potential for asymmetrical power dynamics. Debates over economic policies, such as austerity measures, have at times strained Germany's relationships with its European partners.

4 Poland: An aspiring new Member State trapped on the EU's periphery

4.1 POLAND AS THE OUTER-CORE OF THE EUROPEAN SYSTEM OF DIFFERENTIATED INTEGRATION

By the legal-institutional criteria of differentiated integration (DI) literature, Poland belongs to the outer core of European integration circles. In the logic of economic hierarchies, it belongs to the semi-periphery, trying to escape the dependent market economy status, and the so-called middle-income trap. At the same time, Poland is an example of a peculiar case of discriminatory unilateral self-differentiation (Ruszkowski 2022, pp. 21–45), which is highly counterproductive to Poland's and the whole region's ambitions to be a driver of integration in the future. And because some authors (see for example: Brix & Busek 2022) perceive the two-or-multi-speed Europe as a threat not only to the region but to the whole integration project in general, Poland's place on the map of differentiated integration plays a key role and needs to be understood in detail.

After the end of the East-West divide, which was characteristic for the pre-1989 period (and in which Poland was an unwilling member of the Eastern bloc), the Polish Republic regained its independence and could make its own decisions about its economic future independently of Moscow. Nevertheless, the historical fate of being squeezed between Russia and Germany was reincarnated in new, post-Cold War realities. Poland, which is quite representative of the whole Central European region (that is, often defined as the 'East of the West and the West of the East' at the same time), remains a relatively marginal semi-peripheral economy and must position itself vis-à-vis the heavyweight players, such as its German neighbour.

At the same time, it remains permanently caught between the desire for integration and the omnipresent issue of identity, inseparably tied to the inevitability of the independent nation state. In the complexity of worldviews, visions, values, belonging, and identity, the West's and East's mutual lack of recognition of contributions to freedom and democracy nurtured the feeling of alienation rather than togetherness (Brix & Busek 2022). This issue is reflected in the country's positioning on the map of differentiated integration. Moreover, it is also manifested in the economy's structure and industrial relations. An imitation of the LME did not necessarily lead to a similar imitation of Rhenish style welfare state and other parameters of a specific capitalist model.

The transition to a market economy comprised not only of measures implemented in the neoliberal spirit of the Washington Consensus, such as privatization, commercialisation, or liberalization. It also included elements including stabilization and institutional harmonization – adopting laws, procedures, and norms of Western Europe in order to be a successful candidate with regard to the European Union (still then the European Community at the time of association) (Sachs 2015, p. 115). Westernization, understood as transition towards the model(s) of the West, became a basic, guiding concept for broad-based social-economic transformation. At the same time the *return to Europe* narrative became powerful enough to frame the grand debates in politics and in the society, and to give a sense of direction to guide the millions of citizens. In Poland, the guiding principle – above all others – was its return to Europe, understood as accessing the European Union. The prospect of EU membership provided the reference point. Hardship and uncertainty were tolerated in society if the end point seemed reachable; the ends, in the people's minds, justified the means (Sachs 2015, p. 129). After joining the EU, the insider's perspective started to dominate, and it became clear that EU membership is not a zero-sum game.

There are many levels and dimensions of integration, and various new Member States chose different trajectories in this respect, and there are not only various versions of so-called socialism, but also various variants of post-communism which created specific path dependencies for each and every country. Therefore, it is important to remember that the former Eastern bloc countries constituted a complicated set of various economic models with various policy preferences. Complexity requires a differential diagnosis (Sachs 2015, p. 76). Heterogeneity requires differentiation. No single pattern of governance can be treated as a prescription for development. It should come, therefore, as no surprise that various post-communist states chose different positions on the map of European integration differentiation.

In 2003, the Accession Treaty ratification referendum took place, in which 77.45% of Poles voted to join the EU, 22.55% voted against the motion, and the attendance rate reached 58.85%. Poland joined the European Union on 1 May 2004 as the largest country – in terms of size, population, and economy – as did ten other new Member States. This historical enlargement process took place ten years after the formal application was submitted in 1994. It concluded a four-year-long accession negotiation process (1998–2002) and a ten-year-long association period. Poland joined the Schengen Agreement in 2007 and, at the time of this writing, still has not entered the final stage of the Economic and Monetary Union. Since the moment of enlargement, the new Member States' pro-EU commitment has been questioned many times, and the strongest trend observable in Poland and Hungary is the ostentatious U-turn which they have taken in recent years. It is characterized not only by democratic backsliding and illiberal tendencies, but also by an accompanying display of de-Europeanization. Unsurprisingly for many Eurosceptic political actors such as the Law and Justice party in Poland (*Prawo i Sprawiedliwość – PiS*), the Conservative Party-ruled UK was an important ally. They watched the British case as an illustration of a de-Europeanization process. In this sense, the Brexit process may be perceived as testing the limits of differentiation in Europe. Indeed, it tested the line beyond which differentiation turns into disintegration. Before Brexit, London enjoyed some exemptions from the Eurozone and Schengen Area which had already been quite prominent examples of differentiation. But undermining one of the four freedoms (the free movement of people) – becoming, incidentally, one of the bones of contestation in the Brexit campaign – attacked one of the fundamentals of the integration project and questioned the very idea of European integration at its core. The British case showed that openly opposing the very core of the Single Market turned the direction of the integration trajectory for Britain. Economic theories of international integration inform us that it is not only the free movement of products and services that constitutes a Single Market. The creation and functioning of a Single Market are also conditional on liberalization and free movement of the factors of production: capital and labour. This is why the four freedoms have been treated as inseparable elements of one concept. At least, until 2020, when the UK succeeded in negotiating a status in which it has access to the Single Market but continental Europeans do not have open access to the British labour market (Radunz & Riedel 2024).

For Poland and other EU Member States, the Brexit case is a benchmark and as such it is instructive in terms of the dynamic process of European integration differentiation and fragmentation. In the pre-accession phase, the return-to-Europe paradigm anticipated full and deep membership in the Western structures. In contemporary Central and Eastern Europe, the picture is much more mixed – alongside fully-integrated states belonging to the core of the EU (e.g., the Baltic states or Slovakia) there are reluctant EU members who question the fundamentals of the European integration project, e.g., Poland and Hungary (Riedel 2021). A noteworthy point is that the core period of the Brexit process (2016–2020) coincided with the unprecedented de-Europeanization turn on the European Union's eastern flank. More than ten years after the EU's big bang enlargement, many of the new Member States lost their initial pro-integration impetus and began flirting with Britain and its EU-contesting attitude. After their election success in 2015, Poland's nationalist-conservative government chose the UK as its number one strategic partner in foreign and

EU policies. In the European Parliament, the British Conservatives allied themselves with the Czech Civic Democratic Party (ODS) as well as the Polish Law and Justice (PiS) party as part of the European Conservatives and Reformist group (Radunz & Riedel 2024). However, the UK's decision to leave the European Union highlighted important questions about the consequences and implications for various EU Member States, as well as the Union as a whole. With the UK's withdrawal from the EU, Poland has gained the status of one of the Union's most problematic members. This is because of both the openly Eurosceptic attitude of the ruling party and because of some structural features that characterize the Polish economy. Therefore, the Polish case is interesting in a post-Brexit context, especially in post-pandemic times, when the system of European differentiated integration is dynamically changing. The Russian aggression against Ukraine (2014 and 2022) is also vitally important for Poland's relationship with Brussels, or even Western structures in general. The Russian threat has always functioned as a push-factor for the pro-European attitudes of the Polish citizenry. The unprecedented unity of the West against the Russian aggressor serves the consensus building – at least to some extent – in Polish European politics (Riedel 2018, p. 99). The key question in this context is whether the British experience of leaving the EU, as a benchmark, can act as a good or bad example for other Member States. Potentially, Brexit may lead the nationalist-populist government in Warsaw towards even more sovereigntist attitudes against Brussels. Any perception of British success outside of the EU could support the Eurosceptic voices in Poland, feeding an illusion of Poland becoming the 'second Britain'. Just as the UK was one of the main advocates of the EU's eastern enlargement, its leaving may serve as one of the main arguments for the Eurosceptics' claim that 'there is life outside of the EU' (Riedel 2017, 2023).

Nonetheless, it is difficult to ignore the fact that Poland is not Britain as regards economic strength and potential. In comparison to the UK, Poland is far more dependent on trading with other EU countries (more than 70% of all exports and 80% of all imports are traded with other EU economies). Trade flows are substantially different in the case of the two countries. Not only has the UK traditionally been a key player in the global economy, but the geographical allocation of trade flows differs considerably. The share of the UK's trade with its EU partners was remarkably lower than in the Polish case. For the UK, the first four trading partners are the USA, Germany, Switzerland, and China; in other words, three out of four of the UK's leading trading partners are non-EU states. In contrast, 75% of Polish trade is with EU economies. That said, despite the fact that Germany is Poland's most important partner, theemainns an important market for Polish exports (Riedel 2023a). In a bilateral constellation, we may observe a kind of asymmetry in terms of the importance of the mutual foreign trade between Poland and the UK. The United Kingdom is an important (second largest) market for Polish exports, whereas the Polish market does not seem to be nearly as significant for the UK (11th place). The relatively large trade surplus makes Poland more dependent on exports to the UK than on imports from the UK, which results in Poland being more vulnerable to all sorts of post-Brexit restrictions on access to the British market. It is access to the UK market, much more than the resources coming from it, which makes Poland dependent in economic relations with the United Kingdom (Matysek-Jędrych & Mroczek-Dąbrowska 2021, pp. 299–313).

Similarly to Britain, Poland – which is a latecomer to the European integration process, and not akin to the other founding member states of the European Communities – experienced an EU accession referendum in 2003, which means the Polish political system has already witnessed high political contestation related with European integration. Despite the fact that the referendum ended with the vast majority of Poles voting for accession, the EU debate dominated the political discourse agenda for years before referendum and went on to maintain its position as the central debate topic for years after the fact. In the years preceding the referendum, European integration became the most important line of division in Polish politics, replacing the previous post-communist versus post-solidarity movement divide. Despite the generally broad acceptance for Polish membership in the EU (exceeding 80% in public opinion polls), many related factors need to be taken into account with the utmost seriousness. More and more Polish young people (aged 18–29) claim that Poland would cope better with the challenges of the world if left to do so on its own. Flagship EU policies, such as the green transition or monetary integration, meet strong opposition in Poland. The public discourse is saturated with Euroscepticism along with negative attitudes towards the main EU institutions as well as the largest and leading EU members (predominantly Germany). Poland is on a conflicting trajectory with the EU on most fundamental issues, with the rule of law being a stark example (Matysek-Jędrych & Mroczek-Dąbrowska 2021). The UK (still as an EU member) had been perceived in Poland – especially by the nationalist-populist ruling PiS party – as a natural ally in the European Union. In times of the growing marginalization of Poland, losing such an important partner inside the Union is significantly disadvantageous. In the European Parliament, PiS lost its main ally in the form of Conservative Euro-deputies. In the Council, the UK had a reputation of being a troublemaker, especially at times when Euroscepticism was British policy. That role of troublemaker is now seen as occupied by the illiberal democracies of Central and Eastern Europe, predominantly Poland and Hungary (Radunz & Riedel 2024).

Trying to capture the full picture of the Polish attitude towards the European integration, one needs to recollect the transitory times of the 1990s when the EU association was launched. Poland's status in relation to the European integration process has changed over the past three decades, and dramatically so. In the transition period, Warsaw was treated as a model of successful transformation, democratization, and Europeanization, and – in contrast – after the 2015 elections it evolved into something of a troublemaker, and a troublemaker which would take an illiberal U-turn, i.e., through democratic backsliding and de-Europeanization. In relation to its position on the map of DI, Poland represents the puzzling case of an awkward partner who advocates unity and champions differentiation at the same time. Why is Poland such an interesting case to explore differentiation? As was stated by Agnieszka Cianciara:

> (...) Polish governments of all political colours have been consistently voicing opposition towards differentiated integration labelled as 'two-speed Europe'. Yet Poland's de facto refusal to accede to the eurozone and marked unwillingness to join other enhanced cooperation formats, despite the abilities and capacity to do so, make it one of the champions of internal differentiation in the post-Brexit EU. Thus, on the one hand, the post-accession story of differentiated integration of Member States that joined the EU in the years 2004 and 2007 is a 'story of normalization' (...), where differentiation decreased and new members converged with old members and with established patterns of differentiation. On the other hand, Poland's opt-out from the Charter of Fundamental Rights and persistence outside of the eurozone, together with the growing government's Euroscepticism, make Poland an outlier (...). (Cianciara 2022, p. 538)

This statement is true not only in comparison to the Western European inner core, but also compared to the majority of CEE EU Member States. What is more important, the inner core countries have actually opted for a multi-speed Europe, and rightly so, because they have the only opportunity to move ahead with 'a coalition of the willing', usually termed as enhanced cooperation. While the rhetoric of the Rome Declaration does not identify any preferred scenario, there have still been some preparations for a multi-speed Europe. It is basically a two-speed Europe, although in some policies it can also be multi-speed. The main point for the new breakthrough is constructing a renewed EU around the Eurozone, including fiscal policy and some more integrated social policies (Agh 2017, p. 54).

One of the most important points of reference as regards the positioning of a Member State on the map of European differentiated integration is its attitude towards the supranational monetary union. In this case, what makes the Polish and British societies similar is the lack of appeal of monetary integration on the supranational level. Poles represent an undisputed Euro-positive attitude in general whilst belonging firmly to the Eurosceptic camp when it comes to joining the Eurozone club (Riedel 2018). And this cannot be understood just as an illustration of diversified public opinion typical of all democratic societies. In this case, the same people demonstrate a great deal of sympathy and support for the European Union whilst at the same time being strongly

*Euro*sceptic. In developing these attitudes, they refer to totally different – and very often conflicting – sets of ideas, norms, and values. In Poland, directly after the transformation, there was very strong support for European integration and Polish participation in it. The European Union impressed the Poles as an area of economic prosperity, political stability, and a promised land in general – such high expectations could, however, only lead to disappointment. Once EU accession negotiations started and the EU became much more a set of figures, transition periods, opt-outs, etc., the fairytale picture disappeared. The first disappointments can be observed in the period 1998–2002 (the years of EU entry negotiations). At that time, however, the government launched its informational and promotional campaign before the accession referendum. This stimulated an upward trend in EU support which also continued after the momentous year of enlargement. The enlargement enabled access to the Single Market along with an inflow of cohesion and structural funds. Support for the EU thus reached its peak in 2008. Then the economic crises hit Europe. However – and this is important to note – Poland suffered to a seriously lesser extent. As in many other EU Member States, society started to become more Eurosceptic (Riedel 2017). This downwards trend was broken again in 2014, following developments in Eastern and South-Eastern Ukraine (the Russian annexation of Crimea, and war in the Donbas and Donetsk regions). As an immediate Ukrainian neighbour, and a society formerly belonging to the Eastern bloc, the Poles saw with their own eyes an alternative to their Western orientation. To see this comparison in a sharp contrast it is enough to remind ourselves that directly after the implosion of the Soviet union in 1991, Polish and Ukrainian GDP per capita were very similar. After joining the EU (and still before the war in Eastern Ukraine) Poland's GDP was three times higher than Ukraine's, this happening as a result of Leszek Balcerowicz's shock therapy and the strategic choices undertaken by the post-1989 governments in Warsaw. Poland also was and still is the only EU Member State that has a border both with Russia and Ukraine, making it more exposed to any effects of the Ukrainian-Russian conflict. This critical situation spoke to the imagination of the Polish people to such an extent that their support for the European Union went on to surpass previous (and already high) levels after the first phase of Russian aggression against Ukraine in 2014 (Riedel 2019). This became even clearer after the second phase of the Russian aggression against Ukraine in 2022, when Poland became a front-country vis-à-vis an open military conflict.

Trying to explain the above-mentioned trends, one may refer to various explanatory vehicles. One of them is the economic utility theory which claims that the more a given society, state, or economy gains from the European integration project, the more positive attitudes it reveals about it. In economic terms there are two strong arguments that persuade Poles to be satisfied with their EU membership. One of these is their country's participation in the

Single Market which has stimulated export growth (as an emerging market, the Polish economy is still very much export-dependent). And the second is access to EU funds that boost public investments on an unprecedented scale. Here it is important to note that these two factors may disappear when Poland loses its competitive advantage (based on low labour costs) and when the Polish regions stop qualifying for EU funds. All this suggests that Poland's Euro-enthusiastic attitude may decrease, proportionally. Additionally, other problems are seemingly cumulating inside and outside the EU project. These are – among others – the implications of the refugee/migration crisis, related collective decision problems in the allocation of refugees, not to mention the economic crisis, the Russian-Ukrainian conflict, pandemic-related restrictions, the energy crisis, high inflation, etc. All in all, in the Poles' eyes, the EU is no longer seen as the promised land, a panacea for the inefficiencies of Polish politics and economy, nor as a prize for the so-called transformation *fatigue*. Instead of being a solution, the EU has turned into a problem in the eyes of many Poles. The Euroscepticism of Poland's closest neighbours (such as the Czech Republic) and partners (including Hungary or the UK) is also an important contextual factor. The Brexit context is of the highest importance for Eurosceptic actors – they can point to an example of a country that has left the EU and remained successful in many spheres of socio-economic life. Especially in the case of Poland, whose relations with the UK (trade flows, large diaspora, etc.) are quite special, Brexit is an exceptionally convincing example. Both in Poland and the UK, Eurosceptic parties remain in power – still, in the case of Poland, a worsening in Brussels-Warsaw relations is being witnessed. This may have serious implications in the long term, since the ruling PiS has all sorts of communication tools at its disposal and conducts an openly anti-EU narrative in Polish public discourse. The expression 'Polexit' became de-tabooed and has entered the very centre of the political debate (Radunz & Riedel 2024). Among others, politically biased scholars, who publicly took anti-EU positions, and who sympathize with the Eurosceptic and illiberal government in Poland (2015–2023), heavily criticize federalist visions for Europe (Grosse 2018, pp. 79). The Polexit discourse has become especially loud in the electoral campaign of 2023, and in the context of the evolving debate on the future of Europe.

Evaluating the arguments for and against the various concepts of flexible integration is especially salient in the case of countries such as Poland, where – after Donald Tusk's return to Polish politics (2021) – the pro-/anti-EU cleavage was promoted as being of the most crucial importance in the Polish public debate. This has not been the case since the accession referendum campaign in 2003. The old, and rather personal 'Tusk-Kaczyński' conflict was reactivated in new post-Brexit circumstances and it has manifested in new ways and forms. Bearing in mind the pro-European attitude of the vast majority of Polish society, Tusk and his party have attempted to set the agenda of topics problematic for PiS, including the arguments between Warsaw and Brussels on the issues of green transition, judiciary reforms, rule of law standards, the Article 7 procedure, or the Recovery Fund. The PiS narrative, in return, became even more sovereigntist, and – as a consequence – openly anti-EU. Such a strong polarization in the debate among the political elites may bring about a similar effect among Polish citizens. Pro-EU and pro-Western orientation have been an element of broad political consensus in post-1989 Poland. Contesting and challenging it would mean a Copernican turn in the paradigms of Polish politics. The crisis of 2008 has intensified the process of creating a 'multi-speed' European Union. This policy model is developing an increasingly visible hierarchy between the central and peripheral states (Magone et al. 2016). The central states are larger and stronger within the political system. However, in connection with the intensification of the integration processes and the increase in the number of participants *and* their diversity, the European Union faces the threat of disintegration. The application of flexible integration to the integration process is a necessity (Lasiewicz 2015, p. 100). Nevertheless, the very concept of differentiated integration is highly contested by all sides of the political spectrum in Poland. In general, Poland constitutes a highly puzzling case, in which differentiated integration is delegitimized by all of the major political forces. Whereas Civic Platform used a technocratic narrative to voice limited and conditional justification for differentiated integration in the short term and a mixture of technocratic and populist narratives do delegitimize their main political opponent, Law and Justice used a populist narrative to delegitimize all forms of progressive integration differentiation as well as employing a mixture of populist and technocratic narratives to legitimize uniform disintegration, understood as achieving unity at a lower level of integration: the Single Market, or regressive differentiated integration as the second-best scenario (Cianciara 2021, p. 140). It was expressed most clearly in one of the speeches in the parliament by one of Civic Platform's frontrunners, the former foreign affairs minister Radosław Sikorski: 'Whether we like it or not Europe seems more and more divided into circles of integration and a new European Union emerges, one that is centered around the eurozone; thus it is in Polish strategic interest to join this integration centre: a geopolitical choice for decades' (Sikorski, in Sejm 2013). Another foreign minister from the PiS camp argued that: '(…) the elite-people antagonistic relationship is transformed into antagonism of dominant-and-rich powers versus weaker-and-poorer Member States, where the former are embodied by the Berlin-Paris-Brussels triangle' (Waszczykowski, in Sejm 2013). Therefore, as it was claimed by Krzysztof Szczerski, a PiS-loyal politician, the Law and Justice party '(…) will not allow that the stronger decide for us and control us; we are not going to be a henchman under anybody's leadership ... we should look for allies who do not see their future in a federation ruled by the powerful, but in a community of equal states' (Szczerski, in Sejm 2013).

In this context, it is important to note that the Polish Constitutional Court's 2021 ruling, in which it confirmed the supremacy of the Polish constitution over EU treaties, does not only indicate dissatisfaction with specific EU policies. Instead, it underlines the Polish government's categorical rejection of the EU's founding principles. The court's ruling of 7 October 2021 sent shockwaves across the European Union – the judges declared that the Polish constitution has primacy over some key areas of EU law, including the provision that binds Member States to take 'appropriate measures' to fulfil their obligations under EU law. This unprecedented judicial ruling challenged the fundaments of the EU as a community of law. Some even claim that the so-called Polexit is the only logical consequence of this ruling because the court ruling effectively renders the Polish constitution incompatible with EU treaties. However, far more likely than the various options of a 'hard' or 'soft exit' (Polexit) is a so-called 'dirty remain'. Rather than leaving the Union, the Polish government would then seek to remodel it from within (Hofelich 2021).

While the salience or even awareness of DI has always been low or very low in the Polish public discourse, negative tones prevailed in the discussion on the DI as a potential model for the future of the EU. This relates to the political debate in Warsaw which identifies DI almost universally as a two-speed Europe model and its perception as a recipe for the exclusion of some Member States (supposedly including Poland) from the mainstream of the integration project. However, positions on specific mechanisms and instances of DI such as the Eurozone depended more on various governments' political preferences. For example, already during the 'first' PiS government in 2005–2007, the right-wing authorities opted out of the *Charter of Fundamental Rights*, claiming that the government intended to avoid the possibility of interference from EU law in domestic provisions in the fields of public morality, family law, abortion, and the rights of homosexual persons. As far as entry into the final stage of the monetary union was concerned, PiS always remained sceptical, but other governments proved to be much more positive, although none of them in the end decided to take the final step and actually join the Eurozone (Walecka & Gagatek 2021).

In relation to the dilemmas related with future versions of differentiated integration in Europe, the authoritarian-populist PiS political party manifests two mutually-influencing fears – the fear of deeper integration, and, at the same time, the fear of differentiated integration. The Polish liberal camp was led by the Civic Platform (in Polish – *PO*, meaning *Platforma Obywatelska*), on the other side, it depicts differentiated integration as an inevitable reality that Poland had to adapt to, while possibly co-defining scope conditions and working towards eventually reducing differentiation by joining the Eurozone and the integrative inner core (Cianciara 2021, p. 135). As was formulated by Agnieszka Cianciara:

> Opt-outs and disintegration pressures are typically associated with laggards or proponents of 'less Europe' who do not wish to integrate further, but prefer to maintain the status quo or take a step back. However, differentiation also serves the needs of champions of 'more Europe' who wish to move forward despite lack of unanimous support to do so. Both types of claims are constantly justified and contested as they constitute a deviation from a more traditional and uniform way of 'doing integration' in Europe. (Cianciara 2021, p. 129)

This diagnosis indicates that Poland is politically not eager to act as a leader of integration and equally uninterested in moving to its core. After initial enthusiasm, typical for newcomers and that we in Poland could observe directly after joining the EU, there is no consensus to move the European integration project forward. Economically (see the sections below) Poland is also stabilizing in the semi-peripheral position, with the clear risks of stagnating in the middle-income trap – a position that many of the southern regions found themselves in decades ago.

In the heated debate on a potential Polexit (which would mean Poland leaving the outer core orbit and departing towards the realm of external differentiation), various scenarios are identified. Some question the very idea as unrealistic, some others claim the PiS government is pushing this agenda indirectly by finding itself on a collision course with Brussels at every possible occasion. Yet, some other voices claim that the Polexit is *de facto* happening, since Poland is silently leaving the community of EU shared values, questioning the European legal framework, and cutting itself off from the inflow of EU funding (financial conditionality, e.g., in the case of the Recovery and Resilience Facility). Apart from the Polexit scenario, the 'dirty remain' option should also be identified, in which the Eurosceptic government in Warsaw vandalizes the EU legal order, and devastates the norms and values system agreed supranationally. Poland, after 2015 – ruled by a PiS government – pushed the principle of internal differentiated integration to its limits, albeit in a different way than the UK did. Some scholars have labelled it as an illiberal concept of differentiated integration (Tosiek 2023). However, the illiberal U-turn that Poland took in 2015 refers much more to the socio-political dimension of illiberalism, exemplified by violating the rule of law principles. In the realm of economy, the picture presents itself slightly differently and the evolution of the Polish model of capitalism is presented in section 4.2 below.

4.2 THE EVOLUTION OF THE POLISH WAY TOWARDS THE HYBRID MODEL OF CAPITALISM

Social researchers make a distinct differentiation between 'transition' and 'transformation' (Mieczkowska 2014, p. 76). Transition refers to a planned change with a predetermined trajectory, adapting a system to specific goals. On the other hand, transformation involves systemic reforms without a clear final outcome. In the case of Poland, post-1989 reforms were not targeted at any particular version of capitalism, rather they were a run-away from the bankrupt socialist system.

During the period of systemic shifts, Polish decision makers and even scholars lacked an awareness of various global capitalist models (minor exceptions include, e.g., Kowalik 2002). This lack of awareness extended to Polish public opinion and the political class. Not surprisingly, the selection of a specific path did not undergo comprehensive discussion (Wojtyna 2005, pp. 1–23). The main focus of the discourse was on evaluating the costs and benefits of the reforms, leading to polarization within Polish society (Jarosz 2005; Kotras 2018). Depending on the criteria applied, interpretations of the transformation episode ranged from emphasizing 'taking a civilizational leap' and 'entering the path of growth' (Balcerowicz & Rzońca 2010; Piątkowski 2018) to highlighting collective trauma and reform-related mistakes (Rolski 2013; Długosz 2019). As a result, the debate on the extent of the changes overshadowed discussions about their direction. Also, in accordance with the presented terminology, it can be thus argued that there has been transformation in Poland (i.e., a transition from real socialism to capitalism), but without transition (towards a specific market economy model).

Over time, the dust settled from these reforms, and the collective memory of the challenges associated with them partly faded. A progressively Europeanized and globalized Poland has experienced sustained economic growth for almost three decades. This economic progress has led to a deeper examination of the country's capitalist model. The focus is often on the type of market economy that emerged from the reforms initiated in the late 1980s and the main question asked is whether post-communist Poland's capitalism converges with Western models. For over a decade, there has been growing interest in this topic.

This chapter also aligns itself with the field of comparative capitalism studies within political economics. The aim is to trace Poland's economic evolution since joining the European Union using frameworks that explore different variants of capitalism. This analysis is then complemented by a description of changes in Polish political institutions, which, as argued, provide important context for shaping economic institutions. Some previous works (e.g., Piątek

2023; Szabó 2022) have described Poland's evolution towards illiberal state capitalism. Similarly to the aforementioned works, I understand the notion of the 'illiberal state' (or 'illiberal democracy') in the spirit of important works on this topic from the last two decades (see: Kremnitzer & Shany 2020, pp. 125–152 for a discussion of the characteristics of this phenomenon).

However, this article aims to highlight a less recognized aspect which is that this illiberal model is built upon the foundation of late 20th-century 'neoliberal' reforms (often labelled as such, according to Mączyńska & Pysz 2014, pp. 221–247). Consequently, a distinct model of capitalism is emerging in Poland, characterized by advancing hybridization. The authors refer to this system to as an 'illiberal market economy' (IME) in line with VoC research. This situation raises serious concerns about the long-term effectiveness of this emerging model.

To address the aforementioned questions, it is important to first reconsider whether Poland's variant of capitalism should be analysed using the same criteria that are applied to more 'mature' Western economies. The selection of an appropriate analytical framework is relevant for all the post-communist systems and remains a subject of ongoing debate in the field of political economy (see Rapacki et al. 2020, pp. 565–592). Scholars engaged in comparative economic analysis are divided on this issue. Some studies employ traditional comparative schemas (established originally for developed countries), while others propose modifying or entirely altering the conceptualization of the 'institutional matrix' of post-communist economies. Both approaches find acknowledgement in academic discourse, suggesting that both strategies contribute to a deeper understanding of coexisting economic regimes. The construction of the 'ideal types' of post-communist capitalism by researchers hinges on the conceptualization of fundamental political economic terms (Jasiecki 2018, pp. 328–342).

Poland's institutional arrangement demonstrates traits resembling a blend of elements found in more 'mature' capitalist systems, encompassing not just Western but also Southern European capitalist systems. This characteristic is often referred to as 'hybridity' (Robinson 2013). This is associated with a relatively low level of complementarity between different coordination areas, which, according to VoC assumptions, makes the entire system potentially inefficient. Nonetheless, this provisional structure's adverse effects have been mitigated by factors like the consistent inflow of European Union funds (Maszczyk 2015, pp. 107–122). A comprehensive empirical analysis (Rapacki & Czerniak 2019) conducted within Bruno Amable's DoC framework reiterated this argument about noticeable non-complementarity among various areas. The authors have coined the term 'patchwork capitalism' to describe the emerging institutional order in Central and Eastern Europe. Krzysztof Jasiecki (2020) emphasized Poland's integration with international organizations (primarily the EU, but also NATO and the OECD) in shaping the national variation of capitalism in Central Europe. He argued that involvement in these structures, along with Europeanization, stabilizes Poland's image for foreign investors and creditors. This perspective loosely aligns with the VoC framework, incorporating dimensions such as political context, institutional and entrepreneurial quality, micro- and macroeconomic prospects, and public opinion on the dynamics of systemic changes.

To substantiate the thesis about the distinctive shape of emerging illiberal capitalism in Poland, the authors have employed a literature analysis and empirical data concerning essential institutional areas typically examined from a VoC standpoint. Extensive literature (e.g., Matkowski et al. 2016) points to the ongoing convergence of Poland (and of other countries of Central and Eastern Europe) – not only in a macroeconomic sense, but also an institutional sense. Therefore, the authors consider this approach to be complementary to previous studies in which the VoC matrix was adapted to the specific social, cultural, and economic conditions prevailing in this part of Europe. The authors propose that the dominant coordination type can be situated on a spectrum defined by the market mechanism (common in liberal systems) and the non-market mechanism (typical of coordinated regimes). Then they also look qualitatively with regard to what the coordination is like. They have primarily utilized the established conceptual frameworks put forth by Peter Hall and David Soskice while considering contributions from other researchers including Bruno Amable. Additionally, the author acknowledges the significant features of post-communist capitalism identified over the past two decades (such as economic dependency) (Nölke & Vliegenthart 2009; Drahokoupil & Myant 2016).

Corporate governance configuration is significantly influenced by the cultural and historical trajectory (in other words, it is path-dependent; see: Gutterman, 2020). Since the 1990s, Poland's corporate governance structure has progressively converged towards Western European characteristics. However, it also retains its distinctive traits. The Polish model draws heavily from the German 'dualistic' form of governance, characterized by a clear separation between managerial and supervisory functions. Julian Franks and Colin Mayer's typology (2002, pp. 13–22) also categorizes Poland's corporate governance as 'closed'. This manifests as moderate to high ownership concentration, limited capital mobility, moderate reliance on stock-exchange financing, and relatively low transparency in managerial information disclosure. Owing to its ownership structure, control predominantly rests with company management; enterprises, banks, and oligarchic groups outweigh individual or institutional financial investors in terms of shareholder composition. This model centres on banking, where banks are crucial not only as creditors but also due to their significant stakes in publicly traded companies.

As a result, Poland's corporate governance model closely resembles those found in Germany, Austria, the Netherlands, and even Japan, more so than Anglo-Saxon countries. Consequently, it is evident that Poland's corporate governance conforms to the model prevailing in coordinated capitalism.

In the realm of the financial system, the debate surrounding foreign direct investment's (FDI) role in Central and Eastern Europe (CEE) is noteworthy. This discussion has intensified since Nölke and Vliegenthart's work in 2009. They introduced the term 'dependent market economy' (DME) to expand the binary VoC framework. This is particularly relevant to corporate governance. The authors posited that in DME countries, a distinct coordination mechanism is at play. According to this view, Poland depends on transnational corporations and their internal hierarchies (as do other V4 economies). The adoption of managerial patterns from foreign firms occurred after these economies integrated into global markets in the 1990s. This led to foreign direct investment and foreign capital-involved banking becoming the predominant means of capital acquisition in the Polish economy. The DME discourse emphasizes a harmony between the relatively low individual costs of a skilled workforce and a corporate regime managed from foreign headquarters. It's worth noting the effort made by successive Polish governments since 1989 to attract FDI through the establishment of many 'special economic zones' (Dorożyński & Świerkocki 2022). Also, as a result of the 'repolonization' programme implemented by the government after 2015, the share of foreign ownership in the Polish banking sector is decreasing, and, as a consequence, the share of state ownership is increasing. In addition to nationalization, an important trend in the last decade is the progressive consolidation of banks (Gostomski & Lepczyński 2019). The observed processes are a premise for a thesis about the increasing share of non-market (state) coordination in the Polish institutional order.

However, the singular focus on attracting foreign capital is no longer the defining aspect of Poland's model. It's important to highlight that the net FDI inflow (as a percentage of GDP) was higher in various countries just before the COVID-19 pandemic, both in Southern Europe (Greece) and Northern Europe (Norway). Additionally, Table 4.1 reveals that Poland's reliance on FDI is slightly less than other DME countries, whether in terms of foreign investors' capital in the nation or the value of net foreign credit to domestic companies. Similar to CME countries, bank credit for the private sector is more substantial than stock exchange capitalization. Interestingly, LME countries generally attract the highest average foreign investment inflow.

Poland's reliance on foreign capital is a notable concern, yet its simultaneous dependence on European funds is often overlooked. The convergence of these two factors has fuelled unprecedented growth in the Polish economy over the past two decades (Gorzelak 2014), fostering a broader understanding

Table 4.1 Sources of raising capital (% of GDP)

	Bank credit		Stock market		FDI inward stock	
	2004	2019	2004	2019	2004	2019
Poland	26	51	28	25	28	40
DMEs*	33	49	18	12	53	61
CMEs**	95	91	48	68	17	25
LMEs***	98	73	103	98	43	144

Notes: * average, DMEs represented by the V4 countries (without Poland); ** average, CMEs represented by the typical cases: Germany, Austria, and Japan; *** average, LMEs represented by the typical cases: the UK, the USA, and Ireland.
Source: Authors' own calculations based on World Bank data (bank credit for the private sector and domestic stocks of the listed companies) and OECD (FDIs).

of an 'institutional comparative advantage' within the framework of dependent post-communist capitalism. Nonetheless, the question remains of how to replace this growth engine, especially as Poland is on the brink of becoming a net contributor to the EU. Furthermore, Poland's labour market competitiveness increasingly hinges on productivity growth rather than low costs (see the section on labour relations). Notably, Poland's corporate governance is not solely externally influenced; it has also been notably influenced by the German model (and the broader continental European model).

The practical implementation of these formal (*de iure*) arrangements largely depends on the quality of national political institutions. In the Polish context, a system initially designed to enhance internal corporate oversight (the dualistic management model) has often led to the appointment of politically aligned individuals to supervisory boards in exchange for various forms of support (political corruption, Makowski 2020). This is associated with the substantial presence of state-owned enterprises in the economy (Kozarzewski & Bałtowski 2019) and is primarily shaped by the political-institutional framework. Similarly, the issue of European funds can also become vulnerable to corruption and rent-seeking under illiberal governance, as seen in Hungary's case where the EU suspended structural funds due to the application of the 'conditionality mechanism'. Consequently, rationalizing this area through government action seems advisable, given the importance of these funds to Poland's development model. Nevertheless, political reluctance is evident, as seen in the risky behaviours of authorities in their dealings with Brussels, such as ongoing disputes with the European Commission over post-COVID-19 Recovery and Resilience Facility funds (Serowaniec & Przychodzki 2023). Violating European rule of law standards jeopardizes these transfers and increased corruption could endanger future structural funding as well.

The progress of the Polish economy in its reduction of developmental disparities in relation to the West can be effectively captured through precise indicators such as the median equivalent annual disposable income (expressed in purchasing power parity terms). According to Eurostat, in 2021 Poland had nearly 60% of Germany's result, compared to just slightly over 45% a decade earlier (Eurostat 2023b). Nevertheless, a key aspect for maintaining an appropriate pace of economic growth and improving the country's competitive position is its innovative capacity (Cypher 2014; May & Schedelik 2019). It should be noted that the institutional comparative advantage of DME does not translate into innovation, whether in a 'radical' or 'incremental' sense. These countries do not introduce innovations on a significant scale due to their economic profile centred around semi-standardized industrial assembly for foreign producers, offshoring, and business process outsourcing, among others (Michalski 2014; Stefaniak 2021).

Since the transformation period, successive governments have aimed to attract capital, historically deficient in the Polish economy. Additionally, since joining the EU, the majority of incoming capital funds were allocated for infrastructure investments, which was in line with the advice of international organizations at the time, but to some extent came at the expense of investing in human capital and economic innovation (Biedka 2021, pp. 105–126). It is worth noting that this takes place against the backdrop of a generally low (and on a downward trend since 2008) investment rate in Poland. The main hypotheses explaining this phenomenon are important from the perspective of this article. Ignacy Morawski (2022) lists, among others: the deterioration of the investment climate in connection with the conflict with the EU over the Polish rule of law, low investment effort by the government, shifting from industry to low-capital-intensive business services, supporting consumption by the government, and a large number of small companies (which translates into difficulties in measuring the rate of investment). This catalogue can be supplemented with a factor of dynamic wage growth and the related depletion of the engine of the economy based on low costs.

The peripheral position of Poland in terms of innovation can be examined from various perspectives. The main contributing factors include the insignificant role of R&D in the private business sector, a low number of patent applications, and productivity stagnation (Magone 2020, p. 106). This is reflected in the distant position of the Polish economy in key rankings that track these issues, such as the Global Competitiveness Report and the European Innovation Scoreboard. In the context of the COVID-19 pandemic, the World Economic Forum pointed out the relatively high share of 'jobs at risk of automation' in the employment structure and the 'insufficient progress in enhancing digital skills' (Schwab & Zahidi 2020). On the other hand, a continuation of a long-term trend has been noted, in which Poland's infrastructural gap compared to the richest countries is steadily decreasing, and business adaptation to new technologies is improving.

Although a gradual increase in R&D expenditures as a percentage of GDP can be observed (0.5% in 2004 vs. 1.4% in 2020), it remains significantly below the EU average (which is also steadily increasing and somewhat slipping out of Poland's hands). Studies assessing the effectiveness of Polish pro-innovation actions indicate their inefficiency (Nasierowski 2019). This implies that the outcome achieved from the undertaken investments is lower than anticipated, which in turn implies a low quality of the national innovation system. Reasons for this state of affairs include the lack of consistent and well-defined scopes of specialization for R&D projects. Interestingly, after 2015, the new government proposed addressing this issue by taking actions aimed at occupying niches in electromobility (Morawiecki 2016). In the longer term it will be possible to assess the effects of these policies.

The sources of the low inventive activity of Polish enterprises can also be found in the education system. It is focused on general skills with practically disappearing vocational training. It is not internally consistent; it has elements that both mitigate and reinforce educational inequalities in the population (Bartak 2019, pp. 387–401). Positive factors include a high share of public schools, a high enrolment coefficient, and an easy transition from vocational to academic paths. Negative aspects include low participation in pre-school education, strong differentiation in terms of the teaching quality of middle schools, and the lack of significant material support for students while simultaneously offering free full-time studies (which is mostly used by students from high socio-economic status families).

Interestingly, the Programme for International Student Assessment (PISA) regularly places Polish students above average in each of the three categories tested (mathematics, reading, and science). During the accession period, Poland improved its position in the overall ranking from 16th place in 2003 to 10th place in 2018. This positive result can be attributed to data concerning past public spending per student in relation to per capita income. This precise measure shows that although spending on primary and secondary education in Poland has been lower than in Finland (considered a role model in education), it has also exceeded the average for high-income countries. It may also be the positive effects of the 1997 reform (reversed in 2017) that appear over time. Hence, the biggest challenge for non-academic education in Poland is to protect its relatively good position in the future by securing the 'supply side'. This mainly concerns teachers willing to work in schools despite the instability of the legal environment, low and real declining wages, and negative selection resulting from the declining prestige which was once associated with the education sector.

Another problem is the critically low public funding for higher education in Poland which, throughout the given period, was significantly lower than in wealthy EU countries and only reached their levels in 2016. It is worth noting that the private part of educational investments (amounting to 0.56% of GDP at all three levels of education in 2019) remains clearly below the OECD average (0.83%). The strategy of democratizing (or 'massifying') higher education led to a 20 percentage-point increase in the proportion of people studying at the higher education level within 20 years from 2000. However, a mismatch of supply and demand remains in many sectors of the labour market (see the next section). University-business cooperation is expanding but remains limited, and it is not based on a comprehensive vision of increasing complementarity between the labour market and the education system (Churski et al. 2023). Responsibility for training in specific, narrow areas of skills is mainly taken up by private companies. Thus, it is clear that in this area, Polish institutions have strengthened their similarity to the LME ideal type.

Over the past three decades, the Polish labour market has undergone significant changes. Structural unemployment, which was the major problem in the 1990s, was only 0.6% in 2021. Since 2000, real wages have nearly doubled, and wage inequalities have decreased (Lewandowski & Magda 2023). However, it's important to note that the issue of high unemployment has been replaced in Poland by the problem of a high proportion of fixed-term contracts. Other challenges include relatively low labour force participation rates among women and older individuals, significant gender-based pay differentials, and the lack of a comprehensive migration policy.

Significant changes have also occurred in the dimension of labour market institutions. Recent analyses describe the character of industrial relations in Poland as moderate, positioned between the extremes of statism, corporatism, and neoliberalism. This evolution has taken a convoluted path, from a post-communist 'illusory corporatism' (Crowley & Ost 2001) to an 'embedded neoliberalism' during the transformation period (Bohle & Greskovits 2007). The updated 2020 European Participation Index (EPI) provides comprehensive data on this matter. The composite index includes several measures, such as the coverage of collective agreements, the level of unionization, and employee participation at the management and workplace levels. From 2009 to 2019, Poland remained stagnant between the 18th and 20th places among all EU countries. The importance of raising the standard of work is emphasized in the literature – as suggested by Katarzyna Skorupińska-Cieślak (2018), there is a clear and positive relationship between the results in the EPI along with some socially desirable factors, e.g., low-income inequalities.

Let us examine some variables that contribute to the EPI index. Estimates of unionization rates among Polish workers range from 10.6% of the labour force (according to GUS) to 13.9% (according to CBOS), representing a clear decline since 2000 when it was around 20% (worker-participation.eu n.d.). The main reasons for this decline are privatization and the associated changing economic structure, especially the proliferation of small and medium-sized enterprises. Notably, the conservative party Law and Justice (PiS) and the largest trade union Solidarity (Solidarność) seem to have been intersecting in their views since the mid-2010s. A consensus has formed around lowering the retirement age and more rapid growth of the minimum wage (including its hourly rate, established in 2016). Solidarność actively supports the electoral and political efforts of both President Andrzej Duda and the PiS government, with union leaders officially stating that the promises made to them by the government have been fulfilled.

In contrast, the second-largest trade union, the All-Poland Alliance of Trade Unions (OPZZ), has been actively protesting in recent years, mainly due to growing dissatisfaction among the teaching community. It's worth noting that these two trade unions represent the vast majority of all unionized workers in Poland. Low unionization rates are not the only concern; the scope and scale of collective agreements are also limited. Negotiations generally take place at the company (or workplace) level, and their coverage extends to only about 10% of contracts (which translates to nearly 200,000 workers). This has declined by almost 15 percentage points since the turn of the millennium. Hence, this phenomenon is practically absent in Poland, and prevalent business practices and further legislative changes are weakening it even more. The lack of will to maintain (or revive) the collective bargaining process can be attributed to the two most important political parties that have been governing the country since 2005. Additionally, in 2013, the only institution of social dialogue, the Tripartite Commission, was effectively dissolved. Two years later, it was replaced by a new body, the Social Dialogue Council, but its role has also been gradually marginalized. In conclusion, politicians' attitudes towards industrial relations seem increasingly dismissive, raising questions about the future of the labour market. Undoubtedly, the areas described above are becoming institutionally closer to the LME model, where the unions are weak and a significant part of them is rather subordinate to the government (which also means a bigger role of the state in the coordination mechanism).

These considerations should be supplemented with a few observations on the model of social policy and the welfare state regime shaping itself in Poland since the 1990s. The chronic underfunding of public healthcare and the absence of well-functioning social dialogue in this sector come to the forefront. Public health expenditures *per capita* have been increasing continuously since 2000 but were only US$2,568 in 2021, about 67% of Portugal's level, a country Poland recently overtook in terms of the per person income. Also, this sector struggles with low efficiency and a lack of qualified personnel. On the other hand, since 2015, there has been talk of a 'creeping privatization of public services' (Sześciło 2016, pp. 32–44). This has its roots in the economic populism in the social policy of the PiS government and the rise of direct monetary benefits and indiscriminate support through fiscal policy tools (which also align with regional trends, see Orenstein & Bugarič 2022). This change is significant in terms of the overall functioning of the system. It involves a general shift towards a demand-driven growth model, sustaining consumption (Vukov 2023). Other challenges for public policy include the unresolved housing problem (and its demographic consequences; Lis 2021), persistently fought by successive governments mainly through demand-side measures (such as housing purchase subsidy programmes), as well as a lack of continuity in successive pension reforms (Sawulski et al. 2019). In this last aspect, the most significant threats to the social insurance system result from the 'flexibilization' of the labour market and the lack of comprehensive solutions to improve the demographic situation in the country.

4.3 ILLIBERAL MARKET ECONOMY ON THE EU'S SEMI-PERIPHERY

Since the main purpose of this book is to explain the correlations between the place of a country in the system of differentiated integration and its model of capitalism, in this chapter the authors discuss the Polish case that is the largest (after Brexit) non-Eurozone economy among the EU Member States. It is also an economy that has been in quasi-permanent transformation for more than three decades, taking various turns both vis-à-vis the EU's core and the liberal vs. coordinated model of capitalism. Despite the seemingly 'neoliberal' nature of the initial phases of the Polish transformation, it has not fully developed the LME type of institutions in all areas, at least not in a systematic way. It rather became an 'intermediate' or a 'hybrid' case, combining the characteristics of both the ideal types. The institutional order of the Polish variety of capitalism has been shaped primarily under the 'Washington Consensus' paradigm of the 1990s, but nevertheless failed to create a coherent LME type of capitalism due to the fact that some parts of the matrix were lifted rather from the CME type. As the coordinated parts remain stable, the liberal parts seem to be more and more liberalized (e.g., education, industrial relations).

The Washington Consensus envisaged Westernization on many fronts, including membership in Western structures such as NATO or the EU. And until the moment of the EU accession, the full membership target was not challenged or even questioned by any mainstream political powers in Warsaw. Speaking in DI terms, the shift from the peripheries (non-membership) into the EU's core (membership) went smoothly and undisturbed. Everything changed after accessing the EU in 2004, when Poland faced the dilemma of moving closer to the EU's inner core (i.e., by entering the Eurozone) or remaining on the outer orbit of EU membership. The turbulent Polish EU membership trajectories included joining the inner core, as well as Polexit debates and various forms of *dirty* membership. Equally turbulent was the evolution from the statist post-communist heritage towards some form of market economy, labelled as a hybrid variety of capitalism.

The evolution of Poland's economic and institutional landscape over the past few decades reveals a nuanced and hybrid trajectory, defying the strict confines of an ideal neoliberal framework. Despite the initial neoliberal undertones that characterized the Polish transformation, the national economy's path has deviated from a pure Liberal Market Economy model, giving rise to an intriguing blend of traits from both the LME and Coordinated Market Economy paradigms. During the 1990s, Poland's institutional order underwent a significant makeover under the sway of neoliberal principles. However, this restructuring did not culminate in a seamless LME structure. Instead, elements from the CME framework, such as corporate governance mechanisms, were incorporated into the Polish system. Over time, these coordinated aspects remained relatively stable while the liberal components underwent a gradual process of liberalization. Sectors such as education and industrial relations experienced increasing levels of liberalization, contributing to a transformational shift. This intricate amalgamation of neoliberal and coordinated elements has given rise to what can be labelled the Illiberal Market Economy (IME). This IME model, a product of a post-neoliberal institutional setting, represents a notable departure from the classic neoliberal paradigm. A defining feature of this hybrid variety is the growing prominence of non-market coordination mechanisms, many of which are guided by state interventions. This shift signifies a departure from strict market-driven dynamics and underscores the role of political institutions in shaping and sustaining the IME model. Indeed, the political underpinnings of this model cannot be overlooked. The nature and dynamics of the IME model are inextricably linked with the country's political institutions. These institutions play a pivotal role in either bolstering or hindering the IME's trajectory. Additionally, threats to Poland's continued development are intricately tied to the establishment and functioning of the IME model. The interaction between political structures and economic institutions becomes a crucial lens through which to comprehend the IME's complexities and potential vulnerabilities.

While Poland's integration into the core of the European Union faced challenges due to both its LME-like economic foundations and certain political institutional setbacks, the nation's pro-export orientation and its compatibility with Western industries, notably Germany's, have opened pathways for engagement and integration. This has allowed Poland to occupy a place in the peripheral circles of European integration (called the 'outer core' in this book), where it stands to continue benefiting from the crossroads of economic interdependence and strategic partnerships. In essence, Poland's economic and institutional journey presents a captivating story of deviation from the pure neoliberal model, resulting in the emergence of a hybrid IME. This shift has redefined the role of state intervention, political institutions, and economic coordination, all of which collectively shape Poland's developmental trajectory within the broader European context.

Specifically for the Polish case, in the last part of the conceptual chapter, the authors provide a theoretical vehicle (MIT) that is helpful in shedding some interpretative light on the asymmetrical dependency that binds Poland with the Common Market. The FDI-driven growth and modernisation made the whole economic transition highly dependent on foreign entities and – to a large extent – the structures of the economic institutions, and therefore the model of capitalism was determined by them and their pro-liberal orientation. This external dependency was unavoidable in the face of the deficit of the domestic investment capital (especially in the era of 1990s). And it was consolidated during the time of EU accession, when the Polish market opened widely to Western capital (taking advantage of its cheap labour force). Being trapped in this dependent constellation brought about serious social consequences, such as – for example – a growing societal discontent with the relatively low level of welfare provision offered by the Polish state. Questioning the neoliberal paradigm elevated to power parties such as PiS, which – at the same time – developed their Eurosceptic agenda. Euroscepticism of the ruling party (2005–2007 and 2015–2023) keeps Poland away from the EU's core, but economic dependencies constrain it from leaving the union. At the same time, the Polish economy shows some symptoms of the middle-income trap, similar to the southern peripheries. The low hanging fruits have already been picked, and the relatively low innovation and competitiveness of the Polish economy sets some limits for further catch-up growth. In such circumstances the argument of having one's own currency becomes crucial, especially when devaluations may compensate some deficits in competitiveness. This creates a structural precondition of Poland's remaining on the EU's outer core for the foreseeable future.

Concluding the analysis of the Polish case, one needs to start by noticing that some observers emphasize the gradual but progressing divergence between the inner core and the outer core EU Member States that are labelled as peripheries. The Hungarian scholar Attila Agh claims that since the outbreak of the global crisis in the late 2000s there has been an 'alienation' between the core and the periphery in the EU with marked features in the east's New Member States, such as widespread disappointment of those states' populations with the results of EU membership. Poland together with Hungary have been pioneering in this process of divergence from the EU mainstream and in the emergence of anti-EU populist elites, so those states represent a classic case of Euro-populism in the eastern periphery of the EU (Agh 2017, p. 45).

The Polish industrial relations model does not fit to the European mainstream as regards knowledge, education, nor welfare systems, nor does it fit to the financial market. The labour market, worker participation, and social dialogue resemble the LME type with a lot of flexibility and short-termism. On the other hand, the corporate governance area is based on long-term financing within the banking sector. The aforementioned flexibility, however, does not secure employees, whose voice is becoming ever more weak.

Poland, which, by geographical and geo-economic terms belongs to the EU's eastern periphery, is still characterized by levels of asymmetrical dependency on the developments in the global economy and other major economies of the world. Similarly to southern (semi-) peripheries (see: Magone 2008), it is part of a category of countries that neither belong to the periphery nor to the centre of the global economy. This group of states is labelled as semi-peripheral, because they still represent many peripheral forms of production and struggle to keep up technologically with the more advanced economies of the core (Magone 2008, pp. 237–259). In spite of being a member of the European Union, Poland continues to suffer from asymmetrical dependencies, low knowledge-intensive investments, and a low capacity of research and development.

Moreover, the parliamentary elections results in October 2023 brought about a new situation in Polish politics, also as regards relations with Brussels. The Eurosceptic PiS won the elections, but due to the lack of coalition potential they could not form a majority in the Polish *Sejm* (lower chamber of the parliament). This meant that power went to the hands of a broad coalition led by Brussels-experienced Donald Tusk. One of the unifying elements of the new majority was the pro-European attitude, which predicts a new opening in Poland's relations with Brussels and the EU partners. This does not necessarily need to mean any considerable shift vis-à-vis the analysed economic poles. The liberal Civic Coalition (PO) is moderated by social-democratic and Christian-democratic junior coalition partners, which may result in mixed policy outputs. As regards the question of the future position of Poland on the map of differentiated integration, one may expect the end of the anti-EU trajectory that characterized Polish politics in the period 2015–2023. The political decisions may also influence the economy, mostly by depoliticizing state-owned companies and introducing reforms faster and more decisively in the spirit of the coordinated economy model promoted by the EU (or at least not to delay or dilute the implementation of EU directives). Some of the first actions of the new government include: joining EPPO, undertaking closer cooperation with OLAF (to audit the spending of EU money), as well as declaring a rule of law recovery package (in order to unfreeze the RRF funds).

However, it would be over-optimistic to expect that Poland would move closer to the EU's inner core. This would require a major step, like entering the Eurozone, which is highly improbable in the foreseeable future.

5 Swiss exceptionalism: Integration without membership

5.1 SWISS QUASI-MEMBERSHIP IN THE EUROPEAN UNION

The Swiss Confederation formally remains a country that does not aspire to attain membership in the European Union. This state of affairs is the result of the confluence of several factors discussed in more detail later in the chapter. Yet, one key factor comes to the fore – namely the will of the Swiss citizens. It was in the form of a referendum that the Swiss made decisions on various forms of participation in the process of European integration. At the same time, because various instruments of direct democracy occupy a particularly important position in the systemic solutions of the Swiss Confederation, this form of decision making is the most common and most democratically legitimized formula.

Switzerland, representing the inner periphery of European differentiated integration (DI), is known for its political neutrality and its regular practice of direct democracy in a primary part of the national legislation process (Lavenex 2009). As will be outlined, the direct say of the Swiss people and hence domestic politicization in international relations and agreements has been an element of restriction for parties and government leaders. Only 20% of the Swiss population support Swiss EU accession. Whenever the topic for further European integration spills into the sphere of domestic politics, fierce debates are sparked about Switzerland's cultural heritage and its independence in the international structure. However, the case of Switzerland represents the prototype for dealing with popular demand for Euroscepticism on the one hand and functional pressures in a largely integrated neighbourhood on the other hand – both being a constraint to each other. Switzerland is a non-Member State that is almost entirely surrounded by Member States of the European Union and the Eurozone, with the exception of Liechtenstein (which is much more closely integrated with the EU as a member of the European Economic Area (EEA)). Historically speaking, Switzerland has managed to uphold political neutrality officially since its founding in 1848. Before the era of European integration in the 20th century, it prevailed without any serious material damage through the Second World War. In the post-Second World War era, Switzerland joined and contributed to several integrative treaties and institutions, joining as a founding member of the European Free Trade Association (EFTA) in 1960 and remaining so to this day. The association that also includes Iceland, Norway, and Liechtenstein served as an alternative to the establishing of the European Economic Community (EEC). Switzerland also participated in the negotiations for the European Economic Area (EEA) in 1992 and succeeded with a formal submission of accession to the European Union. In 1992 the EU and EFTA agreed on a common internal market, with the EEA providing for the inclusion of EU legislation regarding the four freedoms in all 30 EEA Members States. However, in a contentious Swiss referendum at the end of the same year, EEA membership was rejected by the Swiss people with a close result (50.3% to 49.7%). The referendum process and its counter-positions strongly reflected a strong cultural divide among the Swiss population, and the formal application was subsequently suspended by the Swiss government. Another federal popular initiative to launch accession-to-EU-membership negotiations with the EU failed, with almost 75% of the turnout voting against the motion. A similar initiative failed in 2001, and only in 2016 was the Swiss application status finally withdrawn. After the first failed referendum on EEA membership, both parties reinitiated negotiations for further bilateral agreements on a sector-by sector basis (Groth 2014). Those talks were also held for the Swiss to safeguard some of the economic benefits that the EU had to offer and to ensure that Swiss companies would not be at a disadvantage in key economic sectors. The negotiations resulted in two waves of ten bilateral agreements overall and several additional referenda that made EU law applicable to Swiss law (Vahl & Grolimund 2006). These mostly concerned technical trade barriers, consumer rights, and the free movement of people. In 2000, the first wave of bilateral agreements was accepted via a referendum, and there were conventional agreements on market access such as the free movement of people, a Mutual Recognition Agreement, a common public procurement market, agricultural policies, overland transport, research, and civil aviation. This was followed by a second wave of bilateral agreements that aimed at harmonizing economic, security, and asylum policies and led to the signing of the Dublin Agreement and Swiss membership of the Schengen zone from 2009. In combination with the existing free trade agreement, the Swiss private sector was given extensive access to the Single European market with its 445 million consumers at that time. As at 2022, the EU was Switzerland's main trade partner, with the Swiss being the fourth largest of all of the EU's trading partners. The bilateral agreements were adopted in a single package, introducing the so-called 'guillotine' clause. They are legally linked to each other, which means that they can only take effect and endure together. Conversely, breaching one agreement signifies the invalidation of all others (Radunz & Riedel 2024).

Swiss integration doctrine evolves under the influence of many variables. However, a set of factors related to the system specificity of Switzerland comes to the fore, including, above all, the cantons' position in the political system, the use of direct democracy mechanisms, and the anchoring of the principle of neutrality in society (as well as in the constitution). The issue of the 'governance of the assembly', i.e., the supremacy of the parliament over the other authorities, is not without significance. As part of the separation of powers in Switzerland, an imbalance between these authorities in favour of the Federal Assembly can be observed. This imbalance means that the Federal Council cannot afford any independent European policy. These factors mean that the official policy of the government – unlike in most EU Member States where participation in the mainstream of European integration was based on the principle of permissive consensus – is determined primarily by public sentiment, both of which are expressed in the form of referenda or election results, and 'between elections' in the form of public opinion polls. The Swiss government, being aware of the permanent risk of taking a popular initiative, referendum, or other forms of direct democracy by one of the Eurosceptic circles, cannot afford to independently formulate a long-term integration policy. It is shaped on an ongoing basis, in the rhythm of subsequent election and referendum decisions of the Helvetians, and with careful listening to public opinion polls in each of the cantons.

It would be expected that small, highly industrialized countries located in the heart of Europe are ideally suited to participate in the mainstream of European integration. However, the example of Switzerland seems to contradict this regularity. Indeed, in the case of Switzerland, the economic theory of integration seems to confirm that if the account of expected profits and losses is positive, then the country enters the integration process, and if the balance is negative, then the country remains outside the mainstream of integration. However, while in the economic calculation the issue of access to the huge Single Market and the competitive pressure it offers is important for relatively small economies such as Switzerland, the decision to join the EU is political in nature and also plays an important role. In Switzerland's case, these are identity and ideological factors. And while they did not seem to be decisive in the case of Bern's political and economic elites, the society itself, which is of decisive importance in the Swiss political system, appreciated them to a much greater extent. At the same time, it should not be forgotten that while in 1992 the Swiss seemed to be almost evenly divided on the issue of European integration, and the vote only minimally indicated the advantage of the opponents of the ratification of the EEA agreement, the voice of the cantons on this matter was already very clear and it was the signal that indicated far-reaching scepticism. This shows the unique, deep, and complex reasons behind the Swiss negation of the integration project.

The reflection on the history and evolution of the Swiss attitude towards European integration started before the 1990s. As early as in 1952 and 1956, when the foundations of a united Europe were being laid, the Swiss Confederation refused to participate in the negotiations on the establishment of the European Communities (the European Coal and Steel Community, the European Economic Community, and the European Atomic Energy Community) on the grounds that it would violate the 'sacred principle of neutrality'. It is *neutrality* that seems to be the key word for understanding Switzerland's relationship with the outside world in general, including the European Union. The problem, of course, is that the European Union has ceased to be the outside world for the Swiss. The process of European integration is so comprehensive, especially in the economic dimension, that Switzerland found itself (not only in geographical terms) in the middle of this element, subject to strong Europeanization pressure. However, this does not change the fact that neutrality is treated in Switzerland not only as a political strategy, but as a value that underlies Swiss statehood and identity. Therefore, in December 1956 the Swiss foreign minister officially declared participation in the common market 'undesirable'. However, as a result of the successes of the functioning of the EEC, in 1961 the government of the Swiss Confederation asked Brussels to consider some form of 'association that would leave intact the principles of neutrality, federalism and direct democracy'. These principles, as can be seen, determine the identity of Switzerland and the Swiss, and as such found themselves in the constitutional order of the Confederation.

Until a certain point, relations between the Swiss Confederation and the European Communities were regulated by the Free Trade Agreement (of 1972), which was completely sufficient from the point of view of access of Swiss goods to the markets of the EEC member countries – and this was actually the basis of the Swiss integration doctrine. However, as the Single Market project developed and services grew in importance to the economy, the framework of the Free Trade Agreement became less and less comfortable and more insufficient. In addition, an agreement on the free movement of capital was not included, which – given the importance of the banking and insurance sector in Switzerland – was a significant drawback. Therefore, the Swiss government's aspiration was to bring about more advanced agreements that would cover all freedoms and more actors – in other words, EEA-like agreements. When negotiating its terms, many of the arrangements were tailored to Swiss needs. However, due to the negative result of the referendum and the decision of the majority of cantons in this matter, Switzerland did not ratify the treaty and eventually found itself outside the EEA. As a consequence of the negative result of the referendum on accession to the EEA in 1992, the Swiss government was forced to abandon activities aimed at obtaining EU membership and to shape relations on the basis of intermediate solutions, which have since become bilateral agreements (in about 20 bilateral sectors). This method is supported by the majority of Swiss society, which in subsequent polls shows a reluctance towards integration based on the principle of full membership. At the same time, economic interests induce and even force the Swiss to remain part of the Single Market. On the other hand, the European Union itself remains open to the application of the Swiss Confederation and would gladly change its current status to that of a full member or at least that of the EEA formula (Radunz & Riedel 2024).

The current formula of EU-Switzerland cooperation is often referred to as 'integration without membership' or 'privileged membership'. Stanisław C. Kozłowski (2009) distinguishes the following phases in Switzerland's relations with the EU (previously the European Communities):

- 1957–1971: This period coincides with the establishment of the European Coal and Steel Community, the European Economic Community, and the European Atomic Energy Community, in which Switzerland consciously – while adhering to the policy of neutrality and distance – did not participate. However, together with other European countries (the United Kingdom, Denmark, Norway, Austria, Portugal, and Sweden), in 1960 it created the EFTA group (European Free Trade Agreement), which was a kind of alternative to the European Communities and consisted of the concept of a so-called 'shallow integration'. In the early 1960s, Bern held talks on association with the EEC, but they did not bring any results, mainly due to such points of contention as, for example, the margin of freedom in adapting the *acquis communautaire* or the competence of the institution of such an association.
- 1972–1987: In 1972, Switzerland concluded a free trade agreement with the EEC (followed by more than 100 different types of trade agreements with the Member States of the then EEC). This solution generally ensured Swiss participation in the continent's economic integration. At the same time, a rule was adopted that each new legal act would be subject to verification in terms of its compliance with the acquis of the European Communities.
- 1988–1992: This period is characterized by the acceleration of the process of European integration (the most characteristic representation of which is the Treaty of Maastricht). This phenomenon naturally generated pressure on the government in Bern and its previous European policy. As a result, Switzerland submitted an accession application in 1992 and at the same time signed an EEA accession agreement in Oporto, perceiving this formula as a kind of intermediate phase on the way to full membership

(which was announced as a long-term goal of the Swiss Confederation's policy).

- Since 1992: The fourth phase begins on 6 December 1992, when the Swiss held a referendum on their EEA membership. To the great surprise of both government circles *and* the European public, the Swiss public rejected EEA membership, albeit with a minimal majority of 50.3%. This event defined the nature of Bern's relationship with Brussels for decades to come.

The foundation of the contemporary integration doctrine of the Swiss Confederation is bilateralism, i.e., a strategy of building relations with the EU on the basis of packages of bilateral agreements regulating particular spheres of social and economic life, each time negotiated bilaterally with Brussels. Bilateralism, as the basis of Switzerland's relationship with the EU, has many important consequences. First of all, it enforces the compatibility of Swiss law with the acquis of the European Union in the part established as the 'minimum common denominator', allowing the Swiss to benefit from access to the Single Market (and vice versa). This is one-sided compatibility; i.e., each proposal for a new legal act in Switzerland needs to be analysed in terms of convergence with EU law in order to avoid discrepancies in both legal systems. At the same time, in the case of new EU legal acts, Switzerland is very often forced to unilaterally adopt them. It can, therefore, be concluded that in this case there is a *de facto* integration, but of a unilateral nature, without an advanced degree of institutionalization. Despite strong economic ties between Switzerland and the European Union (more broadly: the EEA), the Helvetians remain outside the mainstream of European integration.

Bilateral agreements were negotiated and adopted in packages (e.g., the so-called *Bilaterale I* in 1999), which has serious legal consequences. In the adopted package approach, the rule of the 'guillotine clause' (*Guillotine-Klausel*) was applied, which results in the annulment of all contracts in the event that one of the parties terminates any of them. This is a solution reminiscent of the rules of negotiations with the new Member States, in which 'nothing is negotiated until everything is negotiated'. In other words, the success of the negotiations as a whole depends on agreement with regard to every detail. The parties reserve the right to deviate from the whole package of arrangements in a situation where no agreement can be reached in any single sector/area/negotiating chapter. This solution results from the high degree of interconnectedness of individual aspects of the integration process, e.g., the natural connection of the four freedoms (the free movement of capital, people, goods, and services). The issue of participation in the mainstream of European integration has become one of the most controversial for the Swiss. In addition, it is becoming more and more important not only in the structure of social divisions and in the political struggle, but also in the public debate. At the same time, it is impossible not to get the impression that it was Switzerland that had (and still has) unique political solutions, which should be used when designing and building supranational institutional architecture in multicultural, multi-religious, multi-ethnic, and multilingual societies. It is, therefore, a kind of paradox that it is Switzerland – a kind of 'EU in a nutshell' if you will – that shows the attitude of one of the most Eurosceptic countries in Europe. And all the more so because it was Switzerland that was one of the most important centres of pan-European thought at the beginning of the 20th century (see the example of the activity of Richard Nicolaus von Coudenhove-Calergi).

Determinants of the modern integration doctrine of Switzerland are equally complex. The widely understood European policy of Switzerland is determined by the geopolitical, economic, and domestic politics conditions. Geopolitical determinants include, above all, the issue of the location of Switzerland, including its geographical location. Such a hierarchy of determinants is in line with the classical understanding of geopolitics as a field of knowledge that studies the geographical determinants of socio-political phenomena and processes. Used by representatives of international relations, this term defines the relationship between the geographical location of a country and its position in the international community and its policy. The mountainous nature of Switzerland's territory was historically significant from the point of view of its attractiveness as a potential area of expansion for its neighbours (mainly Germany, France, and Austria). The costs necessary to conquer and hold such a difficult territory always outweighed the expected benefits, which is why Switzerland managed to avoid military confrontations. This was of great importance not only from the point of view of the behaviour of the neighbouring countries, but also from the point of view of the systematically built self-perception of the Swiss as a special case of a neutral nation, standing beside the mainstream of history. Nowadays, the neutrality of the Swiss Confederation has not only geopolitical, but also economic significance, i.e., the reputation of the Swiss banking or insurance (or more broadly: financial) sector was built on the basis of its independence (e.g., the most strictly protected rules of banking secrecy). Bern treats all kinds of international obligations with suspicion, which is why the Swiss avoid them if possible. The lack of Switzerland's presence in the Bretton Woods agreements, then in the OECD and many other bodies and organizations, often resulted in partial diplomatic isolation. Nevertheless, the Swiss were ready to pay the price for it, and this position was accepted by both the political elite and the general public. The example of Switzerland shows how classically understood geopolitics is an important variable defining the interests and behaviour of a given political entity in its relations with the outside world (political and economic).

Among other conditions of an economic nature, one should refer to the arguments that appeared during the debate preceding the referendum. On the side of supporters, rhetoric referring to economic demands prevailed – access to the Single Market, economic opening, as well as the fear of potentially cutting off the Swiss economy from its natural markets. It was especially the latter argument which was strongly exposed, mainly due to the pro-export orientation of the Swiss economy. In the opponents' camp, the focus was on identity issues, fear of losing sovereignty, and a lack of trust in the European Union. As a consequence, it was decided that the optimal solution for Switzerland would be the closest possible economic integration, albeit with the most far-reaching political autonomy at the same time. Among the economic reasons, one should also highlight the argument that Switzerland is faring much better than most (if not all) EU Member States. When asked whether the Swiss economy would do better or worse within the EU, the vast majority of respondents believe that not only would it do worse, but membership would undermine the very foundations of the Swiss economic model. The adoption of full membership commitments would require the application of many EU regulations, which, in the liberal model, is combined with greater social liabilities of public finances, increased taxes, and even – as Eurosceptics claim – with increased unemployment and a massive influx of foreigners.

Domestic conditions remain the most complex. Systemic issues come to the fore, including, above all; federalism institutionalized in the constitution of 1848 and attachment to direct forms of democracy, as well as the strong position of the cantons, which fear that the entry of the Swiss Confederation into the EU would undermine their key role in the decision-making process. In addition, identity issues are not without significance, including, for example, the already mentioned principle of neutrality, or the belief in the uniqueness of Switzerland (*Sonderfall*), confirmed by historical experience. Three important principles can be identified at the foundation of Swiss national identity: the principle of neutrality, federalism, and institutions of direct democracy. All three of these principles would undergo a significant transformation (erosion – in the language of Eurosceptics) in the event of Switzerland joining the EU structures. At the same time, it is precisely these elements that built the Swiss identity that caused the Helvetians to remain outside the EU all the time. Further, taking into account that it is in a referendum that the decision on the possible accession of the Swiss Confederation to the EU will be made, it is necessary to look at the evolution of public opinion and the factors of an identity nature that shape it, as well as economic and political determinants.

It can be considered that the European theme has created a new socio-political division on the Swiss political scene. However, this is a division that does not boil down only to different answers to the question of membership in the European Union, but generally to different visions of Switzerland's place in the international community. So, on the one hand, we are dealing with a vision of Switzerland focused on itself, with internal problems, closed off, and based on traditionalist values, while on the other hand, there is another vision of a modern, open, cosmopolitan, export-oriented Switzerland. Switzerland – or more precisely, its political model – is often invoked as a potential role model for the European Union. Remaining a loose union of cantons characterized by far-reaching cultural, religious, linguistic, etc., diversity, Switzerland has developed a specific, functional political system based on consensualism and deliberation. The consequence of such a state of affairs is the fact that the optimal – from the Swiss perspective – model of integration is also a relatively loose and relatively shallow one. The confederal system of Switzerland stands in logical contradiction to the concepts of deep and close integration at the European level. The basic political entity in Switzerland, the canton, is in many respects more loosely integrated into the Swiss Confederation than most EU Member States. Thus, participation in the mainstream of the integration process is perceived from the Swiss perspective not only as an option and an unattractive prospect, but even (especially from the perspective of the cantons) as a threat to independence and neutrality – the superior values of the Swiss.

As a consequence, the Swiss Confederation implements a model of 'integration without membership' or, as other authors define it, the model of 'limited integration'. There are also more pejorative terms, such as Alfred Tovias' 'quasi colonialism' (2006) or Chris Church's 'Swiss Anomaly' (2007). It also seems reasonable to see Switzerland's relations with the European Union through the prism of the metaphor formulated by Ralf Dahrendorf – *Europe à la Carte*. United Europe, in which each participating entity chooses – as on a restaurant menu – its optimal integration set (which policy and to what extent it wants to participate in that policy, and which policy it does not). Admittedly, the founding fathers of the European Communities wanted to avoid such an integration concept, considering it as limiting Europe's integration potential. However, it seems that Switzerland is practising this model of European integration as a result of a functional need. In this way, the Swiss manage to avoid the isolation that would threaten them if they turned their backs entirely on Brussels and actually retained much of the neutrality so valued in Bern. However, the European Union itself, along with growing Europeanization pressure, is perceived as a threat to the Swiss socio-economic model based on liberal economic policy, low taxes, high competitiveness based on innovation, relatively low social protection, and the protection of domestic strategic industries against excessive external regulation. Whether this unique Swiss model of integration will remain only as a kind of relic of the past or rather a model for the future inspired by other countries on the outskirts of the European Union still remains an open question. However, this does not change the fact that visions of an 'ever closer union' are far from the point of view of the Swiss integration doctrine. Taking into account the attitude of Swiss political parties or Swiss society (expressed in public opinion polls, as well as – and perhaps above all – in referenda decisions), even the very foundations of the integration project, such as the four freedoms (the free movement of goods, services, capital, and people) are too far-reaching. In a situation where every citizen of the EU (and the EEA) is forced to apply for a work permit in Switzerland, it is difficult to consider any federalist concepts of European integration at all. Loose economic cooperation is the most that the Swiss really agree with, and visions of a political union with solidarity and redistribution mechanisms seem to be an irrational pipe dream from Bern's perspective.

Switzerland implements a special and specific model of participation in the process of European integration, which is the result of necessity arising from the will of Swiss citizens expressed in electoral or referendum acts on the one hand, and the pragmatism of political and economic elites on the other. As a result, the Swiss reached a rather delicate compromise, allowing them to enjoy access to the Single Market, but without full membership rights. At this price, they managed to satisfy their identity-based needs and avoid the penetration of their political system by strong Europeanization impulses, which would happen in the case of full membership. Such a system has been operating for over two decades and was constructed in an ad hoc mode, after the lost referendum of 1992, as a functional need for a compromise between the needs and conditions of a political and economic nature. This compromise is often shaken under the pressure of Brussels or subsequent popular initiatives (directly or indirectly related to integration issues, e.g., the 2014 referendum), which force Bern into permanent negotiations and flexibility in adapting mandatory EU norms and rules, while respecting Swiss standards in political systems (including the position of regions, federalism, direct democracy, and the principle of neutrality). As Michał Tomczyk notes:

> In the case of accession to the EU, the political system of Switzerland may prevent the transposition of EU law into the Swiss legal order. In this situation, the government will be forced to reform the decision-making process, including limiting the impact of direct democracy. Deepening integration may therefore have a serious impact on its future. Therefore, it can be concluded that the Swiss political system, including direct democracy, turns out to be ineffective and anachronistic, but above all inadequate to the problems and challenges facing Switzerland at the beginning of the 21st century. (2013, p. 8)

The reasons for these and no other relations between Switzerland and the rest of an integrating Europe can, of course, be traced to many factors. Among them, the most important seem to be: the traditional Swiss policy of neutrality, the uniqueness of the political system, a specific political culture built on a strong attachment to the federal state, the dynamics of public opinion, the Euroscepticism of some political elites, and economic interests. But chronologically, one should start with the historical factor. European integration was a project built on the ashes of the Second World War. Economically ruined European countries were looking for a path to reconstruction that would guarantee the avoidance of cataclysms such as the First or Second World Wars. Their motivation was built on the foundation of tragic experiences from the first half of the 20th century. Meanwhile, Switzerland did not have such motivations, because it did not have tragic experiences of the kind that Poland, France, or Germany did. As a neutral country, it did not directly participate in hostilities, its economy remained virtually untouched by the element of the Second World War, and, as a consequence, neither Swiss society nor its elites shared the motivations of Germany or France, which in the 1950s started building economic blocs to link past enemies and thus question the sense of any future aggression. Perceiving this process from the Swiss perspective, one of the most important motives to participate in the project of uniting the Old Continent was missing from the very beginning. For the Swiss, the European Communities and the subsequent European Union never had a security dimension. However, they have always been perceived through the prism of economic interest, as well as through the prism of identity – in the individual dimension, as well as the Swiss political community and its individual, specific features.

5.2 THE HYBRIDITY OF THE SWISS VARIETY OF CAPITALISM

The Swiss model of capitalism is commonly regarded as 'hybrid', a characterization rooted in Switzerland's unique history and the presence of formal and informal institutions with origins in German, French, and Italian socio-economic systems. However, this hybridity differs significantly from that which has recently emerged in Central Europe. Switzerland's market-oriented economic regime has persisted for decades and is deeply ingrained in its cultural identity. Despite efforts to normalize its distinct status, Switzerland remains challenging to categorize within the realm of political economy. It possesses institutional and political conditions that set it apart and can be analysed from various dimensions and theoretical perspectives.

The Swiss Confederation exhibits characteristics of self-determination through trade unions, akin to those in a coordinated market economy (CME) such as Austria and Germany. Simultaneously, it shares traits with a liberal market economy (LME) such as the United States and the United Kingdom, relying on free market mechanisms, particularly in robust export-oriented sectors. This complexity defies simplistic labels like 'welfare state regime' or 'corporatism'. In previous comparative political economy discourse, Switzerland was termed 'democratic corporatism' (Katzenstein 1980, 1987), reflecting its combination of international economic liberalism with substantial compensation through generous social, wage, and employment policies. Gøsta Esping-Andersen found the liberal orientation of the Swiss model perplexing, positioning it between 'liberal' and 'conservative' welfare state regimes (1990). Early comparative capitalism literature was inconclusive as well. The varieties of capitalism (VoC) school initially deemed Switzerland's economy to be a highly coordinated form, yet empirical examinations suggested moderate coordination levels (Hall & Gingerich 2004, p. 479).

Nonetheless, extensive research reveals that in modern times non-market coordination mechanisms play a significant role in various key spheres, including industrial relations, vocational training and education, enterprises, and relations between employers and employees. These mechanisms involve the influence of unions, social networks, and the state in shaping business activities. Despite this, definitive evidence regarding the predominance of non-market coordination in Switzerland's economy remains elusive. Strong liberal features persist, differentiating Switzerland as an anomalous case and a deviation from a highly coordinated model market economy seen in 'classic' CMEs like Germany or Austria. The closest interpretation to reality posits Switzerland as a country that exists between these two types of economies. This approach abstracts from the highly coherent political and economic institutions seen in German-style coordinated economies while embracing a high degree of coordination and elements of collective governance (employee unions, corporate management), distinguishing it from the free-market prototype represented by the United States.

Andrée Mach and Christine Trampusch (2011) present a slightly different perspective on Switzerland's institutional matrix, focusing on its politico-economic features, especially the dominant mode of coordination. Applying a comprehensive historical institutionalism approach, they highlight three distinct peculiarities of the Swiss Confederation that set it apart. These include the dominance of right-wing partisan politics, a reliance on informal institutions and self-regulation within the socio-economic system, and the interpenetration of powerful business associations and the ruling right-wing political class. These factors create what's known as the Swiss bourgeois bloc. These elements explain the direction of major policies and the stability of the Swiss model.

Thus, Switzerland's hybrid capitalism defies easy categorization due to its intricate history and the blending of CME and LME characteristics. Recent changes in business elites and their interactions with globalization may reshape the nation's political and economic landscape. While business elites' instrumental power may have diminished, their structural power has increased, allowing them to shape economic coordination through both formal and informal means. This complex interplay between institutions and ideologies continues to define Switzerland's unique form of capitalism.

The first pivotal aspect is the prevalence of right-leaning partisan politics, coupled with the long-standing marginalization of the left, which has consistently been relegated to 'junior partner' status in the nation's governance since the aftermath of the Second World War. A closely interwoven second factor is the Swiss socio-economic system's reliance on informal institutions and self-regulation, which inherently favour the organized business interests with a traditional advantage of power. The intricate connection between these two factors lies in the symbiotic relationship between influential business associations and the ruling right-wing liberal political class. This intricate interplay forms what academic discourse refers to as the Swiss bourgeois bloc. While the first two factors account for the general trajectory of predominantly pro-business policies, the third factor elucidates the underlying stability of this scenario.

Central to this stability is the idiosyncrasy of the Swiss federal political system, anchored in direct democracy. The central government operates with constrained agency due to its obligation to heed decisions made by individual cantons governing municipalities. This structural configuration, combined with the relatively subdued strength of the left wing, has also contributed to the limited influence of trade unions, positioning them beneath the umbrella of business unions. Major legal alterations encounter multiple *veto points* and *veto players* which, throughout history, have thwarted numerous endeavours to instigate more progressive changes in Switzerland's labour landscape, such as extending citizens' social rights. Although the emphasis on the political right and the constrained political authority of the central government draw Switzerland closer to the liberal model, the extensive collective regulation executed by economic unions and private entities, along with the incorporation of non-market mechanisms for economic coordination, distinctly differentiates the Confederation from the Anglo-Saxon liberal archetype.

Nonetheless, recent explorations into the evolution of Swiss business elites and their potential for coordination (Mach et al. 2021, pp. 17–41) have prompted discussions about potential institutional shifts. In particular, the authors have conceptualized a shift from so-called 'quiet' to more 'noisy' politics. While the former approach was conducted behind closed doors and often relied on informal networks between politicians and business representatives, the latter approach, which has gained momentum since the 1990s, prioritizes transparent policy formulation. This transformation has been motivated by several factors. Notably, there has been a growing divide within business associations, partly catalysed by the ascendance of the nationalist-populist Swiss Popular Party. This transformation has disrupted the hitherto consolidated bourgeois bloc. Moreover, the forces of globalization and heightened internationalization have brought about a transformation within the composition of the business elite. A greater number of foreign individuals now occupy the upper echelons of corporate hierarchy, gender parity has improved, and diverse backgrounds in terms of origin, family history, education, and values have reshaped the elite stratum.

The concept of 'noisy' politics extends to the political elite as well, who have increasingly professionalized their roles in recent decades. A telling example is the augmentation of politicians' remuneration, which has diminished their need to seek external sources of income. This shift signifies a heightened dedication to public service, minimizing potential conflicts of interest stemming from external financial commitments. Does all of the above imply that the influence of business on the coordination mechanisms of Swiss hybrid capitalism has been curtailed? According to existing literature, the answer is a nuanced blend of both yes and no. On the one hand, the so-called 'instrumental' power of informal influence has been curbed by recent developments. However, within the context of the financialized global economy, their 'structural' power has actually expanded. They now engage more actively in 'ideological' work, promoting economic liberalism through allied think-tanks. Yet, the most potent tool in their arsenal remains the prospect of capital relocation and divestment from the national economy if political decisions veer off in an unfavourable direction.

The first set of institutions to be analysed in the VoC framework is the corporate governance and capital markets regime. Switzerland's financial system amalgamates features from both CMEs and LMEs. During the transition spanning the 1990s and the 2000s, Alexander Börsch (2007, pp. 173–194) offers insights into the then-Swiss corporate governance landscape, dissecting it into key components. The initial element revolves around a typically CME-esque structure, characterized by universal, banking-based capital markets for companies. However, unlike Germany, Switzerland's stock market also plays a significant and seemingly expanding role. The Zurich SIX exchange, among the world's most advanced, stands out with an exceptionally high capitalization, constituting a three-digit percentage of GDP (205% in 2004 and 270.5% in 2016). This proportion mirrors the United States more than Germany (134% and 193% respectively versus 42% and 59% for Germany). Strikingly, only 4% of the listed companies' total capitalization is state-owned, marking one of the lowest scores within the OECD. Concurrently, Switzerland boasts one of the highest levels of domestic credit extended to the private sector by banks, progressively rising since the early 2000s and peaking at 170% of GDP in 2016.

Further variances that delineate Switzerland's CME-oriented financial system, rendering it somewhat hybrid, pertain to the significance of institutional investors and the formal structure within corporate entities. The potency of the former can be quantified: the cumulative value of financial assets held by key institutional entities (such as pension funds and insurance corporations) was already substantial in 2004 (158.5% of GDP), and this figure continues to rise, reaching 243% of GDP by 2021. This phenomenon positions Swiss financial capitalism more proximate to Anglo-Saxon regimes than its 'Rhenish' counterparts – Germany's figures are 66% and 90% respectively, while Austria's span less than 40% for the entire period. The latter aspect concerns Swiss corporate law, mandating a one-tier system where the board of directors, oriented towards strategic management, encompasses both external and internal members, with only the latter being executives. This configuration parallels the organizational framework familiar in LMEs. However, there have been notable shifts in board composition and performance since the late 1980s. Scholarly investigation suggests that regulatory pressures, political influences, and proxy advisors' demands led to leaner boards, enhanced diversity, and less burdened directors. Committees, especially for audit, compensation, and nominations, have become prevalent.

Mach et al. (2021) highlights that the preference for managers with a technological educational background has waned, as the significance of business and economics degrees has surged. Furthermore, boards have become more internationally diverse in recent decades. Nevertheless, distinct parallels exist between Switzerland's hybrid financial model and more 'pure' CMEs. Hostile takeovers are notable due to the absence of capital control mechanisms. Stock options as components of executive remuneration, which are infrequently used, separate performance from share prices, a hallmark of LME-esque shareholder value systems. Ownership concentration, traditionally higher in Switzerland compared to more unequivocally liberal systems, remains akin to levels seen in German-speaking countries and Denmark. However, it is lower than what is observed in Belgium (Arthur et al. 2019, pp. 104–132).

Examining the Swiss education and vocational training system brings another set of interesting insights. The skills formation in Switzerland stands as one of the most distinctive elements within its institutional framework of capitalism, offering insights into its unique blend of CME and LME traits. The comparative political economy literature underscores its alignment with the CME ideal type, but its intricacies reveal a dynamic interplay of factors that have shaped Switzerland's approach to fostering a highly skilled workforce.

Switzerland's reputation for hosting a highly skilled workforce, drawn from all corners of the world, serves as a testament to the robustness of its skills formation system. This system thrives on the strong cooperation between educational institutions and employers, particularly evident at the tertiary level, but also extending its reach to lower levels of schooling. Notably, this collaboration finds a particularly illustrative example in the pharmaceutical industry, where the close intertwining of universities and businesses has yielded mutually beneficial outcomes.

A cornerstone of Switzerland's skills formation system is the maintenance of both school-based vocational training (*Fachhochschulen*) and the dual apprenticeship model, which combines firm-based and school-based training. This duality is reminiscent of the systems in Germany and Austria, highlighting the continuity of vocational education in a rapidly evolving economic landscape. Traditionally, employer representatives, predominantly channelled through business interest associations, have steered this system, while unions have held a comparatively limited influence in the process. Yet, despite the system's resilience, challenges have emerged in recent decades. Economic fluctuations during the 1990s and a lack of engagement from stakeholders beyond business associations prompted a reconsideration of the approach. Major corporations even advocated for a restructuring of the system to align it more with a general skills orientation, reflecting the dynamic nature of Switzerland's economy and the need for adaptable skill sets.

Marius R. Busemeyer and his co-authors (2022, pp. 231–250) provide a fascinating case study of how the Swiss state played a pivotal role in revitalizing the vocational education and training system. Employing an 'orchestration' approach that focused on resource mobilization and soft governance, the state reinvigorated a faltering system without direct intervention. Late 1990s legislative initiatives offered financial incentives to both companies and prospective students, promoting vocational training and expanding into promising sectors such as information and communication technology (ICT). Importantly, this revitalization retained the essence of the dual apprenticeship model, ensuring that skills learned were transferable beyond the confines of individual firms.

The historical perspective also unveils Switzerland's journey in adapting its skills formation system to the demands of a knowledge-based global economy. Patrick Emmenegger and his co-authors (2023) have dissected the evolution of vocational education and training in Switzerland dating back to the 1970s. In the face of globalization and the shift towards a knowledge economy, Switzerland's vocational education system faced formidable challenges. These pressures prompted the introduction of the 'upskilling' factor, which emphasized retraining, facilitating access to higher academic education, and nurturing general competencies among vocationally trained individuals.

Contrary to early expectations, the Swiss case reveals an increase in students entering general education at the upper-secondary level, while the popularity of school-based vocational learning has seen a decline. However, the dual apprenticeship model remains appealing, ensuring the integration of theoretical and practical knowledge. Crucially, the number of students pursuing academic pathways has surged, driven by the emergence of specialized and technically oriented universities of applied sciences. This shift showcases Switzerland's capacity to adapt its vocational education system to the evolving demands of the global economy. The country's innovative spirit, coupled with a willingness to collaborate and refine its education ecosystem, has resulted in a dynamic skills formation system that meets the needs of both businesses and students.

Notably, the voluntary nature of the Swiss vocational education and training regime contributes to its adaptability. Due to an absence of significant trade union influence in this domain, firms possess greater flexibility to shape solutions that align with their preferences. Business interest associations, representing a diverse spectrum of companies from large corporations to small and medium enterprises, recognize the value of vocational training. They have steered its enhancement by integrating 'upskilling', thereby ensuring that the Swiss workforce remains versatile and prepared for the challenges of a rapidly evolving economy.

The effectiveness of Switzerland's skills formation system is further underscored by its economic competitiveness. Ranking first in multiple editions of the Global Competitiveness Report since 2005, Switzerland's economy has demonstrated resilience in the face of changing macroeconomic landscapes and external shocks. Its commitment to research and development is also evident in private and public R&D spending, which grew from 2.6% of GDP in 2004 to 3.2% in 2019. These figures consistently surpass the high-income country average, putting Switzerland on par with nations known for their innovation and technology prowess.

In conclusion, the evaluation of Switzerland's skills formation strategy offers a vivid illustration of how the country's predominantly coordinated capitalism aligns with liberal and entrepreneurial principles. Through a blend of historical adaptation, cooperation between stakeholders, and an innovative spirit, Switzerland's skills formation system remains a cornerstone of its economic success and global competitiveness. This intricate balance between coordinated and liberal features showcases Switzerland's ability to thrive in a rapidly changing economic landscape.

Distinctive features of Swiss capitalism are visible also in the realm of the labour market. Switzerland's industrial relations framework epitomizes the intricate interplay between liberal and coordinated elements within its overarching capitalist system. This landscape offers a fascinating glimpse into the nation's unique approach to managing labour dynamics, blending historical traditions with the demands of a modern, interconnected economy. As we delve deeper into the complexities of Swiss industrial relations, we uncover a narrative of adaptation, collaboration, and ongoing transformation.

Historically, Switzerland has stood as a prime example of liberal neo-corporatism, where the coexistence of labour and capital has been meticulously orchestrated to maintain industrial peace. The role of trade unions has often been that of a subordinate partner in decentralized and harmonious industrial relations. As Daniel Oesch (2011, pp. 82–102) eloquently summarizes,

Swiss trade unions have, over the decades, found their niche as collaborative partners, contributing to the nation's steady economic expansion while adhering to an ethos of tranquillity. This environment has been remarkably conducive to productivity, with Switzerland experiencing a dearth of strikes that is virtually unparalleled on the global stage. However, the late 20th century ushered in a wave of transformative changes that disrupted this equilibrium. The emergence of a so-called 'employer's market', coupled with the rise of neoliberal ideologies and the influx of EU immigrants, precipitated a decline in unionization rates. Unions found themselves confronted with the imperative to re-evaluate their strategies, prompting the adoption of more assertive tactics such as strikes, alongside strategic organizational restructuring and mergers.

The empirical data from the International Labour Organization's ILOstat database mirrors this evolution, with union density rates declining from over 20% in 2000 to 14.4% in 2018. While Switzerland's rates have consistently hovered below the OECD average, there has been a convergence of trends, aligning the nation's trajectory with global patterns since the 1980s. Within this framework, Switzerland's labour participation is characterized by a so-called 'dual-channel' model that integrates both trade unions and elected work councils. However, the extent of the impact of work councils is limited, with their role largely confined to information dissemination and consultation, rather than co-determination.

What sets Switzerland apart is the palpable influence wielded by businesses in shaping the labour landscape. Employers' organizations maintain a substantial presence, accounting for approximately 60% of the labour market – an impressively high proportion. This statistic reinforces the idea that Swiss labour dynamics are significantly shaped by the business sector, underscoring the pivotal role these organizations play in influencing labour policies and practices. The evolving nature of organized labour is also reflected in the realm of collective bargaining. Switzerland's experience reveals a resurgence in collective bargaining coverage since the early 2000s, stabilizing at around 50% despite the absence of a statutory minimum wage. This remarkable achievement outpaces historical lows of approximately 40%, positioning Switzerland favourably within the context of international collective bargaining trends. These negotiations primarily take place at the sectoral or industry level, contributing to the maintenance of labour harmony.

Ironically, the process of European integration has played an unexpected role in bolstering Switzerland's collective bargaining tradition. In an intriguing turn of events, business organizations negotiated an enhanced tripartite labour market arrangement in exchange for better access to the European market. This symbiotic arrangement has revitalized collective bargaining and has been instrumental in driving the ascendancy of union-negotiated minimum wages. In parallel, legal reforms since 1994 have engendered a surge in works council engagement within collective agreements, augmenting their role within the broader labour relations framework.

Switzerland's labour market performance since the late 1990s has been robust. Impressively, its performance on key indicators such as employment and unemployment rates, earnings quality, and job security aligns closely with those of top-performing nations. However, persistent gender inequality underscores the challenges that persist within Swiss society. The gender wage gap, though gradually decreasing, remains a notable concern, reflecting the nation's complex blend of liberal, social democratic, and conservative influences. In light of these dynamics, Switzerland's labour landscape navigates a delicate equilibrium. While its historical approach to industrial relations has garnered stability and prosperity, it has not been without its limitations. Gender inequalities and tensions concerning unemployment among foreign workers challenge the nation's commitment to social equity.

In conclusion, Switzerland's industrial relations offer a multi-dimensional portrait of a nation continually striving to balance the tenets of liberal neo-corporatism with the realities of a modern labour landscape. The historical underpinnings, the intricate dance between employer organizations and trade unions, and the impact of European integration collectively weave a tapestry of labour relations that is as nuanced as it is intriguing. Through adaptation, collaboration, and thoughtful transformation, Switzerland's industrial relations remain a testament to the nation's resilience and its ability to harmonize disparate elements within its intricate capitalist system.

5.3 *SONDERFALL* AS INTEGRATION DOCTRINE

Switzerland's unique variety of capitalism, often described as a 'hybrid' model, plays a significant role in shaping the country's position on the map of differentiated European integration. As the authors have explored in the two previous sections, Switzerland's complex blend of institutional features from both coordinated and liberal market economies has profound implications for its relationship with the EU and its broader role in European integration.

Switzerland's political economy defies easy categorization within traditional European integration models. Its combination of self-determination through trade unions and reliance on free market mechanisms places it in a unique position. While Switzerland exhibits characteristics of CMEs such as Austria and Germany, it also shares traits with the LMEs of the United States and the United Kingdom. The Swiss political economy's hybrid nature has implications for its European integration strategy. Switzerland's position as a non-EU member but a key trading partner means it engages in a differentiated form of European integration. It participates in some aspects of the EU's

Single Market through bilateral agreements while maintaining its political and economic independence.

Switzerland's financial system, a blend of CME-like universal banking and LME-like stock markets, reflects its unique position within Europe. Its highly developed stock exchange and strong domestic credit to the private sector indicate its LME-esque attributes. However, the presence of institutional investors and corporate governance reforms align more with CME practices. These financial system characteristics influence Switzerland's approach to differentiated European integration. The country's robust financial sector and stock exchange presence make it a vital player in European financial markets, even outside the EU. Switzerland's access to EU markets through bilateral agreements, especially in the financial sector, demonstrates its ability to navigate DI while leveraging its financial strengths.

The skills formation system, resembling the CME model, emphasizes high-skilled workers and vocational training. However, recent developments have introduced more liberal elements, such as skills portability, reflecting the country's adaptability to changing global demands. Switzerland's strong education and training system contribute to its differentiated European integration approach. Its emphasis on high-skilled labour aligns with the EU's push for a knowledge-based economy. Switzerland's ability to produce adaptable, highly skilled workers positions it favourably within the European landscape, whether engaging in Single Market activities or pursuing innovative collaborations with EU institutions. Industrial relations have traditionally favoured liberal neo-corporatism, with strong employer associations and limited union influence. However, recent shifts, including declining unionization rates and increased collective bargaining coverage, demonstrate the country's ability to adapt its labour market practices. Switzerland's labour market performance and evolving industrial relations play a role in differentiated European integration. The country's flexibility and competitiveness align with the EU's goals for labour market reform and economic growth. Switzerland's ongoing efforts to address gender wage gaps and social policy challenges demonstrate its commitment to shared European values.

In conclusion, Switzerland's unique variety of capitalism, characterized by its hybrid institutional landscape, ensures a significant impact on its position in the differentiated European integration framework. Switzerland has successfully leveraged its economic strengths, including its financial sector and skilled labour force, to engage in selective European integration through bilateral agreements with the EU.

6 The United Kingdom: Free-marketeers and their divorce from the European Union

6.1 FROM 'SPLENDID ISOLATION' TO 'PREFERENTIAL MEMBERSHIP' ... AND BACK?

The British case has been especially informative for the study of differentiated integration (DI) due to London's legacy of exceptionalism present in its European politics as well as, more contemporarily, taking into consideration the Brexit referendum, EU-leaving negotiations as well as their outcomes and results. The first British referendum addressing the question of the UK's participation in the European integration project was held in 1975 and asked whether the country should stay in the European Economic Community. The integration project was still in its infancy and the UK was a freshman in the community. Over a period of 40 years, the EU has acquired a directly elected and influential parliament, substantially reduced the veto power of individual Member States, engaged in civilian and military operations abroad, launched a border-free traffic area and – last but not least – established its own currency thus interconnecting national economic policies even more strongly. According to leave campaigners, the British did not choose to participate in all the above mentioned in 1975 (Glencross 2015, p. 306), but they did, however, participate in the process of the creation of every single element of the European integration project. None of the EU competences appeared in Brussels without the legitimation of the UK. However, after integration advance in the 1990s, followed by 2004's big bang enlargement, as well as subsequent waves in 2007 and 2013, and accompanied with an economic crisis (Schweiger & Magone 2014) which hit the British economy severely, critical mass was achieved and dissatisfaction with membership of the EU advanced in the public discourse. The party system reacted to it on the supply side, giving the Brexit scenario its own dynamics. The Brexit referendum – in its supranational dimension – was not only about Britain's position on the map of the EU, it was also about the future of the integration project as such. The UK switched from an integration-tolerant country to an integration-hostile country, which – by its behaviour and attitude – challenged the very fundaments of the integration process. It produced externalities to be consumed by other Member States and non-members no matter if they were pro-or-anti-integrationist (Riedel 2018, 2023).

The 23 June 2016 referendum was supposed to deal with the renegotiated position of the UK in the EU. The growing public frustrations about UK–EU relations were the result of the long-lasting failure to consult British citizens about Britain's place in Europe and a changing EU that was undermining the relationship between London and Brussels (Cameron 2013). Despite countless vetoes, opt-outs, and constraints, many British governments (both Labour and Conservative) moved Britain's involvement in the European integration project ahead of the British public understanding. With its imperial past and a long-lasting tradition of the so-called 'splendid isolation' logic in its international relations, London has never been an easy partner for continental Europeans (this statement is even more true for the Irish). It is true that the UK, historically speaking, had a specific attitude to the European integration project; however, the Brexit referendum brought about some new quality in the debate on DI in Europe. It used to be one of the most important old Member States (though not the founding member), with one of the most powerful economies and high recognition in international relations. The above-mentioned created relative bargaining power for the United Kingdom and, as a result, an exemptive type of differentiation in the European Union (Schimmelfennig 2014). London's divorce from Brussels provided a strong disintegrative impulse for the whole project. And as such, it has a deconstructive potential for the post-Second World War economic and political order in Europe. The tsunami effect of Britain going out of the EU may be felt not only by the entrepreneurs operating across the Channel, but on the whole Single Market, including the barriers in migration traffic, capital flows, deficits in EU funds, and policies. The Brexit process and its externalities coincided with the pandemic and the Ukrainian war which blurred the picture of the cost-benefit analysis of leaving the EU.

Despite its intentions, the Brexit referendum did not manage to bring stability to the European debate in UK. It was very much the opposite; misunderstandings grew on the sides of both opponents and supporters. The referendum was rather another example of the misuses of direct democracy mechanisms with quite auto-destructive outcomes. The balance of pros and cons related to referendums has been investigated extensively in the literature, and it will suffice here to provide a synthetic overview. On one side, referendums make it possible to confront a problematic issue, spark public discourse, debate arguments, and build the democratic legitimacy of a coming decision. However, on the negative side, referendums very often lead to oversimplifications of an issue in question. They offer binary solutions only, very often to complicated, nuanced problems. Referendum questions can be manipulated, and they get politicized very easily or even used for purely politically strategic (or party) reasons. In the end, the technical problem, i.e., the results of a referendum, will need to be implemented by the representative democracy institutions (like parliament). Quite often the decision makers at Westminster needed to take action against their own will or that of the will of their constituencies (Riedel 2018). In the case of the UK, the 23 June referendum was supposed to refresh the British people's understanding of European integration. As a result, it brought about even more polarization, more myths, and less objective knowledge in general. As happened before in many other EU Member States, such as the Netherlands, France, Ireland, or Denmark, the referendum did not help to bring the EU citizens closer to the EU, but rather sparked Euroscepticism and EU confusions. Instead of offering a solution, the Brexit referendum generated even more problems. Initially, the commitments to hold this referendum had been used to manage tensions within the Conservative Party, i.e., an intra-party problem which spilled over at a nationwide, or even Europe-wide, scale. Even years after the Brexit referendum, polarization among British citizens is high. Simon Hix and his colleagues show that the most preferred option among British voters is still a 'softer' form of Brexit (where the UK applies EU regulatory standards in return for quota-free and tariff-free access to the Single Market). And the most preferred viable option among Leave voters is a much harder trade-off of regulatory sovereignty but limitations on UK exports. The authors highlight how difficult it is to reconcile differences between Remainers and Leavers and how this might also affect the negotiations about the precise contours of the relationship between the EU and UK in the future (Hix et al. 2023, p. 184).

Just as the reform debate on the Future of Europe included internal differentiation as one of the options, Brexit negotiations have put external differentiation in the spotlight. Both in academic deliberations and in real-life politics, DI concepts have offered, so far, a way out from the dichotomous thinking between full membership and full non-membership. The British way of thinking about the UK's participation in the EU closes this way out. This utter kind of opposition to Europe takes an extreme form that cannot be comprehended in existing categorizations (Leruth 2015). The British citizens' decision to leave the EU opened up a new chapter in the discussions about the future forms of DI in Europe and, interestingly, inside the UK as well. Britain ended up diversly integrated with the EU – most parts of it found themselves out of the EU, whereas some others (Northern Ireland) remained inside in the Common Market, and even some others more may be positioned in a so-called 'grey zone' which is to be defined in the upcoming years.

We know that, as they say, there *is* life outside of the EU, and the British now need to seek their answer to the question of what kind life they want to build outside of a united Europe. The other important question is which united Europe; differentiation in Europe has reached such a phase, scale, and depth that it is legitimate to agree to the argument that it is a systematic characteristic of the European integration project as seen in the 21st century. Directly after the Brexit referendum, the inner core of the EU comprising the initial six founding states (Germany, France, Italy, Belgium, Luxemburg, and the Netherlands) met in Berlin in order to discuss the new circumstances generated by the Brexit earthquake as well as to identify the options ahead. Symptomatically, the rest of the EU was called to a meeting in Warsaw a day later for the same purpose. The new divisions in Europe became even more clear in the sharp picture after the British decided to leave. Brexit gave DI new impetus and dynamics. A proper contextualization of the Brexit referendum is vital for a clear understanding of how the general public's preferences are formed and expressed on the topic of options for differentiation available to citizens. In diplomacy, the so-called 'splendid isolation' has been known as a British tradition of being an outsider, which dates back to the country's imperial past. The UK's sitting on the sidelines of integration was not only geographical, but also emotional and political. It has had many manifestations, from *Atlantism*, through pro-*Commonwealthism*, up to *Anglospherism*, but has never been truly isolationism or *desinteresment* (Daddow 2015, pp. 71–88). British imperialist discourses that date back to the 19th century were rather focused on the question of how the UK could influence the world, instead of how to defend itself from external pressures. This reverse of logic suggests that it is also a mental problem nested in the change of UK's position globally. Subordination to Europeanization-based impulses represented the final end of a splendid imperial past. The historical context needs to be supplemented by the most recent history, that is, Margaret Thatcher's attitude to Europe, an attitude which played such a large part in forming Britain's anti-Europeanism. One of the reasons why the UK used to be such an awkward partner in Europe was the distinctive personal influence of the so-called 'Iron Lady', whose individual action and legacy generated and magnified the core dynamics that soured the UK's ties to Europe so bitterly (Fontana & Parsons 2015, p. 89).

More contemporarily, the political force that was the strongest supporter of Brexit was the UK Independence Party (UKIP) led by Nigel Farage. Once a relatively moderate actor on the British political scene, UKIP evolved into a xenophobic, right-wing party, attacking migrants, as well as religious, gender, and ethnic and racial minorities. Its leaders were fully aware of the huge potential of the emotions and fears that were likely to be the deciding factor influencing the British referendum's outcome. Still in April 2016, the Economist Intelligence Unit forecasted that the UK electorate would reject Brexit on the day of the referendum, and it was expected that voters' fears about leaving the EU would rise as the referendum approached and the economic arguments in favour of staying would prevail (Haralambous 2016). On the other hand, we have observed some growing public frustrations in Britain at UK–EU relations which resulted from the long-standing failure to consult UK citizens about their country's place in Europe. Two weeks before the referendum, the opinion polls gave the supporters of Brexit a 10% lead which suggested that quite a safe victory for the isolationists' camp could be predicted. After the murder of Jo Cox, a British politician campaigning for the UK to remain in the EU, there was an observable shift towards support for the membership camp. However, the final results of the referendum showed a moderate 51.9% for leaving and 48.1% for remaining. The binary nature of referendums overshadowed the modest victory of the Leave camp. It was a shock not only in British politics and its economy but also for their European equivalents. The initiator of the referendum, Prime Minister David Cameron, in his speech on the morning after the vote, declared his resignation in the perspective of three months. However, he tried to reassure the panicking markets that the trade of goods and services would continue in the post-Brexit scenario, on a contractual basis similar to the terms that existed when part of the EU. He was proved wrong, and, additionally, Britain no longer has a say in the development of EU laws and regulations. Even though the United Kingdom has always been on the positive side as regards the balance of discriminatory and exemptive differentiations, it appeared not to be enough for quite a portion of the British citizens and political elites. The UK, before the referendum, enjoyed the status of that of preferential membership – the opposite of discriminatory membership (Schimmelfennig 2014) whereby a Member State is exempted from many rights and benefits of integration. The UK was released from many undesirable obligations that most of the other Member States were obliged to take. The rest of the EU was not determined enough to demand the full adoption of EU law. The UK was strong in its Euroscepticism and its economic as well as political power, and, as a result, enjoyed positive discrimination in the community.

It may be too early to ask what consequences Brexit brought about for the system of DI Europe. But early observations allow one to formulate some preliminary conclusions. Firstly, in the long-term, there is the potential strengthening of the centre – the core of integration, which is Germany without any balancing power (taking into account France's downgraded status after the economic crisis). Secondly, an EU without Britain also means an EU without free marketeers – it was the UK – no matter whether ruled by Labour or the Conservatives – that brought the liberal component to the European integration project (a liberal market economy, LME pole – see the following section). Less of Britain in Europe also means fewer liberal ideas. Thirdly, the Brexit process showed us the limits of internal differentiation. Simply speaking, David Cameron overplayed his hand, so to speak, and the British political elites got lost in their attempts to pull Brussels into their domestic politics.

Playing with nationalist interests, Euroscepticism, nativism, and xenophobia spiralled out of control – and as a result Britain extricated itself from the EU. The British exit also potentially widens the circles of external DI. To the already-existing categories of members and non-members, it adds the category of 'former-member', unknown so far in the European studies. After Brexit, the UK circulates on the outer peripheral orbit of the European integration system (Riedel 2023a, p. 296).

Therefore, the authors acknowledge that Brexit symbolizes a milestone in the evolution of the system of European DI. At the same time, the authors treat Brexit as a process, and as an element of the sequence of crises that challenged Europe in the 20th and 21st centuries. The British case is highly informative in understanding the dynamics of differentiation. It was not the demand for differentiation that drove Brexit referendum dynamics. It was the desire to leave the European Union among large parts of the British public and political elites. Historically speaking, London was one of the major driving forces behind increased differentiation. It was treated as a kind of a compromise between the strong, independence-based needs of the British and the consistency of the European project. However, it soon appeared that this was a short-term tactic that did not offer a solid fundament on which the UK's presence in the EU could be grounded (Riedel 2018; Radunz & Riedel 2024). In the case of the UK, it is not the capacities but the preferences that kept London outside of the European core. It simply belongs to the category of less willing countries, together with outsiders such as the quasi-members of Switzerland, Liechtenstein, Iceland, or Norway. Some Member States opt out (internal differentiation), whereas some non-Member States opt in (external differentiation) which results in the need for reconciling heterogeneity inside and outside of the union. Britain is loosely integrated with the EU both horizontally and vertically. Even before Brexit, the UK did not participate in all EU policies (horizontal differentiation) and in some others it participated at its own speed and extent (vertical differentiation). Taking into account the above, logically speaking, it made little sense for the UK to exit the EU in the hope of gaining some greater autonomy; re-entering the Single Market with similar obligations but fewer decision rights (Leruth & Lord 2015). However, renegotiating the UK's membership answered another need – the need for the reconfiguration of the relationship between the UK and the EU. In his January 2013 speech, British Prime Minister David Cameron set out a plan to ask for a mandate from the British people to negotiate a new settlement with Europe (at that time, this operation was seen as a method of strengthening his position in the Conservative Party, but it ended with his resignation after the referendum). At the same time, an audit was launched to calculate the costs and benefits of the UK's membership of the EU. The key issues that David Cameron focused on were the following: allowing the UK to opt out from the

EU's declared ambition to forge an 'ever closer union', restricting access to in-work and out-of-work social benefits to EU migrants (until they had been residents for four years), giving greater powers to national parliaments (in their competences to block EU legislation), and securing explicit recognition that the euro is not the only currency of the European Union.

In this sense, Brexit was not only about Britain's position on the map of the Europe; it was also about the future of the European integration project as such. Brexit produced externalities to be consumed by other Member States and non-members no matter if they were pro- or anti-integrationist. On the other side of the coin, and following the logic of the integration evolution from one crisis to another, it is possible to interpret the Brexit decision as an opportunity to reform of the EU. The reformist impulse of Brexit may enhance European integration in two possible ways. It may help to reform the EU into a more differentiated system which will allow for the accommodation of countries willing to integrate at various speeds and extents. Moreover, having now gotten rid of the major troublemaker and marauder that is Britain, the EU may accelerate towards the aforementioned 'ever closer union' (Riedel 2018). The UK's European question was more than a question of whether or not to be in Europe – it was a question of party politics, identity, political economy, globalization, and, last but not least, a changing Europe. The problem is that it can never be entirely answered (Oliver 2015) because it will come back in a reframed form with every new generation, every new treaty, and every new enlargement. At the same time, Brexit is not a one-day event that simply meant walking out of Europe. Instead, it meant rather the beginning of a lengthy and complex process of negotiations (Bernstein 2016) leading to a new settlement between Brussels and London. Even today, many years after the Brexit process has been concluded, at least in the legal dimension, its socio-economic consequences are far from clear. Preliminary conclusions suggest that the withdrawal of the United Kingdom from the European Union has mutually and significantly changed their relationship. From the point of view of both Brussels and Warsaw, Brexit was not beneficial for the EU due to the financial, economic, and strategic potential of the United Kingdom. For the UK, the balance of advantages and disadvantages looks much worse. The agreement regulating EU–UK economic relations contains many transitional periods, some of which are still ongoing at the time of this writing. The idea was to give companies time to adapt to the new legal environment in bilateral trade. The Global Britain strategy places strong emphasis on cooperation with EU countries, but also includes a clear shift towards strategic partnerships with countries that are culturally and linguistically closest to London. A striking example is the creation of AUKUS, a format grouping Australia, the United Kingdom, and the United States. This alliance is aimed at greater coordination in the Indo-Pacific in the face of a growing and increasingly assertive China.

The Indo-Pacific region, which has become one of the most important economic centres in the world, is now crucial for British trade – which is why London is interested in joining the Trans-Pacific Partnership (CPTTP).

Noteworthily, the Brexit issue tests DI in some new ways. The practicalities of disentangling the UK from its existing membership may form the substance of qualitatively different relations to any in which DI has been used before. Britain may be the first case of differentiated disintegration. Paradoxically, both Britain's exit and it's unrealized staying in would increase the importance of DI. As a result, the EU may need an institutional resettlement that makes its own character as a union of unions explicit (Leruth & Lord 2015, p. 754). When researching the dynamics of DI and its determinants, the United Kingdom is a highly illustrative example. The UK has always been a special case in the European integration project. British exceptionalism has manifested itself in various forms and ways throughout history; 23 June 2016 delivered another culmination point in the story of the stubborn Europeans' relations with its continental partners. The Brexit referendum, which brought about victory for the supporters of the UK leaving the European Union, marked an important milestone in these relations (Riedel 2018; Radunz & Riedel 2024). And even more so concerning the period between 29 March 2017, when the UK officially notified the European Council of its intention to leave the EU (formally triggering Article 50 of the Treaty on European Union), until the United Kingdom withdrew from the European Union on 31 January 2020. Turbulent negotiations and tensions showed how difficult it is to leave the EU *de facto*, even when the political determination to do so is high.

'To flee the chains of Brussels' was the expression used by those who argue that the regulatory burden imposed on businesses by Brussels sapped competitiveness and cost jobs. The economic crisis, followed by long-lasting stagnation, has given a gloss to claims that the UK would do better outside the EU – by expanding its trade with the Commonwealth. Additionally, the fast-growing Asian economies appear to be mirror images of neoliberal Anglo-Saxon ones. In this vision, Great Britannia, reunited with the Anglosphere and trading with Asia, would be simultaneously unchained from Europe and prosperous in its Anglo-Saxon direction (Kenny & Pearse 2016). Most of the analytical reports on the effects of Britain leaving the EU were rather pessimistic (and, in some cases, apocalyptic), suggesting negative outcomes not only for household incomes, but also for economic growth, gross domestic product, and trade (Hodgson 2016). But it is usually not the rational choice that is decisive for the referendum results, but rather political emotions. As was framed by Antony Hilton: 'Brexit is not about economics, it is about the kind of country people think they want to live in and the kind of people they think they are. It is not a factual matter, it is like faith: you believe or you don't – and that's why the outcome is uncertain' (Hilton 2016).

Connecting the deliberations on Britain's changing position on the map of European DI with the VoC debate, it is necessary to focus on the rationale of the 'freeing from the shackles of Brussels' slogans. The framing of so-called 'neoliberals against Europe' is logically problematic in light of the free-marketeers' decision to leave the largest market in the world. Nonetheless, one of the strongest driving forces behind Brexit was the ideology of a so-called 'global Britain' in which Brussels' over-regulation was portrayed as a major barrier in achieving this goal. Free market purity became the slogan of neoliberal Brexiteers. And this tradition has a long-standing pedigree reaching Margaret Thatcher's consistent opposition to any European authority for liberalization. From Thatcher's hostility to the European internal market majority voting in the Single European Act to the Brexiteers' 'Global Britain' discourse runs a very straight, ideational line. Thatcherite neoliberalism always rejected the notion that European-level authority could be good for markets (Parsons 2023, p. 90). The post-Brexit reality shows that it was not liberalization *per se* that was the guiding thought of the Leave camp; it was rather the need to liberalize Britain from the EU's authority while retaining as much access to the Single Market as possible.

Did 'taking back control' effectively mean the need to liberalize? Brexit-related discourse was full of anti- and pro-openness debate. So, economic ideas on how to organize the European Single Market were an important part of this discussion. Paradoxically, directly after Brexit, the UK implemented a series of protectionist policies in the spirit of more regulation; for example: a more restrictive migration system or more free-handed dispersal of state aid. This goes very much against Conservative leaders' promises that leaving the EU would bring more deregulation, free trade, and a liberalization of industrial relations. What is more, post-Brexit practice shows that the leavers' argument that Brexit would deliver liberal hyper-globalization proved untrue.

6.2 MARKET FRIENDSHIP *À LA BRITANIA*

Now that the UK is sailing alone, the liberal pole offers an even brighter lodestar for London, and it is now crucial to identify the evolution of the main elements of the British type of capitalism over the past decades. The British political economy's case can be simultaneously perceived as captivating and disconcerting. Each of these descriptors applies on different levels of understanding. Examining the history of British capitalism proves captivating in terms of research, given that the United Kingdom serves as the birthplace of this economic system and the place where the Industrial Revolution originated. However, from a European perspective, it is also unsettling due to Britain's economic distinctiveness and its selective (*à la carte*) approach to integration, which ultimately resulted in its departure from the EU. Moreover, it holds relevance as it sheds light on the recent dynamics between various Member States' capitalist systems and their interactions with Europe.

Interpreting the British political economy's trajectory over the past six decades, one perspective suggests that following the abandonment of efforts to regain Britain's former global standing, successive governments aimed to reshape the UK into a coordinated market economy (CME). However, these efforts, while not as devoid of success as occasionally portrayed, still fell short of their intended outcomes. This set the stage for a significant policy shift in the 1980s, entailing a departure from endeavours to bring more coordination to the economy or to build a social democratic welfare state. In lieu of these ambitions, a shift occurred towards a renewed reliance on the institutions and regulatory frameworks characteristic of an LME. By the close of the 1990s, this shift in direction was yielding results, evident in a political economy where the principles, including EU membership, were endorsed by major political parties.

For many years, the UK served, in the comparative capitalism scholarship, as the closest empirical example of the 'market-oriented' and 'liberal type' of capitalism in Europe. Most other archetypical LMEs (with the exception of Ireland) were to be found among the non-European, Commonwealth countries (such as the United States, Australia, and New Zealand; Hall & Soskice 2001). The label of an 'European outsider' was thus often developed in the context of the United Kingdom. As befits the homeland of many classical liberal thinkers, the LME characteristics of the British economy traditionally included: highly liberalized labour and finance markets, competitive dynamics between firms and the state, and a focus on the maximization of the 'shareholder value' in corporate governance and capital markets spheres. These attributes, together with an ability to generate some 'radical innovation', are seen as the institutional basis of the British comparative advantage within the varieties of capitalism (VoC) framework. The historical preference for financial over industrial capital and limited private productive investment can be traced back to Britain's dim and distant past. Traditionally, the financial sector, dominated by aristocrats, prioritized short-term profits rather than nurturing close, long-term relationships with local manufacturing industries. Moreover, the British state's institutional path dependencies, coupled with an aversion to public intervention, hindered post-war modernization efforts. As a result, the British economy was weakly organized and relied on limited Keynesian demand-management techniques.

The transformative changes that resulted in this situation occurred no earlier than the latter half of the 20th century. It's evident that prior to that, the British system had a deeply ingrained inclination towards a more liberal direction and historically displayed greater inequality. Nonetheless, during the post-Second World War era, especially under peacetime Labour governments, the system evolved to include certain features reminiscent of a CME. Even the Conservative administrations from 1951 to 1963 were relatively hesitant to dismantle these aspects. However, it was only when The New Right, led by Margaret Thatcher in the 1980s, initiated substantial reforms that these institutions saw significant restructuring. This period saw the erosion of trade union rights and a reduction in welfare support. This era of stringent fiscal conservatism and a partial application of monetarist principles, along with the liberalization of financial markets, marked a distinct new phase of economic growth.

The British economy relied heavily on financial services, constituting nearly 10% of its GDP, and tax revenues from this sector played a vital role in sustaining public finances. Private debt, especially mortgage debt, compensated for declining wage-led demand and reduced government spending. This economic regime has, famously, been labelled as 'privatized Keynesianism' (Schweiger & Magone 2014). In contrast to the German economy, Britain developed favourable labour-market conditions for unskilled service-sector workers. British exports constitute a smaller proportion of the economy and are less sensitive to wage levels, focusing more on high-value financial and business services that don't compete on cost (Baccaro & Pontusson 2016, p. 25). This financialization of the British economy exacerbated pre-existing sectoral and regional imbalances in wealth, investment, and economic dynamism. Following the crash, this fragile financialized model was shored up through extraordinary 'monetary indiscipline'. Reflecting these dysfunctionalities and fragilities, an arresting feature of Britain's growth model has been its ongoing productivity crisis.

In the subsequent sections, the authors explore how the progressive development of the British institutional framework towards a liberal orientation and the consequent growth model gradually reduced the country's disparities with the EU structure. This, in addition to the widely discussed political factors, played a role in facilitating or at least aligning with the conditions that led to the emergence of Brexit. The LME's corporate governance systems are described as being based on stock market financing with low ownership concentration and typically a one-tier company board structure. Over the past 30 years, however, the UK has undergone significant changes in the importance of different categories of shareholders, but the ownership structure remains markedly different from the rest of Europe. In the UK, corporate ownership is widely distributed among various shareholders, which is typical for LMEs and contrasts strongly with continental Europe where ownership and control tend to be concentrated in the hands of one or a few shareholders. Furthermore, in the average UK company, the second- and third-largest shareholders are relatively substantial compared to the largest shareholder, unlike the trend observed in the average company in continental Europe.

And yet, some of the most important trends in terms of the ownership structure include the falling rate of shares owned by individuals, the rising rate of shares owned by foreign investors, and the increasing role of institutional investors. Also, thanks to the legacy of the Great Recession bailouts, government corporate ownership remained higher in 2018 than it had been before the crises. The concentration of ownership grew significantly in the top 100 (from 16% in the 1990s to 78% in the 2010s) and top 20 companies (14% to 68% in the same period). This may be explained by the extraordinarily active market for corporate control (which is typical for LMEs), i.e., frequent mergers and demergers and, as a result, a growing number of the largest companies' subsidiaries among the list of the top companies in the UK. Also, changes in taxation seem to discriminate in favour of institutional shareholders.

The impact of Brexit on corporate ownership in the UK over the coming decades remains uncertain. There is a possibility that Brexit may result in an increase in the number of UK companies being owned by American investors. This could occur due to potential opportunities arising from the opening up and gradual privatization of the UK's National Health Service (NHS). Recent studies have provided initial evidence suggesting that post-Brexit, UK companies may become relatively cheaper targets for takeovers compared to companies in other parts of Europe. This could potentially lead to further increases in the foreign ownership of United Kingdom companies in the future. As the UK establishes subsidiaries within the EU to maintain access to the Single Market post-Brexit, ownership of companies based in the remaining 27 EU Member States held by UK companies may increase. Similarly, companies from the EU Member States may set up subsidiaries in the UK to secure access to the British market after Brexit. These developments could reshape the landscape of corporate ownership both within the UK and across the European continent in the years to come.

Notably, the inception of the world's first corporate governance code of best practice, known as the British Cadbury Report of 1992, was spurred by significant financial scandals. These occurrences prompted the implementation of changes in the British corporate governance system. Alongside subsequent revisions of the code, these reforms encompassed several key modifications. These changes involved enhancing the presence of non-executive directors on boards, curbing the phenomenon of 'CEO duality', and enhancing the involvement of institutional shareholders, encouraging their active participation and voting in investee companies' shareholder meetings. In relation to executive remuneration, the Cadbury Report adopted a so-called 'comply-or-explain' approach, which was later revisited in the wake of the 2008 financial crisis. The assessment affirmed the continuing relevance of the comply-or-explain approach for financial market governance. In contrast, the United States responded to crises with more stringent legislative measures, exemplified by the Dodd-Frank Act (2010) as a response to the Great Recession. This legislation aimed to establish stricter regulations and oversight in the realm of corporate governance.

The aftermath of the economic crash of 2008 had political repercussions that undermined the perception of the New Labour governments' economic competence. The prior endorsement of public spending and state intervention by these governments facilitated the rise of fiscal conservatism, renewing efforts to reduce the size of the state. Characteristics inherent to Britain's LME were reaffirmed. There was limited political willingness to recalibrate the British economy, to downsize the financial sector, to pursue an alternative trajectory, or to adopt a distinct model of capitalism. Simultaneously, as inequality escalated and the wealth of the wealthiest 1% experienced substantial growth, a significant portion of working-class and middle-income individuals observed minimal or no enhancement in their living standards. This group became increasingly dependent on borrowing. While public services and employment safeguards, regarded as the social wage, were sustained during the prosperous periods, they faced ongoing challenges due to austerity measures introduced since the crises.

This credit-driven, consumption-led growth model is worth further evaluation. Alexander Reisenbichler and Andreas Wiedeman (2022, pp. 213–237) identified two distinct pathways through which these growth models generate domestic demand, with the observations applying to both to the LMEs of the UK and the US. Firstly, the 'housing channel' facilitates household borrowing and expenditure by driving up house prices and increasing homeowners' wealth. This, in turn, enhances households' inclination to spend money and improves their ability to borrow against their assets to fund consumption. Secondly, the 'income-maintenance channel' strengthens overall demand by motivating households to access credit markets to uphold their income and economic position during times of stagnant earnings, reduced incomes, and increased personal expenses, particularly within the context of a limited welfare system. As the authors demonstrate, the continuance or renewal of these growth models hinges on a political coalition comprising various actors with policy demands. This coalition encompasses producer groups in the finance, insurance, and real estate service sectors, asset owners, and centre-left and centre-right political parties. They share a mutual policy agenda that revolves around facilitating easy credit access and driving asset price inflation to stimulate consumption.

The future trajectory of such a growth model depends on how policy makers address inherent vulnerabilities related to financial stability and disparities in distribution. Primarily, credit markets play a pivotal role in engendering innovation and sustaining economic growth within this model. Nevertheless, the very forces that propel growth can also yield destabilizing outcomes when financial actors engage in risky behaviours, introduce new financial innovations that disrupt existing markets, or exploit regulatory gaps to maximize profits. Politicians, for their part, possess strong motivations to bolster credit markets to drive growth but might lack incentives to restrain financial capitalism during market overheating. The financial crisis of 2008–2009 exemplified this dynamic, laying bare the internal contradictions of credit-fuelled consumption; while expanding credit facilitates growth, it can also give rise to asset bubbles and financial crises.

Concerns about financial stability persist even in the post-crisis era of ultra-low interest rates and asset price inflation. A second challenge pertains to the distributive repercussions of a credit-driven growth model. Asset price inflation in recent decades has disproportionately favoured asset holders over non-holders, exacerbating disparities in wealth distribution between these groups. This has particularly marginalized younger, low-income, and minority households in housing markets, where soaring house prices have made property ownership unattainable due to inadequate down-payment savings. These inequalities present substantial socio-economic hurdles, given that concentrated income and wealth have been associated with hindrances to economic growth, partially due to the greater propensity of affluent households to save compared to lower-income counterparts. Both the US and the UK, within the OECD, stand out as highly unequal societies. The dampening effects on demand caused by inequality have thus far been mitigated by lenient credit practices and low interest rates. However, this raises the question of how much further housing and income-maintenance avenues can be extended. Moreover, as mounting inequality empowers high-income groups to recycle portions of their expanding wealth as loans to lower- and middle-income groups, this contributes to mounting indebtedness and the potential for financial crises.

Although there are numerous aspects in which Britain maintains its distinctiveness from America, the latter country holds a considerable allure for the British political establishment. Various attitudes, such as those related to welfare, taxation, equity, social justice, public expenditure, and poverty, align more closely with the patterns observed in other European nations. What the two Anglo-Saxon countries share for sure is their credit- and consumption-driven growth models and financialized, LME-type capitalism, which is still being consolidated by the political consensus and which is strongly reflected in their corporate governance regimes.

After the Second World War, the United Kingdom reconstructed its education system through the Education Act of 1944, emphasizing comprehensive development and public responsibility. The Act led to the establishment of local primary schools offering free meals and school healthcare. Although there was criticism about early student selection for further education, this critique saw little change in the subsequent decades. The 1960s witnessed some shifts towards individualized teaching approaches and the growth of independent schools. However, during the 1980s, school autonomy was reduced – with the implementation of the National Curriculum, increased reliance on tests for evaluation, and greater financial accountability through announced rankings. With the advent of the Third Way concept, the promotion of business management methods and school competition continued, which disappointed a significant portion of the electorate aligned with Labour's politics. The education system also underwent changes to involve employers more in running vocational schools.

It is important to acknowledge that education has always been of paramount importance in the United Kingdom, and the country's education system served as a model for many nations, including post-socialist ones. The United Kingdom allocates large amounts of funding to schools, with a substantial share coming from public funds, prioritizing primary education. Notably, however, in the 2010s a negative trend was observed in expenditures relative to GDP in each category of education (pre-school, primary, secondary), except for the tertiary segment (OECD 2023c). For effective reforms, attention should be given to the resources dedicated to education, including intellectual, personnel, and financial investments. In contrast, in other social service institutions such as health and care, business management methods and an internal market system involving private companies were introduced to achieve specific objectives. While this approach has been adopted in other countries, its evaluation remains mixed, and alternative concepts of public management are now being advocated for.

The UK's capitalist system faces a significant challenge in addressing its long-standing issues with technical training infrastructure. As a result, the country continues to produce a mix of graduates with general skills and school leavers with inadequate qualifications, limiting their employment prospects. This aligns with the argument that the UK's economic structure creates a dualistic labour market, where highly educated individuals coexist with minimally trained workers. While some innovative firms thrive, others rely on producing less sophisticated goods and services that require cost-efficient inputs. This structure supports the UK's competitiveness model but creates disparities in skill levels.

The UK's struggle to create high-skilled, high-productivity jobs beyond a limited group of leading firms has negative implications for its productivity and the division between high- and low-skilled employment opportunities. Firms at the upper end can benefit from higher general skill levels, while those at the lower end prioritize cost efficiency. The UK's lower wage and product market regulation become competitive advantages in this scenario. However, this growth model might not be sustainable in the long term, leading to challenges such as current account deficits. The UK's political and electoral alignments also contribute to these challenges. The focus on skills reform is weak, and policies often favour middle-class swing voters over unskilled workers. This creates a widening gap between skilled and unskilled workers, affecting policies related to immigration and skills.

Despite policy makers' efforts to address skill deficiencies, the UK's 'failure to train' isn't due to inadequate policies or political intentions. It's a structural issue rooted in the economy, where sectors rely on inexpensive, low-skilled workers to produce basic goods and services. Firms hesitate to invest in training due to uncertainty regarding the market potential for more advanced products. Even though policies aimed to raise skill levels, the UK's growth in demand for skills has been slow compared to other advanced economies. The UK's training challenge extends beyond skills policies, involving educational and vocational systems. The UK's focus on academic paths rather than vocational ones contributes to these issues. The government's efforts to align skills with a competitiveness agenda, fostered through substantial investments in education and training, have not yielded the desired results. OECD surveys show that the UK's growth in demand for skills is among the slowest among advanced economies. Policy makers are aware of the connection between low-wage sectors and social exclusion, but the UK's focus on apprenticeships and higher education may not fully address the issue.

In conclusion, the UK's approach to addressing skill deficiencies hasn't led to any desired outcomes due to its economic structure, hesitant firms, and political dynamics as it maintains an LME-type approach. The challenges go beyond inadequate policy design and highlight the complexity of addressing skill shortages in a rapidly changing economic landscape. The UK's capitalist system struggles with technical training infrastructure, producing graduates with general skills and underqualified school leavers, leading to a dualistic labour market. Some firms thrive while others prioritize cost efficiency. This impacts productivity, with challenges appearing including current account deficits. Political alignments favour middle-class voters, creating a gap between skilled and unskilled workers. It is a structural issue, as sectors rely on low-skilled workers. The focus on academic paths over vocational paths hinders progress, and investments in education and training haven't yielded the desired results. Policy makers recognize the connection between low-wage sectors and social exclusion, but face challenges in addressing them effectively.

Industrial relations in the LMEs are distinguished by the deregulation of various aspects of the labour market, combined with strict regulation of union activity. Despite the claims made for the 'trickle-down' effects of growth within neoliberal ideology, the United Kingdom experienced a substantial increase in inequality after 1980. The levels of inequality reached were surpassed among industrialized economies only by those observed in the United

States. Since the 1970s, the employment landscape in the UK has undergone significant transformations, impacting workers, the state, employers, and unions. It altered the dynamics between the state and market, and the country has adopted more features of an LME which eroded previous CME-like institutions of post-war origin. Britain became the purest form of the liberal variety of capitalism in Europe.

The Conservative government that came into power after 1979 implemented radical policy changes. These changes included tax reductions and cuts in public spending, which formed the basis for extensive privatization programmes. As a result, the public sector's size and employment levels significantly decreased. The remaining public sector entities were subjected to increasing market influence, as the intention was to shift the balance of power towards employers. Subsequent Labour governments from 1997 to 2010 maintained the fundamental elements of the preceding Conservative policies. However, they introduced the national minimum wage, reversed the opt-out from EU social policy, and implemented a union-recognition procedure. Notably, the composition of the country's labour market has seen substantial changes, including increased female participation, a decline in manufacturing, and a rise in service sector jobs. The 2008 financial crisis and subsequent recession had a major impact on the labour market. Until early 2020, the UK appeared to be economically stable compared to other European nations, with relatively positive employment and unemployment statistics, suggesting successful navigation through the financial crises and the avoidance of massive job losses.

However, concerns have been raised about under-employment, insecure flexible working arrangements, the growth of the 'gig economy', self-employment, austerity measures, cuts in social welfare, and a prolonged wage squeeze for many workers. These changes have also significantly affected employment relations processes, such as unionizing, collective bargaining, and employee participation. Since 1980, the state has overseen unionism, emphasizing more individual labour rights over collective rights, along with labour market deregulation which has diminished employment protections. While some issues were influenced by EU legislation, subsequent Conservative governments implemented radical policies, including severe cuts in public spending and extensive privatization, leading to a reduced public sector and increased market influence. Employers' postures and strategies have varied, with some engaging in union-management partnership agreements, while others have resisted collective bargaining and turned to non-union employee representation controlled by management, resulting in a democratic deficit in many UK workplaces. Some employers have prioritized cost-cutting measures over organizational or employee development, leading to concerns about job quality. The distinction between 'contracts or status' and 'high road versus low road' employment models has become evident in employer approaches to improving economic performance.

Additionally, employers' associations have undergone significant changes in their roles. The decline of unionism in the UK has outpaced that of other Western European countries, posing challenges to the renewal of British unions. Flexibility in the labour market has raised concerns about job quality, particularly with the rise of precarious flexible working arrangements, self-employment, 'zero hours' contracts, and the 'gig economy'. Employment rights and protections depend on how individuals are classified, whether as standard employees, workers, or self-employed. Brexit has introduced further uncertainties, including concerns about offshoring, site relocations, and closures, especially in the manufacturing and industrial sectors. The implications on the labour market, such as the end of free movement of labour between the UK and the EU and the future of EU employment rights in the UK, are still uncertain given the country's political economy context. Moreover, the COVID-19 pandemic, starting in early 2020, has added another layer of uncertainty, profoundly affecting work and employment globally and further complicating the trajectory of employment relations in the UK.

Although the UK had a tradition of voluntarist industrial relations, its employment laws prior to joining the European Economic Community in 1973 already included key provisions such as contracts of employment, minimum statutory notice of termination, redundancy payments, and equal pay for men and women. Some of these rights were enshrined before EU involvement, including the prohibition of racial discrimination in employment. Subsequently, various EU directives have played a significant role in regulating UK labour law and employment relations, particularly in the following two main areas of individual rights and collective information and consultation rights. EU directives have set the minimum floor for individual rights, encompassing aspects such as working time regulations, family and parental leave, equal treatment for part-time workers, and protection for fixed-term contract and agency workers.

Additionally, the EU has enacted legislation for collective representation rights, such as directives on European works councils and information and consultation. However, despite the positive impact of EU directives on workers' rights, their implementation in the UK has been subject to country-specific adaptations by both Labour and Conservative governments. As a result, the full impact of these directives has been somewhat limited, raising questions about their effectiveness in the UK context. The implications of Brexit on employment relations in the UK are significant, with two key questions at the forefront. Firstly, will Brexit put an end to the UK's engagement in the EU's free movement of labour, and if so, what will be the consequences for the UK labour market? Secondly, to what extent will Brexit weaken employment rights in the UK? The termination of free movement of labour with the EU could have substantial effects on the UK labour market, especially in sectors that rely on cheap migrant labour from Eastern Europe. Brexit's emphasis on 'British jobs for British workers' has shaped the discourse on EU immigration and may lead to challenges for UK employers in recruiting labour. Additionally, there is uncertainty regarding the erosion of workers' legal rights post-Brexit. The future trajectory of employment relations in the UK after Brexit remains unpredictable and will depend on the policies and actions of future governments.

In the field of social policy, Britain has long been considered a classic example of the Anglo-Saxon liberal model (flexicurity). However, under the influence of changes implemented in the spirit of third way policies, a mixed regime of the welfare state – called the 'liberal-social hybrid' in the literature – developed. The global economic crisis of 2008 had significant effects on the British welfare state, leading to restrictions and a decrease in social spending over several years. Since the second half of the 1990s, social spending relative to GDP was gradually rising and reached its peak (of 23%) around the outbreak of the global financial crisis in 2009. The trend was reversed then for almost a decade; the spending levels started to recover only in 2017 when the bottom proportion amounted to 19.5% (OECD 2023d).

While the education system was safeguarded, it became a subject of intense debates, teacher protests, and diverse decisions. Various social demands emerged, including calls for providing healthy meals to all children, not raising tuition fees, and improving working conditions for teachers. Ideological demands were also made, such as greater oversight of religious-based independent schools (faith schools) and ensuring equal education opportunities for girls. Additionally, there were appeals for increased innovation in teaching methods and the incorporation of new technologies. The expectations for teachers were raised, introducing performance-based remuneration and encouraging professional development.

During the second decade of the 21st century, the British welfare state faced dual pressures. Some scholars (e.g. Taylor-Gooby 2017, pp. 815–835) referred to this as a 'double crisis of the welfare state', which perhaps appeared to be one of the contributing factors to the Brexit decision. On one hand, it was about increasing benefits due to the growing health and care needs of the aging population, on the other hand, there were constraints urging a focus on innovation and competitiveness in response to the technological revolution and globalization. Attempts to rationalize social spending by cutting and restructuring it to address both sets of pressures were not well received by the older segment of the population, which was more inclined to support Britain's departure from the European Union.

6.3 DIFFERENTIATED DISINTEGRATION – SUMMARIZING BRITAIN'S CIRCULATION ON THE OUTER ORBIT OF THE EUROPEAN INTEGRATION SYSTEM

In conclusion, the UK has undergone significant shifts in its employment relations, labour market dynamics, and welfare state structure. The transition from a CME to an LME, marked by deregulation and increased inequality, has reshaped the relationship between the state, employers, unions, and workers. The UK's journey through these transformations highlights the intricate interplay between economic, political, and social factors. The future trajectory of employment relations and the welfare state in the UK will be shaped by a complex web of influences, including policy decisions, demographic changes, technological advancements, and global events. As the nation navigates these challenges, finding a balance between economic competitiveness and social cohesion will remain a central concern for policy makers, employers, unions, and citizens alike.

Before the Brexit referendum, many assumed that the main threat to the UK's membership of the EU was a single currency it could neither join nor ignore. But what destroyed the UK's membership was the Single Market the UK had enthusiastically promoted. A Single Market is nothing if not a massive exercise in shared law-making (Lord 2023), and British politicians were not ready nor accepting of the shared decision-making procedures in Brussels. The UK moved from internal forms of differentiation to external ones, widening the circles of DI.

Over the decades, the European integration process has expanded in depth and breadth across a range of policy areas and Member States with greatly diversified outcomes, making the European integration process more differentiated. The United Kingdom, already as a member, contributed to the process of differentiation to the greatest extent. As a voluntary non-member or former member (a new category in the EU vocabulary), London is testing the limits of differentiation orbiting on the external circles of differentiation. The historically inspired British leaning towards exceptionalism moved the UK outside the core of the European Union, and now the British need to find out how to establish new relationships with Europe.

An additionally important lesson that one can learn from the Brexit process is that apart from the legal differentiation (*de iure*), what is maybe even more important is *de facto* differentiation, which takes various forms. Non-compliance or other forms of *de facto* differentiation (e.g., flexible implementation, experimental governance, etc.) generally result in a situation in which theoretically equally binding EU rules are implemented differently.

This may develop to the extent in which levelled playing fields (such as the Common Market) are disturbed. Such a heterogenous integration is mainly driven by the growing heterogeneity of the Member States, especially relative to the growing unification of Europe. This gap generates tensions that usually are released by the flexible nature of European integration. Sometimes, however, they are strong enough to extricate a Member State from the EU constellation. In the British case, among many salient factors elaborated above in this chapter, the most important underlying driver was the incompatibility of the preferred version of capitalism between London and Brussels. As the home of liberalism, Britain diverged more and more from the mainstream EU policies that tended to gravitate more and more towards the coordinated market economy model. This has been the case, to a greater or lesser extent, for decades of the British membership of the EU. If the EU promises an 'ever closer union' to its citizens, those not in favour of deepening the integration become outliers. The power of cooperation binds the insiders, and at the same time it pulls out those not willing to cooperate. Notably, the Brexit debacle did not emerge in a vacuum, but rather followed a series of crises. Some of them emerged before the referendum (e.g., the economic/migration crises), some of them after 2016 (e.g., the pandemic, or the war in Ukraine), so Brexit also needs to be seen as an element of overlapping and mutually influencing processes. Crisis situations show some features of a (mis)functioning system in sharp contrast – this was the case of the structural incompatibilities of the British and continental European economies.

7 European differentiated integration and capitalism in a comparative perspective

7.1 EVALUATING THE SHIFTS ON THE CORE-PERIPHERY MAP OF EUROPEAN INTEGRATION

This section wraps up the findings presented in the individual, 'national' case studies. The authors propose to address the issue of differentiated European integration comparatively using the core-periphery model of differentiated integration already presented in Chapter 1. Moreover, they superimpose the concentric circles of differentiated integration (DI) with an appropriate mapping of the varieties of capitalism (VoC) and their evolution in the four selected case countries. Table 7.1 presents a summary of the deliberations presented in the previous chapters in which every analysed case was subject to examining its position on the map of differentiated integration. Three points in time have been provided that represent the three decades that started in the 21st century. Being fully aware that 2000, 2010, and 2020 do not precisely coincide with the specific critical moments occurring in the four states, the authors treat them symbolically as closing a specific phase of European integration, while at the same time opening a new decade.

As can be observed from the summary presented in the bottom row of Table 7.1, the differences between countries occupying various circles of the system of European differentiated integration are enormous. Even within the sphere of internal differentiation, one can notice remarkable differences between EU Member States – Germany represents that of a stable inner core member throughout the decades, whereas Poland changed its status considerably while still remaining on the outer orbit of the EU core. Switzerland is circulating in the sphere of external differentiation, nonetheless representing quite a stable position in the inner periphery. In contrast to that, the United Kingdom, despite its formal membership status throughout the analysed period of time, departed from the internal differentiation domain into the external differentiation and is still searching for its place on the external orbit of the outer periphery. In detail,

Table 7.1 *Differentiated European integration in the 21st century*

	Country/Year											
	DE			PL			CH			UK		
Criterion	2000	2010	2020	2000	2010	2020	2000	2010	2020	2000	2010	2020
Full EU membership	+	+	+	-	+	+	-	-	-	+	+	-
Quasi EU membership (e.g., EEA, *Bilaterale*, Framework agreement)	0	0	0	0	0	0	+	+	+	0	0	-
Participation in the final stage of EMU	+	+	+	0	-	-	0	0	0	-	-	0
Participation in Schengen arrangements	+	+	+	-	+	+	-	+	+	-	-	-
Legal-institutional differentiation	+	+	+	-	-	-	-	-	-	-	-	-
EU attitude among the general population	+	+	+	+	+	+	-	-	-	-	-	-
EU attitude – mainstream political elite	+	+	+	+	+	-	-	-	-	+	-	-
Sum	6	6	6	-1	2	0	-4	-2	-2	-2	-4	-6

Source: Authors' own elaboration.

the specific criteria and how they evolved in the case of the four countries is reflected in the following description.

Starting with the most general yet most obvious criterion, in that EU membership is treated as a zero-sum game, Germany – as the European Communities' founding Member State – remained permanently at the EU's core at the turn of the millennia. Noteworthily, the year 2000 closed a decade in which Germany was still struggling with the efforts of its reunification. This momentous event from 1990 was an extraordinary case of the European integration enlargement, in which no new Member State became a part of the Communities, while at the same time a swathe of new territory and millions of Europeans formerly belonging to the former Eastern bloc (German Democratic Republic) became integrated by West Germany and simultaneously found themselves at the very core of the integration project. In the case of the Polish, it was much a lengthier process and longer metaphorical road to travel. Still, in 2000, Poland was an associated country, negotiating its membership. By 2010 it had formally become an EU Member State, nevertheless with a number of transitional periods still in place (e.g., access to the labour market). In 2020, most of the discriminatory transitional periods expired; however, Poland remains at the outer circle of the EU's core since it did not decide to enter the Eurozone and many other integrative arrangements such as the European Public Prosecutor's Office, which also reflects its issues concerning the quality of the rule of law. Switzerland, throughout the years under scrutiny, has remained outside the European Communities and European Union, positioning itself beyond the core of the differentiated integration system. The United Kingdom, in 2000, ruled by the Labour government, and led by one of the most pro-European prime ministers in British history – Tony Blair – was closest to the EU's core, while remaining at its outer orbit. In 2010, the situation does not change formally, nonetheless this year marks a change of power in Westminster – the new tenant at 10 Downing Street becomes David Cameron who – together with his Conservative Party – started the journey towards London leaving the EU within less than one decade. This moves the UK from the outer core orbit to the periphery of external differentiation. This position places the UK on an even more distant orbit of DI compared to Switzerland. While Switzerland is considered to be a quasi-member despite its rejection of the EEA agreements in 1990s, London's trajectory is different. It divorced the EU in order to stop being a member, including in any quasi- or para-membership form. It constituted a new category of the 'former member', without much will to join any arrangement similar to Norway, Liechtenstein, or Iceland. The UK-EU Trade and Cooperation Agreement, effective from 1 May 2021, placed the UK on the outer periphery, with the exception of Northern Ireland which found itself in the grey zone, with a rather unclear status for the foreseeable future. In the case of Germany and Poland, the situation is very much self-evident – Germany has never considered any other status than full membership, the same for post-communist Poland which became a member on 1 May 2004. Both states participate in the mainstream of the European integration project, but with Poland on a more outer orbit of the core.

The situation looks clearer still in the case of the Eurozone. Only Germany participates fully in the final stage of the economic monetary union (EMU), whereas all the other analysed countries prefer to retain their own currencies and all the inherent consequences as regards the monetary policy and related spheres. Noteworthily, it is *their* will to remain with their own national currencies, since most of the time their economies fulfil the convergence criteria as defined in the Maastricht Treaty, and it is political factors that motivates their reluctance to join the Eurozone. Additionally, it needs to be stated that participating in the final stages of EMU is considered to be one of the most significant cases of differentiation, since Eurozone membership goes far beyond simply pooling competences in interest rate policy, and spills over into fiscal policies and numerous institutional arrangements that generate serious consequences for participating parties and their economies. Even though the supranational institutional changes are not of critical importance, the dynamics of DI within institutions become notably evident through the reforms undertaken in the Eurozone – ranging from the establishment of the European Stability Mechanism to the creation of the Banking Union. These reforms have contributed to the reinforcement of institutional disparities between Member States within the Euro area and those outside of it (Schimmelfennig & Winzen 2019, p. 1172) and therefore between the inner and outer core of the European DI system.

Legal differentiation boils down to opt-ins in the case of the EU Member States (internal DI) and opt-outs in the case of non-members (external DI). Differentiation in primary laws boils down to the cases of differentiation to be identified in the treaties. In the case of this criterion, Germany remains constantly at the core, deciding not to take advantage of the differentiation opportunities that treaty revisions offer. All the remaining States either negotiated some opt-ins (such as Poland before accession in 2000, or the UK after 2020) or opt-outs (Poland after accession, the UK after Brexit). Swiss arrangements differ substantially in this respect since Switzerland's participation in the Common Market was based on a system of sectoral bilateral agreements (later transformed into a framework solution which has constantly remained under 'work-in-progress' negotiations) that allowed the Swiss to selectively opt in. As a non-member, Switzerland could not participate in inter-governmental conferences with voting powers. In the case of the secondary legislation (e.g., directives) the situation is slightly different, however; it echoes primary law differentiation. On becoming a member in 2004, Poland gains a place at the decision-making table in Brussels, and London loses theirs in 2020 which changes their bargaining power considerably. Germany and Switzerland remain stable in the case of this criterion, being, however, on opposite poles. Schimmelfennig and Winzen (2019) found that three factors have been driving this form of integration at least from the time of the Maastricht Treaty: the heterogeneity of wealth and identities; pre-existing differentiation; and integration in core state powers (Schimmelfennig & Winzen, 2019). According to them, the primary factor behind differentiation at the treaty level can be attributed to post-functional dynamics (featuring political polarization, identities, and attitudes towards European integration), while differentiation on the policy level is predominantly influenced by functional logics (Schimmelfennig & Winzen 2014). They further argue that the functional pressure from the increasing interdependence leads to 'reintegration'. This implies that while formal opt-outs may exist in specific policy domains, Member States actively seek ways to foster convergence with EU policies in practice (Schimmelfennig & Winzen 2014, 2020).

The next criteria visible in Table 7.1 go beyond the legal-institutional or political instances of differentiation, but they are nevertheless equally salient for the process and system of DI. Attitudes towards European Union and European integration in general determine the positioning of a specific country *vis-à-vis* Brussels. And vice versa, being outside or inside the EU influences people's perceptions on key issues of European integration. European integration as such, and DI in particular, raise numerous controversies across and within the Member States. This is articulated directly – such as in the case of treaty ratification referenda – or indirectly – through national elections. Sometimes opinions are formed directly on specific EU policies and decisions (e.g., austerity measures or the climate-energy package), and sometimes they are mediated and expressed indirectly (e.g., attitudes towards migration). EU citizens disagree on the scope and depth of specific policies as well as on the speed of their implementation. These individual-level preferences define the collective integration constraints. From this point of view, EU citizens' polarized opinions and ideological stances are important for their directly and indirectly formulated attitudes towards various aspects of European integration. In the case of this criterion, one may observe a clear division between Member States and non-Member States. In Germany and Poland, the general public is constantly supportive towards the European integration project (though with different underpinnings), whereas in the case of the UK and Switzerland, the public remains notoriously more Eurosceptic. This is similarly the case with attitudes towards the EU among the members of the mainstream political elite. In Germany, it is legitimate to state that the main political parties, and their leaders, remain constantly pro-EU (even the AfD's rising popularity did not alter this picture in 2020). In the case of Poland, the post-1989 political elites are generally very pro-Western and supportive towards the European integration project – which is the case even for the post-communist politicians and parties. This changes, however, when the national-populist PiS political party gains power – to a lesser extent in 2005–2007 and much more seriously in 2015–2023, when Law and Justice, with its coalition partners, turns from soft Euroscepticism towards hard Euroscepticism. In the period under analysis, the Swiss political establishment remains pragmatic towards the European integration themes, but the three decades are marked by the growing power of the SVP, which evolved from a small agrarian party into a fully-fledged catch-all party with a distinct Eurosceptic characteristic. The UK case is slightly different, generally speaking, especially in comparison to their continental counterparts; the British politicians (with the noticeable exception of the Scottish) are more sceptical towards various instances of European integration. Nevertheless, post the remarkable electoral victory in 1997 the governmental majority in London is formed by the Labour Party, led by the pro-European Tony Blair. This period ends in 2010 when Gordon Brown steps down after losing the general election to the Conservative Party. Thus begins the process that cumulated in 2016's Brexit referendum and ended with the UK leaving the European Union.

The above-mentioned constellations show how DI may facilitate the integration process and serve as an alternative to stagnation or disintegration. This is the case because countries with more integration-friendly governments (e.g., Germany) can widen and deepen their integration and cooperation while countries with more Eurosceptic governments can distance themselves from that and preserve their status quo (Schimmelfennig & Winzen 2020). The absence of differentiated integration would entail a situation where no agreement is reached at all. States could use their right to veto and block agreements, as they do when unanimity is needed for a decision. This is the case for policy areas that 'the Member States consider to be sensitive', e.g., foreign and security policy, citizenship, EU membership, social security and protection, finances, and taxation (in part) (European Council & Council of the European Union 2022).

7.2 THE EVOLVING DISTRIBUTION OF COORDINATION FORCES

In this sub-section, the authors discuss the more quantitatively oriented approach to the varieties of capitalism framework in order to cognitively complement the qualitative, mostly historical-institutional case studies they have conducted in this book's previous chapters. Namely, the authors will trace the evolution of the distribution of different forces in the coordination mechanisms of the four economies concerned. Although they have already used some statistical resources in order to evaluate the vectors of change in the discussed economies' capitalistic systems, it is also important to re-evaluate the comparisons in a more systemic way.

The concept of a coordination mechanism (the 'input side' of the system) is crucial for determining the variety of capitalism prevailing in a country's economy. As the authors have previously indicated, it cannot be understood as a phenomenon resulting from only one source, as it is rather the result of many different forces which are sometimes mutually competitive. The authors are aware that it is not possible to empirically cover all of these forces but – following the spirit of the key comparative capitalism literature – they have attempted to capture four different types (or actors) of the coordination process in the economy.

The authors model their take on coordination on what is essentially a 'diamond' consisting of two axes. In the first axis, they have juxtaposed the market type of coordination (which they assume is closer to the business world embodied by enterprises and employers) with the non-market type of cooperation preferred by the world of labour (employees, unions, etc.). The greater strength of the first measures results in the institutional environment as being more competitive. For a change, the higher the score of the latter, the more cooperative ways of coordination prevail in the system. The second axis also opposes a more market-oriented and non-market type of coordination. The embodiment of the former are the transnational corporations (TNCs), which are increasingly the key players in many economies in the globalized world. On the other side, the latter force is represented by the state type of coordination. Such a combination attempts to capture the conflict between the market-oriented, private, and foreign capital and the intervention-inclined national state.

Two important remarks must be made at this point. Firstly, although this could be sensible, the authors do not treat the share of coordination on either axis as a zero-sum game. This means that simultaneously both two juxtaposed actors can gain or lose on their importance in coordinating the economic realm. Nevertheless, it is interesting to explore whether these trade-offs actually occur. Secondly, the authors perceive their investigation as one which looks at the same issue of coordination, but from different angles. While one angle concentrates on the nexus between the local world of labour and business and embodies a competitiveness-cooperativeness conflict within a modern capitalism, the second angle focuses more on the external (international) dimension of a globalized economy.

Table 7.2 presents the set of variables which the authors used in order to bring the four economies of interest to a common denominator. One variable has been chosen for each of the three actors on each of the three institutional areas (which are in line with the case study analysis and include: (1) corporate

Table 7.2 *Variables used for creating coordination diamonds with data sources*

Force of coordination	Area of coordination		
	Corporate governance and capital markets	Industrial relations and the labour market	Knowledge system
Business (market)	Ratio of stock market capitalization, % GDP to domestic credit to private sector by banks, % GDP (authors' own calculation based on World Bank data)	Business freedom * (Heritage Foundation)	R&D spending in business enterprise sector, % GDP (authors' own calculation based on OECD and World Bank data)
Labour (non-market)	Work councils structure and negotiations, average (authors' own calculation, ICTWSS)	Labour freedom † (Heritage Foundation)	Collective bargaining coverage (ILOstat)
State (domestic capital)	Credit to government and state-owned enterprises, % GDP (World Bank)	Labour market programme spending, % GDP (OECD)	Public spending on education, % GDP (World Bank)
TNCs (foreign capital)	Net primary income, % GDP ‡ (authors' own calculation, World Bank)	Precarious employment, % employees (Eurostat)	FDI net inflow, % GDP (World Bank)

Notes: * A composite measure including variables concerning the ease of entering or exiting the market (the number of procedures, time required, and costs). † A composite measure including variables concerning the labour market institutions' quality from the perspective of the employees (e.g., the ratio of the minimum wage to the average value added per worker, mandatory severance pay, rigidity of hours, etc.); ‡ The number was reversed so that the more positive the result, the bigger the amount of foreign assets is in the given country.
Source: Authors' own elaboration.

governance and the capital markets, (2) industrial relations and labour markets, and (3) the skills and knowledge creation system).

The logic of choosing different indicators follows the above considerations. For example, the bigger the ratio of stock market capitalization to bank credit, the more short-term and market-oriented is the financial system. Similarly, the strength of the employees in the field of corporate governance and capital markets can be assessed by looking at the work councils' rights that the employees have been granted by law. The role of TNCs for employee knowledge and skills creation can be approximated with the scope of foreign direct investment net inflows to the host economy, often associated with technology transfer; public spending on labour market programmes shows how active the state is in the area of the labour market and industrial relations, and so on.

The three indicators were then standardized, aggregated into one composite 'index of strength' and scaled to the values of between 1–10. Due to the insufficient data availability, it was not possible to perfectly match the time period of the authors' case studies with this empirical endeavour. Nevertheless, to capture a dynamic nature of coordination mechanisms in each country the authors present the results in two points or, more precisely, in two sub-periods, the first of which is the pre global financial and Eurozone crisis perspective and covers the average of the years 2001–2006, and the second is a post-crisis insight and concerns the period 2014–2019.

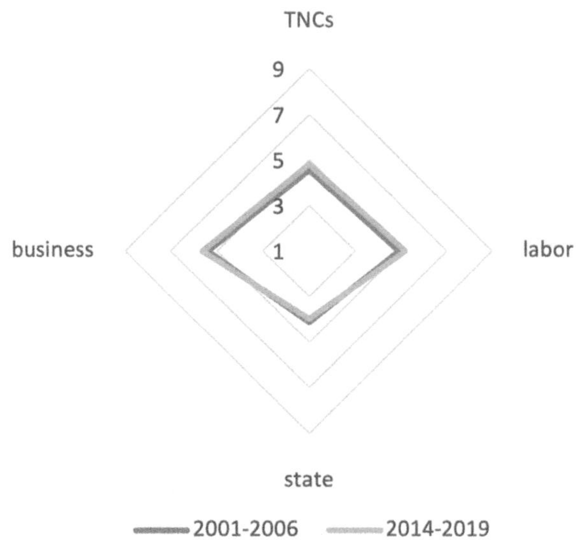

Source: Authors' own elaboration.

Figure 7.1 *Switzerland's coordination diamonds*

Figure 7.1 presents the coordination diamonds for Switzerland during the two specified time periods, offering insights into the evolution of its coordination landscape. Switzerland's coordination dynamics reveal several noteworthy trends, one of which is that the business sector consistently emerges as the dominant actor, scoring the highest among all actors in both periods, with scores of 5.4 and 5.6 respectively. This finding aligns with the 'employers' bias' observed in comparative capitalism scholarship. Interestingly, Switzerland maintains a remarkably balanced distribution of coordination among the key actors. While the business sector holds a prominent position, other actors also play substantial roles. Labour, with scores of 4.9 and 5.2, demonstrates active participation and influence in the coordination process.

The state's role remains relatively stable, scoring 4.1 and 4.0, indicating its consistent but limited agency within Switzerland's unique political system and indirect democracy. Notably, TNCs exhibit a steady increase in coordination strength, with scores of 4.6 and 4.8, highlighting their growing influence in shaping coordination efforts. Overall, the Swiss coordination landscape appears to be characterized by a balanced distribution of power, with the business sector at the forefront. The stability of the institutional order and the nuanced role of the state are consistent features. These findings underscore the resilience and adaptability of Switzerland's coordination mechanisms, reflecting its distinctive political and economic context.

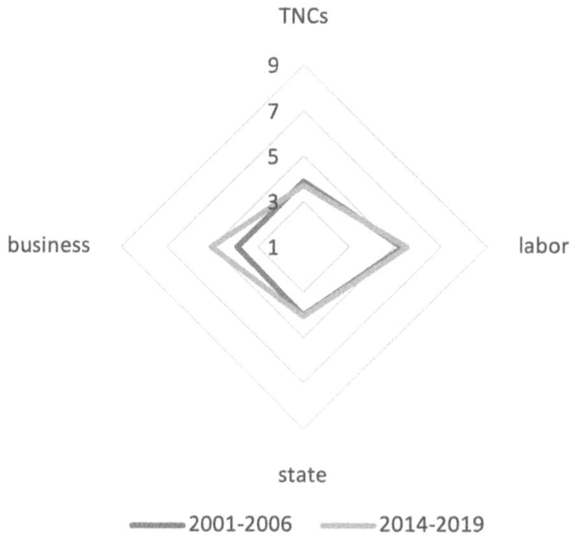

Source: Authors' own elaboration.

Figure 7.2 *Germany's coordination diamonds*

Figure 7.2 evaluates the change of coordination patterns in terms of the German economy. In this case, a comprehensive analysis of coordination dynamics in the pre-crisis and post-crisis periods reveals interesting insights. From the 2001–2006 perspective, Germany exhibited moderate coordination strength across all key actors. The business sector scored 3.9, indicating a relatively modest level of influence in shaping policies and practices. Labour, with a score of 5.3, demonstrated a slightly stronger coordination presence during this period, reflecting its active involvement in negotiations and policy discussions. The state, with a score of 4.0, played a stabilizing role, maintaining a balanced influence. TNCs, at 3.9, showed a relatively small engagement in coordinating efforts. Transitioning to more recent optics, there is evidence of increased coordination in Germany; business saw a notable rise in its coordination strength, reaching a score of 5.0, suggesting an amplified role in policy discussions and decisions. Labour maintained its strength, scoring 5.5, indicating continued active participation and influence. The state's score slightly increased to 4.1, affirming its role as a stabilizing force in coordination. TNCs experienced a marginal decline to 3.7, but remained engaged in the coordination landscape.

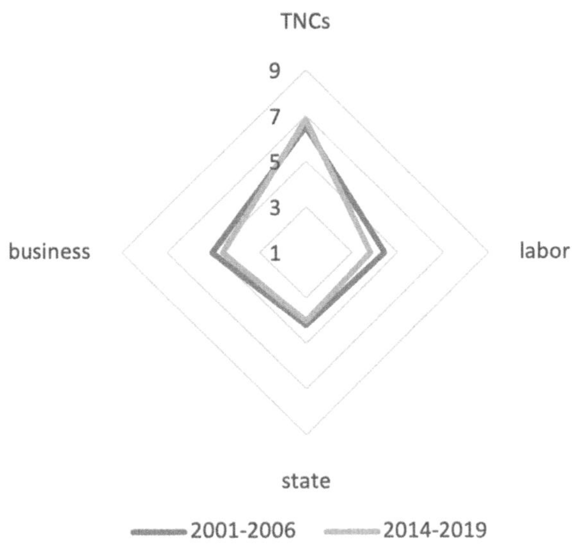

Source: Authors' own elaboration.

Figure 7.3 *Poland's coordination diamonds*

Analysing the coordination dynamics for Poland in the two given time periods also offers valuable insights into the evolution of its coordination patterns (see Figure 7.3). From a pre-crisis perspective, Poland demonstrated a moderately coordinated environment across all key actors. The business sector scored 5.1, indicating a relatively strong presence and influence in policy discussions and decisions. Labour, with a score of 4.4, showcased active participation but at a slightly lower level compared to the business sector. The state, scoring 4.2, played a significant role in maintaining coordination balance. The increase in the role of the state coordination that the authors have found in the Polish case study is not yet visible since the data series ended in 2019 and the events that occurred after this date seem to be significant. TNCs exhibited a high coordination strength of 6.5, indicating their substantial influence in shaping policies. From a post-crisis perspective, there were noteworthy changes in Poland's coordination landscape. The business sector saw a modest decline, scoring 4.6, while labour experienced a more significant decrease, with a score of 3.8, suggesting reduced influence and participation in coordination efforts. The state's score remained relatively stable at 4.0, maintaining its role as a stabilizing force. TNCs even displayed a slight increase in coordination strength, with a score of 6.8, indicating sustained influence.

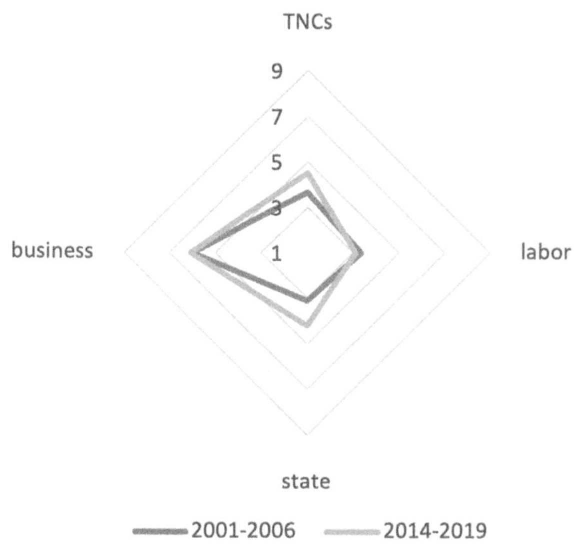

Source: Authors' own elaboration.

Figure 7.4 The United Kingdom's coordination diamonds

Figure 7.4 presents the coordination diamonds for the United Kingdom during the two specified time periods, shedding light on the evolution of its coordination mechanism. In the UK's coordination dynamics, several significant trends become apparent, one being that the business sector consistently emerges as the dominant actor, scoring the highest among all actors (and among all countries) in both periods, with scores of 6.0 and 6.1. This dominance aligns with the prevalent influence of employers and market type of regulation in the

Table 7.3 The distribution of different forces' share in the coordination mechanisms

Pre-crisis (2001–2006)	CH	DE	PL	UK
TNCs	4.6	3.9	6.5	3.7
Labour	4.9	5.3	4.4	3.3
State	4.1	4.0	4.2	3.1
Business	5.4	3.9	5.1	6.0
Post-crisis (2014–2019)	CH	DE	PL	UK
TNCs	4.8	3.7	6.8	4.5
Labour	5.2	5.5	3.8	3.1
State	4.0	4.1	4.0	4.2
Business	5.6	5.0	4.6	6.1
Δ	CH	DE	PL	UK
TNCs	0.3	*-0.2*	0.3	0.8
Labour	0.3	0.2	*-0.6*	*-0.2*
State	*-0.2*	0.1	*-0.2*	1.1
Business	0.2	1.1	*-0.5*	0.1

Source: Authors' own elaboration.

comparative capitalism scholarship. Labour, on the other hand, exhibits lower scores of 3.3 and 3.1, indicating a comparatively weaker position and influence in the coordination process. This reflects a challenging landscape for labour coordination in the UK. Interestingly, the state's role undergoes a notable transformation, with scores increasing from 3.1 to 4.2 between the two periods. This suggests an enhanced role of the state in coordination mechanisms during the post-crisis perspective, signifying potential shifts in government policies or strategies. TNCs also experience an increase in coordination strength, with scores of 3.7 and 4.5.

Table 7.3 presents a summary table of all the coordination actors' scores in all countries in both sub-periods given. Initially, two important observations come to mind when looking at these results. Firstly, the shapes of the economies' institutional orders seem to be strongly path dependent as the shifts in coordination strengths are rarely significant. Secondly, there is a clear and observable heterogeneity among different countries, as their coordination mechanisms are biased towards different forces. The results obtained from this quantitative analysis are, in general, concise with the findings of qualitative case studies. Interestingly, one cannot claim the existence of any vivid trade-off between the forces that were juxtaposed on one axis (business–labour, state–TNCs) suggesting that empirically there is a kind of zero-sum game in this dimension. The only case when such a trade-off actually occurs is the nexus between national and foreign capital in terms of Poland, Switzerland, and Germany. Business and labour tend to follow the same direction of change (except for, interestingly, the United Kingdom, where employees are weakened at the expense of employers).

Nevertheless, beyond these remarks of a general nature, the connections between the evolution of the countries' different varieties of capitalism and their position on the core-periphery map of European integration is not clearly unambiguous. Yet, just like in the original VoC dichotomic schemes, one can note the essential differences between the representatives of the two extreme poles: Germany, the core economy and the typical CME, and the United Kingdom, the LME on the EU's outer periphery. Across the two periods the TNCs played a small (comparatively the smallest) role in Germany, labour was strong, and the business sector's role was either equal or only modestly bigger than that of the state. Inversely, the UK's economy witnessed a significant growth of TNC influence, and a further decline in labour's strength (which, in both periods, was already the weakest among all the analysed countries). Additionally, across the timeframe of evaluation, the business sector remained more important than the regulation of the state.

Somewhat in between these two extremes are Poland and Switzerland, a position which reflects their hybridity. The Swiss institutional order was subject to the least number of changes which correlates with the qualitative finding that the Swiss political system conserves the economic one. Although the 'business bias' can be vividly seen, labour also remains strong. Looking on the second axis, foreign capital dominates over domestic capital. On the other hand, the Polish case resembles the British case more closely. The two market-oriented forces (of business enterprises and foreign corporations) clearly outweigh the non-market actors (of state and employees).

What makes the German case the most specific is that it is the only country where the inward forces of globalization seem to be tamed by policy – the role of TNCs (already the smallest) further decreased. Furthermore, the German model seems to be the most 'balanced' one. Additionally, and noteworthily, in the UK the growth of the TNC's role was significant after the global financial crises. These empirical facts reflect the splitting growth models of the two varieties of capitalism: the German pro-export way of development, and the British pro-consumption and pro-import mode. The big drop in strength of labour has been recorded in the UK, while in Germany it remained rather stable. Yet, the erosion of employees' voices in Poland was even more significant. Poland, although generally export-oriented, shares the TNC's influence characteristic with Britain. It maintains and deepens enormous exposure to the forces of globalization due to its dependence on transnational corporations and external capital.

7.3 CONCLUSIONS: WHAT DOES THE COMPARATIVE APPROACH REVEAL?

In the previous two sub-sections, the authors individually introduced indices for measuring the level of (differentiated) integration of each country in three points of time, as well as for the evolution of their coordination mechanisms – which is the essence of their market economy types – in two sub-periods (pre- and post-crises). We can now elaborate on the relationship between the two variables when seen from such a methodological perspective. We are aware that this remains complicated and concerns multiple feedback loops, rather than a simple, one-sided causality. Nevertheless, focusing simply on the evident correlation allows the authors to theorize from different theoretical perspectives.

The dynamic picture of European differentiated integration shows how the selected Member States positioned themselves at various points in time on the concentric circles of the inner and outer core and the inner and outer periphery. Some of them present much more stable positions – namely, Germany at the inner core and Switzerland on the inner periphery – whereas some other countries travel across the map of DI much more dynamically and in the opposite directions. Poland became a Member, but at the same time still shows little prospect for joining the inner core of the EU. The UK departed the outer core and found itself on the outer periphery of the DI system. Yet, this book is intended to look at the economic fundaments of the European DI map. While in the previous chapters a case-by-case perspective was taken, in the section below the authors have tried to apply a more comparative approach which enables some generalizations. The dynamic picture of DI as described above will be supplemented by a dynamic picture of the evolving systems of coordination in European economies.

The complementarities typical for a specific variety of capitalism constitute important so-called 'tectonic plates' on which the socio-political processes take place, including those of a European integration nature. Moreover, these plates are unstable and the specific countries 'move', not only on the map of DI, but also *vis-à-vis* the economic poles. Figure 7.5 summarizes the aforementioned, along with this entire chapter. It reflects the movements of the national economies in question in relation to the liberal market economy pole and its coordinated market economy equivalent. The correlations of these shifts with the movements in the system of DI suggest that they are intertwined. Since the EU's core – understood both as the supranational polity and the inner core Member States – becomes more and more that of a coordinated market economy, the more likely it becomes that the more liberally oriented economies find themselves on the outskirts of the European integration system. This economic fit and misfit is not the only driver of DI; nonetheless, it remained largely neglected in the previous studies. This is why the authors have tried to contribute to the debate on Europe's various speeds and depths of integration with economic determinants.

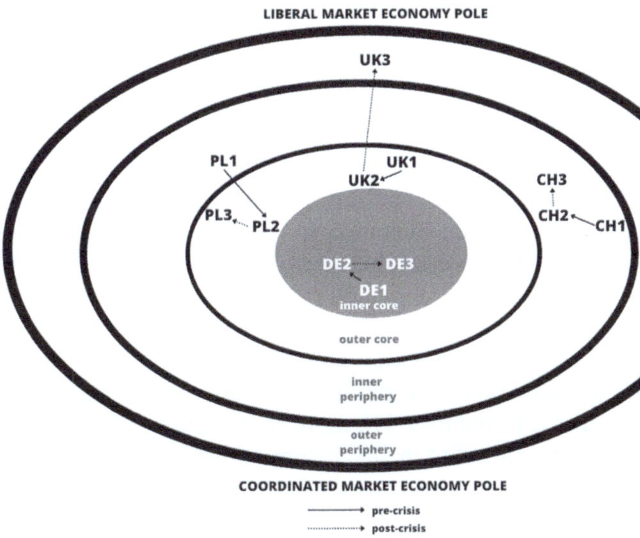

Source: Authors' own elaboration.

Figure 7.5 *The core-periphery scheme of European integration and capitalism*

The results obtained thanks to creating the two indices are a rather fine fit with regard to the authors' previous theoretical assumptions. In Figure 7.5, the solid arrows indicate the shifts that have occurred since the 1990s and on until the global financial crisis (starting in 2007–2008) and the Eurozone sovereign debt crises (of 2010–2012). This period was marked by the neoliberal paradigm in public policy and the tenets of the Washington Consensus and this direction was followed also by integratory efforts pursued by the European Union which favoured the more LME-like oriented economies. Based on the authors' analysis, each of the four countries was liberalized at that time so they were 'going with the flow' of the mainstream integration. The situation changed drastically in the post-crisis period, represented in Figure 7.5 by the dotted arrows. Here, the authors assume that the EU switched back to promoting capitalism leaning more towards CMEs. Countries that were further liberalizing their economies (or not restoring the coordinated institutions) 'move out' from the EU's core. This is the case of the majority of the evaluated economies, the first of which being the United Kingdom and Poland. Switzerland became a state leaning more and more towards that of an LME, but at the same time it has rebuilt some of its CME components (which reflects its integratory stagnation). Germany proved its stable position in the EU core as the one always 'going with the flow' of the European mainstream (while at the same time constituting the main element of the mainstream) in the logic that the authors have presented. In the later post-crisis period, it was the most (relatively) coordinated economy, which allowed it to better fit to the changing nature of European integration.

The superimposition of the concentric circles of DI with the adequate mapping of the VoC and their evolution in the four selected case countries shows a remarkable correlation of the type of capitalist model they develop on one side, and the orbit of DI on which they circulate on the other side. The differences between the countries occupying various circles of the system of European differentiated integration are considerable. Moreover, they are dynamic, and this evolution also parallels the movements representing the changes in their market economies. The more coordination in the economy, the closer the state positions itself to the EU's core. The more liberal the capitalist system, the more the state departs from the EU's core.

8 Concluding the journey through diversified Europe in the post-Brexit era

The main goal of the authors' publication is to bring together the scholarship on differentiated integration (DI) and varieties of capitalism (VoC). As a result, the authors explore DI from the perspective of political economy, which has been largely neglected in the earlier studies on various forms of flexible integration. Until recently, they had observed rather isolated ways of theorizing European DI – from a political science perspective or from an economic perspective. The substantial difference between the two ways of thinking about European integration provides fertile ground for comparative analysis – the two perspectives provide a rich enough diversity for studying European diversity in its full scale and depth (Spolaore 2015; Ter-Minassian 1997). The political economy framework shows that a well-designed cross-case study analysis has great potential to provide insightful knowledge about the European integration process and significant insights about its determinants (Zielonka 2007). Various separate intradisciplinary ways of theorizing European integration have evolved in entirely different sets of circumstances (Schimmelfennig & Winzen 2019, pp. 1172–1191). Yet, the lessons learnt from diversified theoretical vehicles can inform one another (Riker 1964; Inman & Rubinfeld 1992) and deliver a better understanding of the state of the art (Rodden 2003; LaCroix 2010) through the cross-fertilizing effect of mutual learning.

Thus, this book provides a multi-dimensional perspective, starting with a critical literature overview of European differentiated integration, then moving on to an analysis of specific VoC-related theories – both the classical approaches and the more contemporary perspectives. While explaining the dynamic background of multiple crises that affected the EU in the 21st century, the empirical heartland of the publication is focused on four countries (Germany, Poland, Switzerland, and the United Kingdom) that represent critical cases from inside and outside the European Union. The study examines differentiated integration in Europe and provides incisive analyses of economic determinants. It not only updates our knowledge on European integration differentiation, but it also enhances a better understanding of some key determinants affecting the current trajectory of the European integration project.

In other words, in this publication the authors consider the extent to which tendencies towards European differentiation are rooted in the development of economic ideas and practices, and in specific institutional path dependencies. In particular, they ask whether some normative claims about the economy and appropriate modes of economic governance have been coded into the system of differentiated integration in Europe. Furthermore, the authors have provided some possible explanations as to *why* this has been taking place, by looking at varieties of capitalism poles that are present and evolving in contemporary Europe, and how selected European economies are positioning themselves vis-à-vis these poles.

Differentiation increases and generates implications and externalities that require further academic exploration – the related scientific discourse needs verification, enhancement, and updating. At the same time, the proposed interdisciplinary approach delivers new perspectives on the most important dynamics of today's European integration process. Such an analysis is not intended to provide any normative stances postulating specific scenarios – be this more unitary or differentiated integration (Bolton et al. 1996; Inman 2003), or judging whether a furthering of the federalization of the EU is a desirable goal or not (Rosamond 2000). In addition, it is not targeted on proving the state-like qualities of the EU in opposition to its Member States' attributes (Kelemen & McNamara 2022). Rather, this book is focused on investigating the similarities and differences between the political and institutional dimensions of DI on one side, and the socio-economic dimensions on the other (Sinn 1994), and explaining them through the prism of political-economy lenses (Wellisch 2000). Such a broad research agenda includes a number of sub-topics that are investigated in this book. One of them analysed here is the way that European diversity is managed politically and economically (Oates 1972; Brennan & Buchanan 1980; Riedel 2023b). This under-studied topic reveals some fruitful potential for further interdisciplinary approaches (Ahmad 2006). Until now, the economic perspectives focused almost solely on economic theoretical vehicles (Wildasin 2004), such as the theory of optimum currency areas. Conversely, a number of political scientists have exclusively explored intra-disciplinary theoretical prisms. Occasionally, some other lenses, including federalism (Frey & Eichenberger 1999) and confederalism have been debated in the political realm (Burges 2000). The political economy approach (Smith 1776; Spolaore 2015) allows for the integration of a great number of available theories and mixed methods into a coherent research design (Oates 2005), which is an added value for an enhanced understanding of the full picture of the system of integrative differentiation in Europe.

This book also adds to the existing scholarship in several respects. Firstly, it provides a novel, empirically-grounded take on the EU as a political-economic order, in which the two dimensions – those of the political and economic – are intertwined. The authors seek to substantiate the claim that in order to understand the EU that has emerged from the polycrisis, we need to develop the notion of the EU as an entity promoting a specific variant of market economy. And, consequently, that some national economies fit more whereas others fit less with regard to the dominating VoC model. Secondly, the book brings our thinking about differentiation forward, in that it not only incorporates the role of political-economic ideas and ideologies but also considers how these ideas and ideologies are structurally conditioned and, at the same time, how they condition structures and institutional arrangements. A key contribution of the book is to understand how the dynamic interaction of ideas and ideologies on the one hand, and structural-institutional factors on the other, shape the very nature of a complex system such as the EU in its contemporary form. Finally, the book takes explicit account of Europe's political-economic diversity and the different conception of Europe that exists by focusing not only on the EU level but also within the EU Member States.

The authors explain the position of specific European states on the map of internal and external differentiated integration by looking at how their economy's internal institutional complementarities and the dominant economic ideology together constitute the variant of market economy that a given state chooses to build. Such a political economy approach is complementary towards the previously dominating political-science perspective. In the political realm, it seems that the idea of the European integration process towards an 'ever deeper' Union has come to a halt. However, it has not been halted by a mysterious intangible force but by politicians, parties, and 'the people'. Scholars from various disciplinary perspectives have tried and are still trying to advance our understanding of the dynamic phenomenon of European integration and its different profiles. Thus, studies on differentiated integration in Europe, both inside and outside of the European Union, have burgeoned in recent years. Relatively less attention has been put on non-political determinants for this phenomenon, and even less focus has been on the political economy of European integration. In this research, the authors have attempted to fill this gap by analysing the varieties of capitalism as explanatory vehicles.

By superimposing two maps, one presenting a dynamic picture of DI, and the other a dynamic picture of the evolving systems of coordination in European economies, one may observe some important intertwining. The complementarities typical for a specific variety of capitalism constitute important 'tectonic plates' on which socio-political processes take place, including those connected to European integration. Moreover, they are not stable, and the specific countries 'move' not only on the map of DI but also vis-à-vis the economic poles. The movements of the national economies in question in relation to the LME pole and the CME pole overlap with the movements of the same states on the map of DI. The correlations of these shifts with the movements in the system of DI suggest that they are interrelated. The authors argue that the EU's core – understood both as the supranational polity and the inner core of Member States – moves closer and closer to a coordinated pole. Consequently, the more likely it becomes that the more liberally oriented economies find themselves on the outskirts of the European integration system. The authors are fully aware that there is no simple causality mechanism to be identified. Rather, they see it as a mutually influencing process in which the economic conditions shape the state's choices as regards its European politics, and, at the same time, it is the EU policies that influence the structure of the European economies. This two-directional process keeps the more CME states closer to the core and the more LME-esque economies on the peripheries of the DI system. This economic fit and misfit is not the only driver of DI; nonetheless, it had remained largely neglected in previous studies. This is why the authors have tried contribute to the debate on Europe's various speeds and depths of integration with the economic determinants by providing a political-economy perspective.

The authors connect this to the second argument that the EU, as an organizational entity and as a cluster of economies, evolves periodically towards the pro-LME or pro-CME poles. While after the ratification of the Single European Act (1986) they observed a wave of deregulation that stimulated more liberal *negative integration* in Europe, the authors' analysis of the 2000–2020 period shows an opposite trend. Focusing on the 21st century's developments, they captured not only the consequences of the Maastricht Treaty (1993), which finalized monetary integration, but also enhanced the EU's social policies. Moreover, the economic crisis, as well as other accompanying crises (e.g., the COVID-19 pandemic-related lockdowns), triggered more interventionist economic policies both at the supranational and national levels. This translated into more state presence on the market, but also more European Union. Additionally, Brexit eliminated the UK and its liberal ideology from the EU's core, therefore limiting the liberal ideas in the EU's policies. By showing the evolution of economic systems in four selected countries, the authors position them also vis-à-vis European mainstream tendencies. The CMEs' convergence animates the promotion of *Sozialmarktwirtschaft* at the community level. The thesis that the authors seek to substantiate is that the EU is in the process of becoming a more coordinated market economy for two reasons, the first of which is that the dominant majority (especially after Brexit) of the EU's Member States follow various versions of the CME model. The second reason is that EU policies orient themselves more and more towards coordinated solutions. An important research challenge is to spell out in advanced detail how the distinctive features of a system of DI in Europe overlap with the map of VoC, which the authors have elaborated upon in the previous chapters of this book.

A critically important contextual variable that is present in this book is the acknowledgement of the overlapping crises that shape the European integration project. This polycrisis also determines the evolutionary trajectory of DI trends. Crises have revealed the fragility of EU regimes but have also highlighted their plasticity, even in the face of intense politicization. At the same time, crisis situations create space for the interaction of political and economic rationale. Tensions between sovereignty practices and European integration did reach a climax, but they ultimately led to new sovereignty practices. EU leaders were able to reform existing institutions while carefully attending to Member States' highly politicized concerns (Jabko & Luhman 2019, p. 1052). Few events over the past few decades have given rise to such a large amount of debate and speculation concerning the state of the European Union and the future of European integration as the previously mentioned series of cascading crises (Ioannou et al. 2015). This has resulted in the application of European integration theories to interpret crisis-led policy-making processes and integration outcomes in the EU. A great number of analysts have attempted to interpret this crisis-induced momentum of institutional innovation in the EU through the lenses of old and new theories of European integration (Jones et al. 2016; Zeitlin 2016; Genschel & Jachtenfuchs 2018; Schimmelfennig 2024). Different theories (Krueder-Sonnen 2016; Schimmelfennig 2018; Niemann & Speyer 2018) have varying potential in explaining crisis policy making in the EU depending on the specific nature of the crisis pressures to which EU polity is subject (Ferrara & Kriesi 2022). Crises, understood as critical junctures, allow one to see the mechanisms and driving forces of differentiated integration evolution in sharper relief. In particular, the authors' guiding objective is aimed at investigating the determinants and drivers for differentiation arising from economic underpinnings. Therefore, the overarching questions to be challenged are: What can we learn from a comparative analysis of the core and periphery of European integration through insightful investigation into the selected countries' political conflicts and economic systems?

In 2016, Jean-Claude Juncker (the then-President of the EU Commission) spoke of a polycrisis that the EU faces. The question remains as to whether it differs from previous times of trouble – whether we are observing a business-as-usual series of crises, a type of quasi-permanent crisis in which European integration process is immersed, or whether this time it is different, and the polycrisis Europe has been experiencing in the past years is rather a type of 'perfect storm' situation – an unprecedented cumulation of overlapping crises that create a critical mass that presents a danger to Europe. Some authors (Brack et al. 2020) claim that 21st-century crises are potentially destructive for the European integration system as such – specifically, they ascribe distinctive features when considering the period from 2009 onwards. This pessimism is justified by the following argumentation; firstly, it is because of its multi-dimensionality, that is, 'a crisis that touches upon multiple sectors of European integration. Whereas previous crises would deal with one aspect, such as defense or budgetary issues, the current crisis affects numerous policies, ranging from migration to trade and economic governance' (Brack et al. 2020). Secondly, it is no longer about peripheral issues, as all sub-crises emerging in the last decade touch on 'key elements of European integration: free movement (the Schengen crisis and Brexit), common currency (the Eurozone crisis), identity (Brexit and illiberal challenges), key values of European integration (illiberal challenges), and borders (Brexit and the Schengen crisis)' (Brack et al. 2020). A third, distinctive feature of this multi-crisis period is the complex character and so its longevities, i.e., 'determining when a crisis has begun and ended is an inherently subjective exercise [...]. Since 2008, the EU has been experiencing crisis after crisis and even when the main threat seems to have passed, the consequences are long lasting' (Brack et al. 2020).

Since that series of cascading crises was induced and embedded both in political and economic circumstances, their interaction becomes a focus point in order to properly understand crises as contextual variables. Nikolas Jabko and Meghan Luhman (2019) claim that politicization, in situations of crisis, can accelerate the reconfiguration of fragile sovereignty practices, or, in other words, that the logic of European integration in crises deviates from the expectation that politicization hinders integration.

> After a crisis reveals the vulnerability of existing sovereignty practices, EU leaders search for integrationist remedies, incorporate sovereignty concerns as key reform ingredients, and coalesce to marginalize sovereignty claims that threaten integration. This logic calls into question the widespread view that politicization necessarily carries dismal prospects for integration. (Jabko & Luhman 2019, p. 1037)

Much earlier (in 1970), Philippe Schmitter proposed a model of crisis-induced decision-making cycles. In an article written four decades ago, Schmitter incorporated the notion of intrinsic crisis into a revised understanding of the basic neo-functionalist paradigm developed by Ernst Haas (1968). Schmitter's argument rested on the assumption that treaty-based international organizations, whether regional or global, were especially prone to entropy – they would settle into a self-encapsulating 'zone of indifference' based on their initial task endowment and resources, and simply continue to perform the circumscribed tasks assigned to them with as little impact as possible upon either their Member States or other international organizations – until a crisis forced them to revise their practices (Schmitter 2012). In times of crisis, there are alternative strategies that actors (nation-state level, supranational, cross-national parties, interest associations, market participants, or social movements) can adopt. The resulting outcome of their conflicts, if the crisis is sufficient, forces the regional organization out of its entropic zone of indifference. This may enhance either the scope of its tasks or the level of its authority. And, under some favourable conditions, a package deal can emerge that accomplishes both, an outcome labelled as 'spillover', as the authors know it from neo-functionalist theorizing. The argument has a temporal structure and consists of decision-making cycles induced by successive crises. Each time the European Communities and the subsequent European Union have expanded competences, the stakes in the game have involved ever more complex packages of policies whose interactive effects and emergent properties have proven more difficult to predict (Lefkofridi & Schmitter 2015, pp. 5–6). In such a non-deterministic evolutionary path, shaped by a quasi-permanent crisis, the European integration project developed into the system of differentiation as we know it today.

One of the crises that carried special salience for the system of differentiated integration was related to the UK's decision to leave the EU. The answer to the question regarding what consequences Brexit brings about for a differentiated Europe remains an open one. Nonetheless, provisionally it is legitimate to formulate some preliminary conclusions, the first of which is a potential strengthening of the centre – the core of integration, which is Germany without any balancing power (taking into account France's status after the economic crisis). Secondly, an EU without Britain means also an EU without free-marketeers – it was the UK (no matter whether ruled by Labour or the Conservatives) which brought the liberal component to the European integration project. Less of Britain in Europe also means fewer liberal ideas. Thirdly, the authors have learnt the limits of internal differentiation. Simply speaking, David Cameron overbid. The British political elites got lost in their attempts to pull Brussels into domestic politics – by playing with egoistic interests, nationalisms and xenophobia spiralled out of control, and, as a result, Britain placed itself outside of a united Europe. The British exit potentially also widens the circles of differentiated integration. It goes beyond the known schemes of the inner and outer core as well as the inner and outer peripheries. To the already-existing categories of Members and non-Members, it adds the category of the former-Member, unknown thus far in European studies. Specifically, from the political-economy perspective, a noteworthy observation is the liberal characteristic of the British economy that was a poor fit as regards the EU's mainstream. Without marginalizing the political factors (such as the Euroscepticism which became the paradigm of British politics), the authors recognize that economic factors play a significant role in shaping the European policies of specific countries. Since the UK represents the liberal market economy pole among the European states, it found itself on the outer periphery of the system of differentiated integration. This happened in the time of the EU's core pulling more and more towards the coordinated market economy model.

In this study, the notion of differentiated European integration serves as a heuristic device for understanding and empirically analysing how differentiation is associated with the political economy of core and periphery relations inside and outside the EU. John Erik Fossum developed the notion of *differentiation configuration* as the relevant source of benchmarks for discerning dominance. The term refers to how territory, function, hierarchies, and citizens' rights and obligations are configured and combined (Fossum 2021). Differentiation configuration is about the (multi-level) system's structural-institutional make-up, with particular emphasis on what this entails in differentiation terms (Fossum 2023). While the Norwegian scholar deals with the political dimension of differentiation (polarization, contestation, and legitimacy), the authors focus their attention on the economic system complementarities and their relation to DI configuration.

Most often, DI is described as 'a tool for managing heterogeneity among EU Member States to enable the integration progress' (Tekin 2016, p. 184). It leads towards a flexible institutionalization of cooperation between EU Member States, and the strong ties of economic interdependence are so significant that it is unlikely that the EU would disintegrate (in contrast to differentiated integration, Schimmelfennig (2018) defines differentiated disintegration as 'the selective reduction of a state's level and scope of integration'; Schimmelfennig 2018, p. 1154), or at least it would be extremely difficult for it to do so (Webber 2014, p. 358). It is predominantly the functionalist theorizing (including neo-functionalism and post-functionalism) that stresses the importance of functional pressures for more European integration. The main idea behind neo-functionalism is that European integration is primarily driven by feedback processes, spillover, and path dependency (Haas 1968, pp. 283–317; Hooghe & Marks 2019, p. 1115). Functional spillovers arise from interconnection between policy areas – when a particular policy area is integrated at the European level, it often results in the integration of closely-related areas as well, so as to avoid negative externalities. The integration of only one of two connected policy areas may undermine national policy but cannot be corrected at the national level. Therefore, it is desirable to regulate similar policy areas at the same level to maximize the benefits of integration (Schimmelfennig 2020, p. 14). Institutional spillovers are also closely linked to the supranational institutions of the EU. Neo-functionalists assume that these institutions have a vested interest in achieving greater European integration, as their continued existence depends on it, among other things. Hence, during negotiations, these institutions play a critical role in identifying common interests and reaching compromises (Haas 1961, p. 368; Niemann et al. 2021, p. 4; Schimmelfennig 2020, p. 15). Moreover, integration reinforces interdependencies between states that are difficult to unravel or have negative consequences if unravelled (Schimmelfennig 2020, p. 16).

Neo-functionalist logic, which is closely connected with the line of argumentation of this book, claims that the consequences of path dependency and spill-over effects for European integration vary widely. Firstly, neo-functionalism, based on its assumption that integration generates spillover effects, implies that those insiders (the inner core) who are more deeply integrated will experience stronger spillover dynamics compared to outsiders (Schimmelfennig 2016, p. 487). Secondly, when it comes to uniform integration, path dependency tends to foster greater uniformity. However, if the starting point is already characterized by differentiated integration, path dependence is likely to result in further differentiation due to the high costs associated with switching paths (Pierson 1996; Schimmelfennig 2016). Ultimately, the varying constellations of preferences along with the will to integrate within insider and outsider groups have significant implications. Insiders tend to be more open and willing to pursue further integration, while outsiders exhibit greater reluctance. This dynamic can result in a scenario where insiders continue to advance in their integration efforts, making it increasingly unlikely for outsiders to choose to join in, which leads to a widening gap between insiders and outsiders (Jensen & Slapin 2012; Schimmelfennig 2016). The core becomes more and more united (*an ever-closer union*), whereas the peripheries become more and more diverse. This logic includes the ideas and practices of economic activity – the market-building processes are more homogenous the closer to the EU's core one gets. Neo-functionalists suggest that integration within the EU will continue to progress and reinforce itself. This is driven by spillover and path-dependency processes. These processes are particularly effective when initial integration leads to strong transnational interdependence and grants autonomy to supranational actors.

Apart from the functionalist rationale, the other grand theory of European integration also offers some explanatory potential in generating a better understanding of the interaction between DI outcomes and the ways in which the market economy is organized in a given state. Liberal inter-governmentalism focuses on the heterogeneity of mainly economic national preferences. For Moravcsik (1993), there are two sources of this heterogeneity: there is the heterogeneity coming from the divergence of interests regarding market-making and market-correcting EU policies, and the heterogeneity arising from variations in state capacity (Moravcsik 1993). Concerning the first factor, states aim for protectionist policies or policies supporting market liberalization, depending on the position of their regional producers. Domestic producers that benefit from an open European market will demand market expansion, while producers who fear the competition with other EU countries will demand a more protectionist policy. Furthermore, countries with a highly regulated national economy will prefer a similar level of European regulation to offset the competitive advantage of economies with a less regulatory burden (Moravcsik 1993, p. 19).

Various concepts of differentiated integration are no longer treated as an aberration of the European integration process, but rather as its legitimate mainstream. However, it should be applied wisely and carefully since it carries some risk of disintegration for the European Union project. There are different scenarios identified towards which the European Union could be headed in the future. Concerning the EU's future, there are already a number of different scenarios in place. The European Commission presented its White Paper on the future of Europe (2017), detailing five scenarios exploring how the European Union might develop in the future until 2025. Scenario number three of the White Paper resembles and matches differentiated integration the most, and is where the coalition of the willing, which is different sub-groups of the EU Member States, would agree on specific policy areas. The advantage of such a scenario is based on the assumption that differentiation produced a net gain in European integration as a whole. However, the relationship between the crises and DI remains unclear. The crisis-related politicization heightened political contestation, and tensions among Member States and their citizens may drive membership further apart and therefore reinforce differentiation (Schimmelfennig 2022). The debate on the future of Europe should take into account that the problem of differentiated integration is not purely a technocratic one of a legal-institutional nature. It also has an important political economic dimension – as such, the debate should take into account both political factors as well as economic complementarities so as to articulate the normative claims for and/or against differentiation. The last argument contributes to the pioneering nature of this book project. Not only are integrative approaches (inclusively treating economic, political, social, and legal-institutional dimensions) rare in EU studies, but nor are they applied in the study of differentiated integration. The theoretical discourses about European integration evolve in isolation without much dialogue between or among the disciplines. This phenomenon is connected to the fact that very few academics represent competence in political science, the economy, or legal studies at the same time. The theme of differentiated integration is perfectly suited for interdisciplinary approaches since it pools the social, political, economic, and legal problems of today's Europe within one context. The confrontation of economic, political, and legal ways of thinking about differentiated integration promises the delivery of added value to scientific discourse in that field.

References

Agh, A. (2017). The 'populist explosion' in the west and its effect on the NMS. The Polish and Hungarian blind alley of populism compared. *Czech Journal of Political Science* 1, 45–67.

Ahmad, E. (2006). *Handbook of fiscal federalism*. Edward Elgar Publishing.

Albert, M. (1993). *Capitalism vs. capitalism: How America's obsession with individual achievement and short-term profit has led it to the brink of collapse*. New York: Four Walls Eight Windows.

Amable, B. (2003). *The diversity of modern capitalism*. Oxford: Oxford University Press.

Andersen, S., & Sitter, N. (2006). Differentiated integration: What is it and how much can the EU accomodate? *European Integration* 28(4), 313–330.

Andreoni, A., & Tregenna, F. (2020). Escaping the middle-income technology trap: A comparative analysis of industrial policies in China, Brazil and South Africa. *Structural Change and Economic Dynamics* 54, 324–340.

Andrianjaka, R. R., & Rougier, E. (2019). What difference does it make (to be in the middle income trap)? An empirical exploration of the drivers of growth slowdowns. *Structural Change and Economic Dynamics* 51, 225–236.

Anusik, J., & Riedel, R. (2023). Differentiated European integration and the changing type of capitalism in Central Europe. *Studies in European Affairs/Studia Europejskie* 27(2).

Aoki, M. (1994). The contingent governance of teams: Analysis of institutional complementarity. *International Economic Review*, 657–676.

Aoki, M. (2001). *Toward a comparative institutional analysis*. The MIT Press.

Applebaum, A. (2020). Zmierzch Demokracji. Zwodniczy powab autorytaryzmu, Agora S.A. Warszawa.

Archibugi, D., Held, D., & Koehler, M. (1998). *Re-imagining political community. Studies in cosmopolitan democracy*. Polity Press.

Arthur, N., Chen, H., & Tang, Q. (2019). Corporate ownership concentration and financial reporting quality: International evidence. *Journal of Financial Reporting and Accounting* 17(1), 104–132.

Baboš, P. (2010). Varieties of capitalism in Central and Eastern Europe: Measuring the co-ordination index of a national economy. *SEER: Journal for Labour and Social Affairs in Eastern Europe*, 439–458.

Baccaro, L., & Pontusson, J. (2016). Rethinking comparative political economy: The growth model perspective. *Politics & Society*, 44(2), 175–207.

Backhaus, T., & Müller, K. U. (2023). Can a federal minimum wage alleviate poverty and income inequality? Ex-post and simulation evidence from Germany. *Journal of European Social Policy* 33(2), 216–232.

Balcerowicz, L., & Rzońca, A. (2010). Systemy instytucjonalne a siły napędowe gospodarki. Zagadki wzrostu gospodarczego. Siły napędowe i kryzysy–analiza porównawcza, eds L. Balcerowicz, A. Rzońca. Warszawa.

Barcz, J. (2018). Spójność Unii Europejskiej w dobie zmian. *Sprawy Międzynarodowe* 2, 21–39.

Barro, R. J. (2016). Economic growth and convergence, applied especially to China. NBER Working Paper No. 21872. Cambridge, MA: National Bureau of Economic Research.

Bartak, J. (2019). Instytucjonalne uwarunkowania nierówności szans edukacyjnych w Polsce. Nierówności społeczne a wzrost gospodarczy (57), 387–401.

Batora, J., & Fossum, J. E. (2020). Introduction. In *Towards a segmented European political order. The European Union's post-crisis conundrum*, eds Jozef Batora & John Erik Fossum. Routledge, 1–21.

Beck, U. (2013). Niemiecka Europa. Warszawa.

Becker, U. (2009). *Open varieties of capitalism: Continuity, change and performances*. Springer.

Benassi, C., Durazzi, N., & Fortwengel, J. (2018, June). The political economy of skill formation along fragmented supply chains. In 30th Annual Meeting, SASE.

Bernstein, A. (2016). To Brexit or to Brexit? *News Extra*, April, 7.

Biedka, W. (2021). Inwestycje w kapitał ludzki w ramach polityki spójności a rozwój regionalny. Prace Geograficzne (164), 105–126.

Blome, N., Böll, S., Kuntz K., Kurbjuweit, D., Mayr, W., von Rohr, M., Scheuermann, C., & Schult, C. (2015). 'The Fourth Reich': What some Europeans see when they look at Germany. http://www.spiegel.de/international/germany/german-power-in-the-age-of-the-euro-crisis-a-1024714.html (accessed: 22.06.2015).

Börzel, T. (2005). Mind the Gap! European integration between level and scope. *Journal of European Public Policy*, 12/2, 217–236.

Bohle, D. (2018). European Integration, capitalist diversity and crises trajectories on Europe's eastern periphery. *New Political Economy* 23(2), 239–253.

Bohle, D., & Greskovits, B. (2007). Neoliberalism, embedded neoliberalism and neocorporatism: Towards transnational capitalism in Central-Eastern Europe. *West European Politics*, 30(3), 443–466.

Bolton, P., Roland, G., & Spolaore, E. (1996). Economic theories of the break-up and integration of nations. *European Economic Review* 3(40), 697–705.

Bongardt, A., & Torres, F. (2022). The European green deal: More than an exit strategy to the pandemic crisis, a building block of a sustainable European economic model. *JCMS: Journal of Common Market Studies* 60(1), 170–185.

Borowski, J., Czerniak, A., & Farkas, B. (2022). Diverse models of capitalism and synchronization of business cycles. *Comparative Economic Studies*, 1–32.

Börsch, A. (2007). Institutional variation and coordination patterns in CMEs: Swiss and German corporate governance in comparison. *Beyond Varieties of Capitalism: Conflict, Contradictions, and Complementarities in the European Economy*, 173–194.

Bottenberg, K., Tuschke, A., & Flickinger, M. (2017). Corporate governance between shareholder and stakeholder orientation: Lessons from Germany. *Journal of Management Inquiry*, 26(2), 165–180.

Bousquet, N. (1980). From hegemony to competition: Cycles of the core. In T. Hopkins, & I. Wallerstein (eds), *Processes of World System*. Beverly Hills.

Brack, N., Coman, R., & Crespy, A. (2020). Sovereignty conflicts in the European Union. In *Theorising the crises of the European Union*. London: Routledge.

Bratke, J. (2016). Die Erklärungskraft neuer Cleavage-Ansätze. Eine Analyse des AfD-Ergebnisses bei der Bundestagswahl 2013, Geschwister-Scholl-Institut für Politikwissenschaft: Bachelorarbeit.

Brennan, G., & Buchanan, J. M. (1980). *The power to tax: Analytical foundations of a fiscal constitution*. Cambridge: Cambridge University Press.
Bresser-Pereira, L. C., Araujo, E. C., & Peres, S. C. (2020). An alternative to the middle-income trap. *Structural Change and Economic Dynamics* 52, 294–312.
Brix, E., & Busek, E. (2022). *Central Europe revisited. Why Europe's future will be decided in the region*. Routledge.
Brousseau, E., & Glachant, J. M. (2008). *New institutional economics*. Cambridge University Press.
Bulman, D., Maya, E., & Ha, N. (2014). Transitioning from low-income growth to high-income growth – is there a middle-income trap? World Bank Policy Research Working Paper No. 7104.
Burges, M. (2000). *Federalism and the European Union*. Routledge.
Busemeyer, M. R., Carstensen, M. B., & Emmenegger, P. (2022). Orchestrators of coordination: Towards a new role of the state in coordinated capitalism? *European Journal of Industrial Relations* 28(2), 231–250.
Busemeyer, M. R., Neubäumer, R., Pfeifer, H., & Wenzelmann, F. (2012). The transformation of the German vocational training regime: Evidence from firms' training behaviour. *Industrial Relations Journal* 43(6), 572–591.
BWP (2013). Will income inequalities cause a middle-income trap in Asia? Breugel Working Paper, Brussels.
Callaghan, H. & Höpner, M. (2005). European integration and the clash of capitalisms: Political cleavages over takeover liberalization. *Comparative European Politics*, *3*, 307-332.
Callaghan, H. J. (2006). *European integration and the clash of capitalisms: British, French and German disagreement over corporate governance, 1970–2003*. Northwestern University.
Cameron, D. (2013). The future of the EU and the UK's relationship with it. https://www.gov.uk/government/speeches/eu-speech-at-bloomberg (accessed 20 June 20-16).
Cernat, L. (2002). Institutions and economic growth: Which model of capitalism for Central and Eastern Europe? *Journal for Institutional Innovation, Development and Transition* 6, 18–34.
Chang, Ha-Joon (2016). *23 rzeczy, których nie mówią ci o kapitalizmie*. Wydawnictwo Krytyki Politycznej, Warszawa.
Chiocchietti, P. (2023). A quantitative analysis of legal integration and differentiation in the European Union, 1958–2020, *JCMS* 2023.
Church, C. (2007). Continuity within change: The background of Swiss relations with Europe. In *Switzerland and the European Union: A close, contradictory and misunderstood relationship*, ed. C. Church. London: Routledge, 186–202.
Churski, P., Geodecki, T., Gomola, A., Hausner, J., Kolegowicz, K., Lenart-Gansiniec, R., Oleksy, P., & Woźniak, D. (2023). Współpraca uczelni z biznesem: Polska na tle wybranych krajów Unii Europejskiej. [University-business cooperation. Poland in comparison with selected EU countries].
Cianciara, A. (2021). (De-)legitimating differentiated (dis)integration in the European Union: Between technocratic and populist narratives. *Journal of Contemporary European Research* 17(2), 128–146.
Cianciara, A. (2022). Poland as the (new) awkward partner: Differentiated integration or differentiated disintegration? In *The Routledge handbook of differentiation in the European Union*, ed. Benjamin Leruth, Stefan Gänzle, & Jarle Trondal. London and New York: Routledge, 537–550.

Clift, B., & Mcdaniel, S. (2021). *Capitalist convergence ? European (dis ?) integration and the post-crash restructuring of French and European capitalisms.* Taylor & Francis.

Coates, D. (2000). *Models of capitalism: Growth and stagnation in the modern era.* Cambridge: Polity.

Colomer, M. (2011). The building of the American and European empires. *Journal of Political Power* 4/3, 395–411.

Cromme, G. (2005). Corporate governance in Germany and the German corporate governance code. *Corporate Governance: An International Review* 13(3), 362–367.

Crowley, S. (2005). East European labour, the varieties of capitalism, and the expansion of the EU. In Annual Meeting of the American Political Science Association, Washington DC.

Crowley, S., & Ost, D. (eds). (2001). *Workers after workers' states: Labor and politics in postcommunist Eastern Europe*. Rowman & Littlefield.

Cypher, J. M. (2014). *The process of economic development.* Routledge.

Czerniak, A. (2014). Poland. How it avoided the middle-income trap. *Polityka Insight.*

Dabus, C., Tohme, F., & Caraballo, A. (2016). A middle income trap in a small open economy: Modelling the Argentinian case. *Economic Modelling* 53, 436–444.

Daddow, O. (2015). Interpreting the outsider tradition in British European policy speeches from Thatcher to Cameron. *Journal of Common Market Studies* 3/1, 71–88.

Dahrendorf, R. (1979). Speech delivered at the European University Institute (http://aei.pitt.edu/11346/2/11346.pdf).

De Neve, J.-E. (2009). The European onion? How Differentiated integration is reshaping the EU. *European Integration* 29/4, 503–521.

Dehio, L. (1955). Deutschland und die Weltpolitik im 20. Jahrhundert. Oldenbourg, München.

Derviş, K. (2012). World economy convergence, interdependence, and divergence: Growth in emerging market and developing economies is less dependent on advanced economies over the long run, but in the short run they dance together. *Finance & Development*, 49(003).

Destatis (n.d.). *Women in executive positions: Germany below EU average*. Retrieved 17 October 2023 from https://www.destatis.de/Europa/EN/Topic/Population-Labour-Social-Issues/Labour-market/Female_Executive.html

Długosz, P. (2019). Trauma transformacji w Europie Środkowo-Wschodniej. Środkowoeuropejskie Studia Polityczne 1, 95–121.

Dorożyński, T., & Świerkocki, J. (2022). Specjalne strefy ekonomiczne w Polsce. Doświadczenia i perspektywy. Wydawnictwo Uniwersytetu Łódzkiego.

Drahokoupil, J., & Myant, M. (2016). Dependent capitalism and employment relations in East Central Europe. In *Labour and social transformation in Central and Eastern Europe* (pp. 56–73). Routledge.

Drazen, A. (2000). *Political economy in macroeconomics*. Princeton University Press.

Drucker, P. (1997). The global economy of nation-state. *Foreign Affairs* 76/5, 159–171.

Duttle, T. (2016). *Differentiated integration at the EU member state level. An empirical comparison of European integration theories*. Baden Baden: Nomos.

Eichengreen, B. (2000). The EMS crisis in retrospect. In: National Bureau of Economic Research (8035).

Eichhorst, W., Hemerijck, A., & Scalise, G. (2022). Welfare states, labor markets, social investment, and the digital transformation. *Digitalization and the Welfare State* 64.

Eilstrup-Sangiovanni, M. (2006). *Debates on European integration.* Palgrave Macmillan.

Eisl, A., & Fabry, E. (2020). Is Brexit a game changer for EU external differentiated integration? Power Europe Policy Brief, June 2020, Notre Europe – Jacques Delors Institute.

Ellguth, P., & Kohaut, S. (2019). A note on the decline of collective bargaining coverage: The role of structural change. *Jahrbücher für Nationalökonomie und Statistik* 239(1), 39–66.

Emmenegger, P., Bajka, S. M., & Ivardi, C. (2023). How coordinated capitalism adapts to the knowledge economy: Different upskilling strategies in Germany and Switzerland. *Swiss Political Science Review.*

Eriksen, E. O. (2019). *Contesting political differentiation. European division and the problem of dominance.* Cham: Palgrave Macmillan.

Esping-Andersen, G. (1990). *The three worlds of welfare capitalism.* Princeton University Press.

European Commission (2017). *White paper on the future of Europe and the way forward.* Retrieved from https:// ec .europa .eu/ commission/ white -paper -future -europe-reflections-and-scenarios-eu27_en.

European Council & Council of the European Union (2022, 26 October). *Unanimity.* https://www.consilium.europa.eu/en/council-eu/voting-system/unanimity/.

Eurostat (2023a). Gender pay gap in unadjusted form (indicator). Accessed October 2023.

Eurostat (2023b). Mean and median income by age and sex – EU-SILC and ECHP surveys (indicator). Accessed October 2023 from: https:// ec .europa .eu/ eurostat/ databrowser/view/tesem180/default/table?lang=en.

Fabry, A. (2019). Neoliberalism, crisis and authoritarian–ethnicist reaction: The ascendancy of the Orbán regime. *Competition & Change* 23(2), 165–191.

Farkas, B. (2016). Models of capitalism in the EU. In *Key Debates in New Political Economy.*

Feldmann, M., & Popa, M. (2022). Populism and economic policy: Lessons from Central and Eastern Europe. *Post-Communist Economies* 34(2), 219–245.

Ferrara, F. M., & Kriesi, H. (2022). Crisis pressures and European integration. *Journal of European Public Policy* 29(9), 1351–1373.

Filipe, J., Kumar, U., & Galope, R. (2017). Middle-income transitions: trap or myth? *Journal of the Asia Pacific Economy* 22(3), 49–453.

Fontana, G., & Parsons, G. (2015). One woman's prejudice: Did Margaret Thatcher cause Britains' Anti-Europeanism? *Journal of Common Market Studies* 53(1), 89–105.

Fossum, J. E. (2015). Democracy and differentiation in Europe. *Journal of European Public Policy* 22(6), 799–815.

Fossum, J. E. (2021). EU Constitutional models in 3D. Differentiation, dominance and democracy. EU3D Working Papers 15/2021.

Fossum, J. E. (2023). The Norway Model and the UK post-Brexit. In *Handbook on the European Union and Brexit.* Edward Elgar Publishing, 362–383.

Franks, J., & Mayer, C. (2002). Corporate governance in the UK: Contrasted with the US system. In *CESifo Forum* 3(3), 13–22. München: ifo Institut für Wirtschaftsforschung an der Universität München.

Frey, B. S., & Eichenberger, R. (1999). *The new democratic federalism for Europe: Functional, overlapping, and competing jurisdictions.* Cheltenham: Edward Elgar.

From, J., & Sitter, N. (2006). *Europe's nascent state. Public policy in the European Union. Essays in the honour of Kjell A. Eliassen.* Oslo: Gyldendal.

Gänzle, S., Leruth, B., & Trondal, J. (2019). *Differentiation, differentiated integration and disintegration in a 'post-Brexit-era'.* Routledge.

Gänzle, S., Leruth, B., & Trondal, J. (2021). A differentiated European Union. In *The Palgrave handbook of EU crises*, 687–706.

Genschel, P., & Jachtenfuchs, M. (2018). Introduction: Beyond market regulation. Analysing the European integration of core state powers. In *Beyond the regulatory polity? The European integration of core state powers*, eds P. Genschel & M. Jachtenfuchs. Oxford: Oxford University Press, 1–23.

Giddens, A. (2013). *The third way and its critics*. John Wiley & Sons.

Giddens, A. (2015). The politics of climate change. *Policy & Politics* 43(2), 155–162.

Gill, I., & Kharas, H. (2007). *An East Asian renaissance: Ideas for economic growth.* Washington, DC: World Bank.

Glawe, L., & Wagner, H. (2020), China in the middle-income trap? *China Economic Review* 60, 2–26.

Glencross, A. (2015). Why a British referendum on EU membership will not solve the Europe question. *International Affairs* 91(2), 303–317.

Goergen, M., Manjon, M. C., & Renneboog, L. (2008). Recent developments in German corporate governance. *International Review of Law and economics* 28(3), 175–193.

Gorzelak, G. (2014). Wykorzystanie środków Unii Europejskiej dla rozwoju kraju– wstępne analizy. Studia regionalne i lokalne 15(57), 5–25.

Gostomski, E., & Lepczyński, B. (2019). Zmiany struktury własnościowej sektora bankowego w Polsce. Polityka państwa wobec sektora bankowego w Polsce, 51.

Gräbner, C., & Hafele, J. (2020). *The emergence of core-periphery structures in the European Union: A complexity perspective* (No. 6). ZOE Discussion Papers.

Grosse, T. G. (2015). Czy 'zróżnicowana integracja' może prowadzić do federacji w Europie? *Przegląd Zachodni* 354(01), 21–36.

Grosse, T. G. (2016). Tragedia państw peryferyjnych, czyli o geopolitycznych dylematach Polski w Unii Europejskiej. In *Polska jako peryferie*, ed. Tomasz Zarycki. Warszawa: Wydawnictwo Naukowe Scholar, 25–50.

Grosse, T. G. (2018). Federacja w Europie, czyli dążenie do utopii? In Z. Czachór, T. G. Grosse, & W. Paruch (eds), Integracja europejska – polska perspektywa. Warszawa: Wydawnictwo Sejmowe.

Groth, F. (2014). Influence of European Union law on Swiss law: An analysis of Switzerland's integration process into the EU legal order. Maastricht European Private Law Institute Working Paper 13.

Gugler, K., & Peev, E. (eds). (2023). *The European corporation: Ownership and control after 25 years of corporate governance reforms*. Cambridge University Press.

Gutterman, A. S. (2020). *Sustainability and corporate governance: A guide to law and practice*. Routledge.

Haas, E. B. (1961). International integration: The European and the universal process. *International Organization* 15(3), 366–392.

Haas, E. B. (1968). *The uniting of Europe: Political, social, and economic forces 1950–1957* (reissued). Stanford University Press.

Habermas, J. (2015). In the favour of a strong Europe – what does it mean. *Juncture* 21/1, 82–88.

Hall, P. A., & Gingerich, D. W. (2004). Varieties of capitalism and institutional complementarities in the macroeconomy: an empirical analysis. MPIfG Discussion Paper, No. 04/5, Max Planck Institute for the Study of Societies, Cologne.

Hall, P. A., & Soskice, D. (eds). (2001). *Varieties of capitalism: The institutional foundations of comparative advantage*. Oxford: Oxford University Press.

Hall, P. A., & Thelen, K. (2009). Institutional change in varieties of capitalism. *Socio-economic Review* 7(1), 7–34.

Hampden-Turner, C., & Trompenaars, A. (1993). The seven cultures of capitalism: Value systems for creating wealth in the United States, Britain, Japan, Germany, France, Sweden and the Netherlands.

Haralambous, D. (2016). How will Brexit affect EU and China? *China Daily 12*, 2016-12.

Harding, H. (2020). Forty years of reform and opening: From the 'economic miracle' to the middle-income trap. *Issues & Studies: A Social Science Quarterly on China, Taiwan, and East Asian Affairs* 56(1), 1–5.

Hassel, A. (2007). What does business want? Labour market reforms in CMEs and its problems. In *Beyond varieties of capitalism: Conflict, contradictions, and complementarities in the European economy*, 253–277.

Hilton, A. (2016). Statement in the *London Evening Standard*, 25 February.

Hix, S., van der Linden, C., Massie, J., et al. (2023). Where is the EU-UK relationship heading? A conjoint survey experiment of Brexit trade-offs. *European Union Politics* 24(1), 184–205.

Hodgson, P. (2016). Complying with Brexit. *Complience Week*, May, 53–55.

Hofelich, T. (2021). De facto differentiation in action: Why Poland will stay in the EU, with or without the blessing of Brussels. LSE European Politics and Policy (EUROPP) blog.

Holst, C., & Molander, A. (2020). Epistemic worries about economic expertise. In *Towards a segmented European political order. The European Union's post-crisis conundrum*, eds Jozef Batora & John Erik Fossum. Routledge, 72–92.

Hooghe, L. (2003). Europe divided? Elites vs. public opinion on European integration. *European Union Politics* 4(3), 281–304.

Hooghe, L., & Marks, G. (2019). Grand theories of European integration in the twenty-first century. *Journal of European Public Policy*, 26(8), 1113–1133.

Höpner, M., & Schäfer, A. (2007). A new phase of European integration: Organized capitalisms in post-Ricardian Europe. MPIfG Discussion Paper, No. 07/4, Max Planck Institute for the Study of Societies, Cologne.

Höpner, M., & Schäfer, A. (2012). *Integration among unequals: How the heterogeneity of European varieties of capitalism shapes the social and democratic potential of the EU.*

Hopt, K. J. (2015). Corporate governance in Europe: A critical review of the European Commission's initiatives on corporate law and corporate governance. *New York University Journal of Law & Business*, 12(1), Fall, 139–213.

Iammarino, S., Rodríguez-Pose, A., Storper, M., & Diemer, A. (2020). Falling into the middle-income trap? A study on the risks for EU regions to be caught in a middle-income trap. Report for the EU Commission, Brussels.

Iankova, E. A. (2002). *Eastern European capitalism in the making*. Cambridge University Press.

ILOstat (n.d.). *Country profiles*. Retrieved 17 October 2023 from https://ilostat.ilo.org/data/country-profiles/.

Im, F. G., & Rosenblatt, D. (2015). Middle-income traps: A conceptual and empirical survey. *Journal of International Commerce, Economics and Policy* 6(3), 1–39.
Inman, R. P. (2003). Transfers and bailouts: Enforcing local fiscal discipline with lessons from U.S. federalism, In J. Rodden et al. (eds), *Fiscal decentralization and the challenge of hard budget constraints*. Cambridge, MA: The MIT Press, 35–83.
Inman, R. P., & Rubinfeld, D. L. (1992). Fiscal federalism in Europe: Lessons from the United States experience. *European Economic Review* 36, 654–660.
International Labour Organization. ILO modelled estimates and projections database (ILOEST). ILOSTAT. Accessed 5 September 2023.
Ioannou, D., Leblond, P., & Niemann, A. (2015). European integration and the crisis: Practice and theory. *Journal of European Public Policy* 22(2), 155–176.
Jabko, N., & Luhman, M. (2019). Reconfiguring sovereignty: Crisis, politicization, and European integration. *Journal of European Public Policy* 26(7), 1037–1055.
Jackson, G., & Sorge, A. (2012). The trajectory of institutional change in Germany, 1979–2009. *Journal of European Public Policy* 19(8), 1146–1167.
Jarosz, M. (ed.). (2005). Wygrani i przegrani polskiej transformacji. Oficyna Naukowa.
Jasiecki, K. (2018). The strength and weaknesses of the varieties of capitalism approach: The case of Central and Eastern Europe. *International Journal of Management and Economics* 54(4), 328–342.
Jasiecki, K. (ed.). (2020). Variations of Market Economy Comparative Study. 16 Countries of the Region. China-CEE Institute Nonprofit Ltd.
Jensen, D., & Slapin, J. (2012). Institutional hokey-pokey: The politics of multispeed integration in the European Union. *Journal of European Public Policy* 19(6), 779–795.
Johnson, C. (1982). *The developmental state*. Cornell University Press.
Johnston, A., & Regan, A. (2018). Introduction: Is the European Union capable of integrating diverse models of capitalism? *New Political Economy* 23(2), 145–159.
Jones, E., Kelemen, R. D., & Meunier, S. (2016). Failing forward? The Euro crisis and the incomplete nature of European integration. *Comparative Political Studies* 49(7) 1010–1034.
Kasjanovs, I. (2015). Is part of the Latvian economy already in the middle-income trap? *World Economics* 16(1), 1–12.
Katzenstein, P. J. (1980). Capitalism in one country? Switzerland in the international economy. *International Organization* 34(4), 507–540.
Katzenstein, P. J. (1987). *Corporatism and change: Austria, Switzerland, and the politics of industry*. Cornell University Press.
Keiro, O., Yuki, H., & Tetsuchi, S. (2017). Middle-income traps in East Asia: An inquiry into causes for slowdown in income growth. *China Economic Review* 46, 53–S16.
Kelemen, R. D., & McNamara, K. R. (2022). State-building and the European Union: Markets, war, and Europe's uneven political development. *Comparative Political Studies* 55(6), 963–991.
Kenny, M., & Pearse, N. (2016). After Brexit. The Eurosceptic dream of an Anglosphere. *Juncture* 22/4, 304–307.
Keohane, R. O. (2002). *Power and governance in a partially globalized world.* Psychology Press.
King, L. P., & Sznajder, A. (2006). The state-led transition to liberal capitalism: Neoliberal, organizational, world-systems, and social structural explanations of Poland's economic success. *American Journal of Sociology* 112(3), 751–801.

Kıran, J. (2018). Expanding the framework of the varieties of capitalism: Turkey as a hierarchical market economy. *Journal of Eurasian Studies* 9(1), 42–51.
Kirsch, A., & Wrohlich, K. (2020). More women on supervisory boards: Increasing indications that the effect of the gender quota extends to executive boards. *DIW Weekly Report* 10(4/5), 44–49.
Kölliker, A. (2001). Bringing together or driving apart the union? Towards a theory of differentiated integration. *West European Politics* 24(4), 125–151.
Kotras, M. (2018). Narracje i strategie argumentacyjne w dyskursie IV RP jako narzędzia wyznaczania granic wspólnot w polskim społeczeństwie. Kultura i Społeczeństwo 62(1), 141–165.
Kowalik, T. (2002). Jaki kapitalizm dla Polski? Prawo i Gospodarka (94), 8–9.
Kozarzewski, P., & Bałtowski, M. (2019, May). Return of state-owned enterprises in Poland. In Seventh Annual Conference of the Leibniz Institute for East and Southeast European Studies 'Firms and Social Change in Eastern and South-Eastern Europe. Historical, Political and Economic Perspectives', Regensburg.
Kozłowski, S. C. (2009). Konfederacja Szwajcarska a proces integracji europejskiej. Kontrowersje między Bernem i Brukselą dotyczące reżimów podatkowych w kantonach szwajcarskich. *Studia Europejskie* 2, 57–58.
Kremnitzer, M., & Shany, Y. (2020). Illiberal measures in backsliding democracies: Differences and similarities between recent developments in Israel, Hungary, and Poland. *Law & Ethics of Human Rights* 14(1), 125–152.
Kreuder-Sonnen, C. (2016). Beyond integration theory: The (anti-) constitutional dimension of European crisis governance. *JCMS: Journal of Common Market Studies* 54(6), 1350–1366.
Krpec, O., & Hodulák, V. (2019). The Czech economy as an integrated periphery: The case of dependency on Germany. *Journal of Post Keynesian Economics* 42(1), 59–89.
Kundnani, H. (2015). *The paradox of German power*. Oxford University Press, USA.
Lachmann, L. M. (1979). *The legacy of Max Weber*. London: Heinemann.
LaCroix, A. (2010). *The ideological origins of American federalism*. Cambridge, MA: Harvard University Press.
Lane, D. (2005). Emerging varieties of capitalism in former state socialist societies. *Competition & Change* 9(3), 227–247.
Lane, D., & Myant, M. (2007). *Varieties of capitalism in post-communist countries*. Palgrave Macmillan.
Larcker, D. F., & Tayan, B. (2016). Chairman and CEO: The controversy over board leadership structure. Rock Center for Corporate Governance at Stanford University Closer Look Series: Topics, Issues and Controversies in Corporate Governance No. CGRP-58, Stanford University Graduate School of Business Research Paper, 16–32.
Lasiewicz, E. (2015). The crisis and its effect on disparities in the European Union. *Annales Universiattis Mariae Curie-Skłodowska Lublin – Polonia Sectio K*, XXII/1, 91–101.
Laursen, F. (1995). The *political economy of European integration*. Martinus Nijhoff Publishers.
Lavenex, S. (2009). Switzerland's flexible integration in the EU: A conceptual framework. *Swiss Political Science Review* 15(4), 547–575.
Lee, J.-W. (2019). Convergence success and the middle-income trap. *The Developing Economies* 58(1), 1–34.
Lefkofridi, Z., & Schmitter, P. (2015). Transcending or descending? European integration in times of crisis. *European Political Science Review* 7(1), 3–22.

Leruth, B. (2015). Operationalizing national preferences on Europe and differentiated integration. *Journal of European Public Policy* 22(6), 816–835.
Leruth, B., & Lord, C. (2015). Differentiated integration in the European Union: A concept, a process, a system or a theory? *Journal of European Public Policy* 22(6), 754–764.
Leuffen, D., Rittberger, B., & Schimmelfennig, F. (2013). *Differentiated integration. Explaining variation in the European Union*. Basingstoke: Palgrave.
Leven, B. (2019). Middle-income trap: The case of Poland. *Business and Economic Research Journal* 10(5), 1029–1038.
Lewandowski, P. M., & Magda, I. (2023). *The labor market in Poland, 2000–2021*. IZA World of Labor.
Lewicki, G. (2019). Hansa 2.0. A return to the Golden Age of trade? Polski Instytut Ekonomiczny. https://pie.net.pl/wp-content/uploads/2019/02/Hansa-2.0.pdf.
Li, Y., & Cheng, Z. (eds). (2019). *China's reform to overlap the middle-income trap*. Springer Singapore.
Lis, P. (2021). Wspólnie czy indywidualnie? Na własność czy wynajem? Wszystkim czy wybranym? Dylematy współczesnej polskiej polityki mieszkaniowej. Studia BAS (2), 35–50.
Lord, C. (2020). Integration through differentiation and segmentation. The case of one Member State from 1950 to Brexit (and beyond). In *Towards a segmented European political order. The European Union's post-crisis conundrum*, eds Jozef Batora & John Erik Fossum. Routledge, 243–264.
Lord, C. (2023). Exit as legitimacy? In John Erik Fossum & Magdalena Góra (eds), Report on differentiation, dominance and democracy. *ARENA REPORT* 7/23, 119–132.
Mabbett, D. (2023). In the shadow of hierarchy: Minimum wage commissions in the UK and Germany. *Socio-Economic Review*, mwad027.
Mach, A., & Trampusch, C. (2011). The Swiss political economy in comparative perspective. Switzerland in Europe. In *Continuity and change in the Swiss political economy*, 11–26.
Mach, A., David, T., Ginalski, S., & Bühlmann, F. (2021). From quiet to noisy politics: Transformations of Swiss business elites' power. *Politics & Society* 49(1), 17–41.
Mączyńska, E., & Pysz, P. (2014). Liberalizm, neoliberalizm i ordoliberalizm. Ekonomista (2), 221–247.
Magone, J. M. (2008). A semi-peripheral economy in the European Union. In *Contemporary Spanish politics*. Routledge, 237–259.
Magone, J. M. (2020). The dissension over the logic of European cohesion policy. The core-periphery divide and the impact on European integration. *Europa* XXI, 38, 97–117.
Magone, J.M., Laffan, B., & Schweiger, C. (2016). The European Union as a dualist economy: Understanding core-periphery relations. In *Core-periphery relations in the European Union: Power and conflict in a dualist political economy*, eds José M. Magone, Brigid Laffan, & Christian Schweiger. Routledge.
Mahoney, J., & Goertz, G. (2006). A tale of two cultures: Contrasting quantitative and qualitative research. *Political Analysis* 14(3), 227–249.
Majone, G. (1994). The rise of regulatory state in Europe. *West European Politics* 17(3), 77–101.
Makowski, G. (2020). Szykując grunt pod 'wielką korupcję': działania (anty) korupcyjne władz w latach 2015–2019. Fundacja im. Stefana Batorego.
Maszczyk, P. (2015). Ewolucja modelu kapitalizmu w Polsce 41(41), 107–122.

Matkowski, Z., Prochniak, M., & Rapacki, R. (2016). Real income convergence between Central Eastern and Western Europe: Past, present, and prospects. Centre for International Research on Economic Tendency Surveys, Copenhagen.

Matysek-Jędrych, A., & Mroczek-Dąbrowska, K. (2021). Brexit and its potential consequences for Poland – the perspective of Single Market Principles. In Anna Visvizi, Anna Matysek-Jędrych, & Katarzyna Mroczek-Dąbrowska (eds), *Poland in the Single Market: Politics, economics, the euro*. Series: Europa – Perspectives on the EU Single Market. London and New York: Routledge, 299–313.

May, C., & Schedelik, M. (2019). Comparative capitalism and innovation policy: Complementarities and comparative institutional advantage. *Journal of Economic Policy Reform* 24(4), 456–471.

McMenamin, I. (2004). Varieties of capitalist democracy: What difference does East-Central Europe make? *Journal of Public Policy* 24(3), 259–274.

Menon, A., & Schain, M. A. (eds). (2006). *Comparative federalism: The European Union and the United States in comparative perspective*. Oxford: Oxford University Press.

Menz, G. (2008). *Varieties of capitalism and Europeanization: National response strategies to the single European market*. Oxford University Press on Demand.

Michailidou, A., & Trenz, H.-J. (2020). European solidarity in times of crisis. In *Towards a segmented European political order. The European Union's post-crisis conundrum*, eds Jozef Batora & John Erik Fossum. Routledge, 132–151.

Michalski, B. (2014). Umiędzynarodowienie sektora mid-tech na przykładzie wymiany handlowej sektora samochodowego w Polsce w latach 2004–2012. Ekonomia Międzynarodowa (06), 63–80.

Michalski, B. (2018). Looking for evidence of the middle-income trap. The case of Polish trade in high-tech goods with Germany. *Post-Communist Economies* 30(3), 405–420.

Mieczkowska, M. (2014). Transformacja czy tranzycja? Szkice definicyjne. Acta Politica Polonica (30), 71–80.

Molina, O., & Rhodes, M. (2007). The political economy of adjustment in mixed market economies: A study of Spain and Italy. In *Beyond varieties of capitalism: Conflict, contradictions and complementarities in the European economy*, 223–252.

Monnet, J. (1976). *Memoirs*. Paris: Fayard.

Moravcsik, A. (1993). Negotiating the Single European Act: National interests and conventional statecraft in the European Community. *International Organization* 45(1), 19–56.

Morawiecki, M. (2016). Plan na rzecz odpowiedzialnego rozwoju. Warszawa: Ministerstwo Rozwoju.

Morawski, I. (2022, 6 czerwca). Zagadka niskich polskich inwestycji. Puls Biznesu. AccessedOctober2023fromhttps://www.pb.pl/zagadka-niskich-polskich-inwestycji-1152507.

Muenkler, H. (2015). Macht in der Mitte: die Neuen Aufgaben Deutschalnds in Europa. Hamburg: Koerber Stiftung.

Mykhnenko, V. (2007). Poland and Ukraine: Institutional structures and economic performance. In *Varieties of capitalism in post-communist countries*. London: Palgrave Macmillan UK, 124–145.

Nasierowski, W. (2019). Techniczna sprawność działań proinnowacyjnych w Polsce z perspektywy Unii Europejskiej. Gospodarka Narodowa. *The Polish Journal of Economics* 300(4), 79–104.

Nedergaard, P. (2013). The influence of ordoliberalism in European integration processes – a framework for ideational influence with competition policy and the economic and monetary policy as examples.

Nee, V., & Swedberg, R. (2005). Economic sociology and new institutional economics. In *Handbook of new institutional economics*. Boston, MA: Springer, 789–818.

Nelson, R. R. (1956). A theory of the low-level equilibrium trap in underdeveloped economies. *The American Economic Review*, 46(5), 894-908.

Niemann, A. (2021). Neofunctionalism. In *The Palgrave handbook of EU crises*, 115–133.

Niemann, A., & Speyer, J. (2018). A neofunctionalist perspective on the 'European refugee crisis': The case of the European border and coast guard. *Journal of Common Market Studies* 56(1), 23–43.

Niemann, A., Edwards, G., & Jakobi, P. (2021). Still not yet obsolete? A neofunctionalist account of Brexit. *Mainz Papers on International and European Politics (MPIEP)*, 25.

Nölke, A. (2019). Comparative capitalism. In *The Palgrave handbook of contemporary international political economy*, 135–151.

Nölke, A., & Vliegenthart, A. (2009). Enlarging the varieties of capitalism: The emergence of dependent market economies in East Central Europe. *World Politics* 61(4), 670–702.

Oates, W. (1972). *Fiscal federalism*. Harcourt Brace Jovanovich.

Oates, W. E. (2005), Toward a second-generation theory of fiscal federalism. *International Tax and Public Finance* 12, 349–373.

OECD (2023a). *Education at a glance 2023: OECD indicators*. Paris: OECD Publishing.

OECD (2023b). Unemployment rate (indicator). Accessed on 17 October 2023 from https://data.oecd.org/unemp/unemployment-rate.htm.

OECD (2023c). Public spending on education (indicator). Accessed on 17 October 2023.

OECD (2023d). Social spending (indicator). Accessed on 24 October 2023.

Oesch, D. (2011). Swiss trade unions and industrial relations after 1990. *Switzerland in Europe*. London: Routledge, 82–102.

Oliver, T. (2015). To be or not to be in Europe: Is that the question? Britain's European question and an in/out referendum. *International Affairs* 91(1), 77–91.

Olsen, J. (2010). *Governing through institution building. Institutional theory and recent european experiments in democratic organization*. Oxford University Press.

Orenstein, M. A., & Bugarič, B. (2022). Work, family, Fatherland: The political economy of populism in central and Eastern Europe. *Journal of European Public Policy* 29(2), 176–195.

Parsons, C. (2023). Brexit and economic ideas. In *Handbook on the European Union and Brexit*, eds John Erik Fossum & Christopher Lord. Edward Elgar Publishing, 85–103.

Paus, E. (2020). Innovation strategies matter: Latin America's middle-income trap meets China and globalization. *The Journal of Development Studies* 58(4), 657–679.

Pavlínek, P. (2016). Whose success? The state–foreign capital nexus and the development of the automotive industry in Slovakia. *European Urban and Regional Studies* 23(4), 571–593.

Peck, J., & Zhang, J. (2013). A variety of capitalism … with Chinese characteristics? *Journal of Economic Geography*, 13(3), 357–396.

Piątek, D. (2023). The illiberal model of state capitalism in Poland. Ekonomia i Prawo. Economics and Law, 22.

Piątkowski, M. (2018). *Europe's growth champion: Insights from the economic rise of Poland.* Oxford University Press.

Pierson, P. (1996). The path to European integration: A historical institutionalist analysis. *Comparative Political Studies* 29(2), 123–163.

Pontusson, J. (2005). *Inequality and prosperity: Social Europe vs. liberal America.* Cornell University Press.

Princen, S., Schimmelfennig, F., Sczepanski, R., Smekal H., & Zbiral, R. (2022). Different yet the same? Differentiated integration and flexibility in implementation in the European Union, West European Politics.

Próchniak, M. (2019). Product market competition. In *Diversity of patchwork capitalism in Central and Eastern Europe*. Routledge, 67–83.

Puchala, D. (1972). Blind men, elephants and international integration. *Journal of Common Market Studies*, 10.

Quinville, R. (2022). Germany's Zeitenwende: New era, new language. Wilson Center (accessed: 20.11.22).

Radunz, A., & Riedel, R. (2024). *Differentiated integration beyond Brexit – Revisiting cleavage perspective in times of multiple crises*. Routledge.

Rapacki, R., & Czerniak A. (eds). (2019). *Diversity of patchwork capitalism in Central and Eastern Europe*. Taylor & Francis, 239.

Rapacki, R., Gardawski, J., Czerniak, A., Horbaczewska, B., Karbowski, A., Maszczyk, P., & Prochniak, M. (2020). Emerging varieties of post-communist capitalism in Central and Eastern Europe: Where do we stand? *Europe-Asia Studies* 72(4), 565–592.

Regan, A., & Brazys, S. (2018). Celtic phoenix or leprechaun economics? The politics of an FDI-led growth model in Europe. *New Political Economy* 23(2), 223–238.

Regini, M. (2006). Political economy. In International *encyclopedia of economic sociology*, eds Jens Beckert & Milan Zafirovski. Routledge.

Reisenbichler, A., & Wiedemann, A. (2022). Credit-driven and consumption-led growth models in the United States and United Kingdom. In *Diminishing returns: The new politics of growth and stagnation*, 213–237.

Riedel, R. (2016). Ekonomia polityczna jako interdyscyplinarne podejście do studiów nad integracją europejską (Political Economy as an Interdisciplinary Approach in European Integration Studies). *Rocznik Integracji Europejskiej*, nr 10/2016, 37–50.

Riedel, R. (2017). The evolution of the Polish Central Bank's perspectives on the Eurozone entry. *Post-Communist Economies* 29(1), 106–116.

Riedel, R. (2018). Great Britain and differentiated integration in Europe. In *Brexit – History, reasoning and perspectives*, eds Troitiño David Ramiro, Kerikmäe Tanel, & Chochia Archil. Springer (Professional) International Publishing, 99–112.

Riedel, R. (2019). Russian threat as a push factor in the European integration discourse in Poland. In *Russia and the EU. Spaces of interaction*, eds Thomas Hoffmann & Andrey Makarychev. Routledge – Taylor & Francis Group, 154–170.

Riedel, R. (2020). Undermining the standards of liberal democracy within the European Union: The Polish case and the limits of post-enlargement democratic conditionality. In *Towards a segmented European political order: The European Union's post-crises conundrum*, eds John Erik Fossum & Jozef Batora. London and New York: Routledge, 175–198.

Riedel, R. (2021). *Poland and the middle income trap*. In *Poland in the Single Market, economics, the euro*, eds Anna Visvizi, Anna Matysek-Jędrych, & Katarzyna

Mroczek-Dądrowska. Series: Europa – Perspectives on the EU, Single Market. Routledge.

Riedel, R. (2023a). De-Europeanization of eastern peripheries or testing the limits of differentiation – Poland in the post-Brexit European Union. In *Handbook on the European Union and Brexit*, eds John Erik Fossum & Christopher Lord. Edward Eldgar Publishing, 296–308.

Riedel, R. (2023b). Environmentalism and differentiated European integration. In *Natur – Geist und Macht. Aspekte des vielgestaltigen Phänomens*, eds Beata Giblak & Krzysztof Żarski. Harrassowitz Verlag, 411–422.

Riedel, R., & Gierlich, C. P. (2021). Between differentiation and (dis)integration – Theoretical explanations of a post-Brexit European Union. *Studies in European Affairs* 25(2), 7–28.

Riker, W. H. (1964). *Federalism: Origin, operation, significance*. Boston, MA: Little, Brown, and Company.

Robinson, N. (2013). Economic and political hybridity: Patrimonial capitalism in the post-Soviet sphere. *Journal of Eurasian Studies* 4(2), 136–145.

Rodden, J. (2003). Reviving Leviathan: Fiscal federalism and the growth of government. *International Organization* 57, 695–729.

Rokkan, S., & Urwin, D. W. (1983). *Economy. Territory, Identity: Politics of Western European Peripheries*, London.

Rolski, M. (2013). Krytyka Planu Balcerowicza w ujęciu Grzegorza Kołodki oraz Tadeusza Kowalika. *Studia Ekonomiczne*, 130, 88–100.

Röpke, W. (2008). *The German question*. Ludwig von Mises Institute.

Rosamond, B. (2000). *Theories of European integration*. The European Union Series. Palgrave.

Ruszkowski, J. (2022). Regresywna koncepcja Unii Europejskiej na przykładzie dyskursu prowadzonego przez Prawo i Sprawiedliwość. *Rocznik Integracji Europejskiej*, nr 16, 21–45.

Sachs, J. (2015). The end of poverty. Economic possibilities for our time. New York: Penguin Books.

Sapir, A. (2006). Globalization and the reform of European social models. *JCMS: Journal of Common Market Studies* 44(2), 369–390.

Saucedo-Acosta, E. J., Salinas Aguilar, D. Y., & Díaz Pedroza, J. (2019). The Balkans as a hierarchical market economy. *European Journal of Interdisciplinary Studies* 11(2).

Sawulski, J., Magda, I., & Lewandowski, P. (2019). Czy polski system emerytalny zbankrutuje. IBS Policy Paper (2).

Scharpf, F. W., & Schmidt, V. A. (eds). (2000). Welfare and work in the open economy: Volume I: From vulnerability to competitiveness in comparative perspective. Oxford: Oxford University Press.

Schimmelfennig, F. (2014). EU enlargement and differentiated integration: Discrimination or equal treatment? *Journal of European Public Policy* 21(5), 681–698.

Schimmelfennig, F. (2016). European integration in the euro crisis: The limits of postfunctionalism. In *Coping with crisis: Europe's challenges and strategies*. Routledge, 127–143.

Schimmelfennig, F. (2018). Brexit: Differentiated disintegration in the European Union. *Journal of European Public Policy* 25(8), 1154–1173.

Schimmelfennig, F. (2020). The conference on the future of Europe and EU reform: Limits of differentiated integration. *European Papers – A Journal on Law and Integration* (2), 989–998.

Schimmelfennig, F. (2022). Differentiated integration has been of limited use in the EU's polycrisis. *Policy Briefs*, 2022/31. Integrating Diversity in the European Union (InDivEU). http://hdl.handle.net/1814/74520 (retrieved from Cadmus, EUI Research Repository 04.12.2022).
Schimmelfennig, F. (2024). Crisis and polity formation in the European Union. *Journal of European Public Policy*, 1–25.
Schimmelfennig, F., & Winzen, T. (2014). Instrumental and constitutional differentiation in the European Union. *Journal of Common Market Studies* 52(2), 354–370.
Schimmelfennig, F., & Winzen, T. (2019). Grand theories, differentiated integration. *Journal of European Public Policy* 28(8), 1172–1191.
Schimmelfennig, F., & Winzen, T. (2020). Ever looser union? Differentiated European integration. Oxford University Press.
Schimmelfennig, F., Leufen, D., & Rittberger, B. (2015). The European Union as a system of differentiated integration: Interdependence, politicisation, differentiation. *Journal of European Public Policy*, 22(6), 764–782.
Schmitter, P. (2012). European disintegration? A way forward, *Journal of Democracy* 23(4), 39–48.
Schneider, B. R. (2013). *Hierarchical capitalism in Latin America*. Cambridge University Press.
Schneider, B. R. (2015). The developmental state in Brazil: Comparative and historical perspectives. *Brazilian Journal of Political Economy* 35, 114–132.
Schoellgen, G. (1992). Die Macht in der Mitte Europas. Stationen Deutscher Aussenpolitik von Friedrich dem Grossen bis zur Gegenwart. Munchen: Verlag Beck.
Schoellgen, G. (2003). Der Aftritt. Deutschlands Rueckkehr auf die Weltbuehne. Propylen Verlag.
Schönberger, C. (2012). Hegemon wider Willen. Zur Stellung Deutschlands in der Europäischen Union. *Merkur* 66 (2012), 1–8.
Schwab, K., & Zahidi, S. (2020, December). Global competitiveness report: Special edition 2020. World Economic Forum.
Schwarz, H.-P. (2005). *Republik ohne Kompass, Anmerkungen zur deutschen Aussenpolitik*.
Schweiger, C. (2014). *The EU and the Global Financial Crisis*. Edward Elgar Publishing.
Schweiger, C., & Magone, J. (2014). Differentiated integration and cleavage under crisis conditions. *Perspectives on European Politics and Society* 15(3), 259–265.
Seeleib-Kaiser, M. (2016). The end of the conservative German welfare state model. *Social Policy & Administration* 50(2), 219–240.
Sejm (2013). *Informacja ministra spraw zagranicznych o założeniach polskiej polityki zagranicznej w 2013 r.* Online: http://orka2.sejm.gov.pl/StenoInter7.nsf/0/48239696DF9135D8C1257B350004E792/%24File/36_a_ksiazka.pdf (accessed 29 August 2020).
Serowaniec, M., & Przychodzki, M. (2023). The introduction of the National Recovery and Resilience Plans in the light of the Visegrád Grup Countries' Experience. PRAWO i WIĘŹ, 1(44), 49–58.
Shelburne, R. (2016). Long-run economic growth: Stagnations, explosions and the middle income trap. *Global Economy Journal* 16(3), 433–458.
Shiraishi, T., & Sonobe, T. (eds). (2019). *Emerging states and economies. Their origins, drivers, and challenges ahead*. Springer Singapore.

Shonfield, A. (1965). *Modern capitalism. The changing balance of public and private power*. Oxford University Press.
Sinn, H.-W. (1994). How much Europe? Subsidiarity, centralization and fiscal competition. *Scottish Journal of Political Economy* 41, 85–107.
Skorupińska-Cieślak, K. (2018). Stosunki przemysłowe w krajach Europy środkowo-wschodniej. Perspektywa porównawcza. Studia Prawno-Ekonomiczne (109), 303–326.
Smith, A. (1776). *An inquiry into the nature and causes of the wealth of nations*. Bottom of the Hill Publishing (2019 edition).
Snyder, T. (2019). Droga do niewolności. Rosja Europa Ameryka, Znak Horyzont Kraków.
Spolaore, E. (2015). The political economy of European Integration. Working Paper 21250/NBER. National Bureau of Economic Research.
Staehr, K. (2015). Economic growth and convergence in the Baltic States: Caught in the middle-income trap? *Intereconomics* 5, 274–280.
Statista (n.d.). Largest stock exchange operators worldwide as of July 2023, by market capitalization of listed companies. Retrieved 17 October 2023 from https://www.statista.com/statistics/270126/largest-stock-exchange-operators-by-market-capitalization-of-listed-companies/#:~:text=The%20New%20York%20Stock%20Exchange,What%20is%20a%20stock%20exchange%3F.
Steenbergen, M. R., Edwards, E. E., & De Vries, C. E. (2007). Who's cueing whom? Mass-elite linkages and the future of European integration. *European Union Politics* 8(1), 13–35.
Stefaniak, J. (2021). Znaczenie udziału Polski w Jednolitym Rynku Europejskim: rynek usług.
Stephens, P. (2013). Germany should face the German question. *Financial Times*, 18 April 2013.
Strange, S. (2011). *The retreat of the state: The diffusion of power in the world economy*. Cambridge University Press.
Streeck, W. (1992). National diversity, regime competition and institutional deadlock: Problems in forming a European industrial relations system. *Journal of Public Policy* 12(4), 301–330.
Stubb, A. C. G. (1996). A categorization of differentiated integration. *JCMS: Journal of Common Market Studies* 34(2), 283–295.
Szabó, J. (2022). Political economy of illiberal capitalism in Hungary and Poland. Politická ekonomie 2022(5), 617–637.
Sześciło, D. (2016). O powikłanej decentralizacji. Instytucjonalny krajobraz systemu usług publicznych w Polsce. Zarządzanie Publiczne (38), 32–44.
Taylor-Gooby, P. (2017). Re-doubling the crises of the welfare state: The impact of Brexit on UK welfare politics. *Journal of Social Policy* 46(4), 815–835.
Tekin, F. (2016). Was folgt aus dem Brexit? Mögliche Szenarien differenzierter (Des-) Integration. *Integration* 39(3), 183–197.
Ter-Minassian, T. (1997). *Fiscal federalism in theory and practice*. IMF.
Thelen, K., & Busemeyer, M. R. (2012). Institutional change in German vocational training: From collectivism toward segmentalism. In *The political economy of collective skill formation*, 68–100.
Tindemans L. (1975), Report by Mr. Leo Tindemans, Prime Minister of Belgium, to the European Council (sent 195). Bulletin of the European Communities, Supplement 1/76, (commonly called the *Tindemans Report*).

Tomczyk, M. (2013). Polityka Szwajcarii wobec Unii Europejskiej, Wydawnictwo Uniwersytetu Łódzkiego, Łódź.

Topal, M. H. (2020). The middle income trap: Theory and empirical evidence. *Bogazici Journal Review of Social, Economic and Administration Studies* 34(1), 51–75.

Tosiek, P. (2023). Poland's EU vision: Towards an illiberal concept of differentiated integration? Presentation at the ECPR General Conference, Charles University – Prague, 4–6 September 2023.

Tovias, A. (2006). Exploring the 'pros' and 'cons' of Swiss and Norwegian models of relations with the European Union: What can Israel learn from the experiences of these two countries? *Cooperation and Conflict* A/2, 203–222.

Tranoy, B. S., & Schwartz, H. M. (2020). Illusions of convergence: The persistent simplification of a wicked crisis. In *Towards a segmented European political order. The European Union's post-crisis conundrum*, eds Jozef Batora & John Erik Fossum. Routledge, 47–71.

Tugcu, C. T. (2015). How to escape the middle income trap: International evidence from a binary dependent variable model. *Theoretical and Applied Economics* 1(602), 49–56.

Ülgen, S. (2022). *Rewiring globalization*, 1–166. https://carnegieeurope.eu/2022/02/17/rewiring-globalization-pub-86308.

Umiński, S. (2017). The pros and cons of integration vs. disintegration scenarios for Europe. *European Integration Studies* 11(2017), 8–18.

Vahl, M., & Grolimund, N. (2006). Integration without membership: Switzerland's bilateral agreements with the EU. Brussels.

Vitols, S. (2009). European Works Councils: An assessment of their social welfare impact. ETUI Working Paper 2009.04.

Vukov, V. (2023). Growth models in Europe's eastern and southern peripheries: Between national and EU politics. *New Political Economy*, 1–17.

Walecka, K., & Gagatek, W. (2021). The politics of differentiated integration: What do governments want? Country Report – Poland. *EUI Working Paper* RSC 2021/31.

Wallerstein, I. (1974). *The modern world-system: Capitalist agriculture and the origins of the European world economy in the sixteenth century*. New York: Academic Press.

Webber, D. (2014). How likely is it that the European Union will *dis* integrate? A critical analysis of competing theoretical perspectives. *European Journal of International Relations* 20(2), 341–365.

Wellisch, D. (2000). *Theory of public finance in a federal state*. Cambridge: Cambridge University Press.

Wildasin, D. E. (2004). The institutions of federalism: Toward an analytical framework. *National Tax Journal* 57, 247–272.

Wojtyna, A. (2005). Alternatywne modele kapitalizmu. Gospodarka Narodowa. *The Polish Journal of Economics* 202(9), 1–23.

Wolf, S. (2004). *The German question since 1919: An analysis with key documents*. Praeger Frederick Publisher.

worker-participation.eu (n.d.). *Poland*. Retrieved 17 October 2023 from https://www.worker-participation.eu/national-industrial-relations/countries/poland.

World Bank (2023). Market capitalization of listed domestic companies (% of GDP) [Data set]. Accessed October 2023 from https://databank.worldbank.org/source/world-development-indicators/Series/CM.MKT.LCAP.GD.ZS

Ye, L., & Robertson, P. (2016). On the existence of a middle-income trap. *Economic Record* 92(297), 173–189.

Zeitlin, J. (2016). EU experimentalist governance in times of crisis. *West European Politics* 39(5), 1073–1094.

Zhang, Q., Nakatani, R., & Valdes, I. G. (2022). Fiscal decentralization improves social outcomes when countries have good governance. IMF Working Papers 2022/111, International Monetary Fund.

Zheng, Z. (2020). *Middle-income trap. An analysis based on economic transformations and social governance*. Palgrave Macmillan, Tsingua University Press.

Zielonka, J. (2007). Europa jako imperium. Nowe spojrzenie na Unię Europejską. PISM, Warszawa.

Zoch, G., & Schober, P. S. (2018). Public child-care expansion and changing gender ideologies of parents in Germany. *Journal of Marriage and Family* 80(4), 1020–1039.

Index